VOICES OF THE PEOPLE!

Expressions of Life, Love & Legacy
Captured by The Avenue Bakery,
Baltimore's Game Changer

James Hamlin

Photo credits/Photo Inserts:
Hamlin Family Collection
Medley Management and Prose, Inc.
The Royal Theater & Community Heritage Center (TRTCHC)

Book Cover Design: *Visions That Transcend*

ISBN 979-8-218-47728-8 (Paperback)
ISBN 979-8-218-47727-1 (ebook)

Printed in the United States of America

This Book is Dedicated to Entrepreneurs — Past, Present, and Future. And the message is to never be discouraged, never give up, and always keep the faith!

"Our greatest weakness lies in our giving up. The most certain way to succeed is always to try just one more time." —Thomas Edison

Contents

Mission

The Avenue Bakery Vision Statement:
The Avenue Bakery's vision is to influence the development and unification of "The Pennsylvania Avenue" community while providing desired quality goods and services.

Mission Statement:
"The mission of The Avenue Bakery is to be the pioneer of reforming the current state of our historic Baltimore community and restore it back to its once vivacious and culturally rich history that once was *Historic Pennsylvania Avenue*. It is our priority to instill pride and respect that will transform into the longevity of numerous black-owned businesses. We believe The Avenue Bakery will spearhead the revival, growth, and profitability of the Baltimore community by offering distinctive homemade and exclusive rolls, pastries, and beverages to our valued customers in Baltimore and its surrounding areas; therefore, promoting and advocating for other black-owned businesses to come back to our historic community to make it once again profitable. By treating our employees as family and co-pioneers to our revitalization efforts, we strive to create a welcoming atmosphere that is reminiscent of the Historic Old West Baltimore."

The Avenue Bakery
Home of Poppay's Rolls

ROYAL
ALWAYS
A
GOOD SHOW
ROYAL
NOW PLAYING
ROYAL
ALWAYS
A
GOOD SHOW
Passing

The Avenue Bakery's Legacy Logbook Backstory: The Beginning

As you view our Legacy Logbooks, you will see that we have hosted people from all over the country. We've also welcomed folks who have traveled from as far away as Canada, Sweden, and France—and as they say, the hits keep coming.

The initial idea to furnish The Avenue Bakery's lobby with an open-wide and beckoning logbook, atop a sturdy wooden podium, came out of the trials, the tribulations, and the lessons learned from the Bakery's inaugural year, 2011. It was also our desire to know what our customers thought of us and our ability to change quickly based on their opinions.

Anyone who knows the Avenue Bakery knows that its mission is trifold: to provide the community and visitors with something they can't get from anywhere else; to spearhead the revitalization of Baltimore's Historic Pennsylvania Corridor with commerce and happy foot traffic; and to educate and entertain the public by vividly showcasing Baltimore City's rich African American history, culture, contributions and potential to again become the place to be.

Today, tourism is the third largest industry in Baltimore City, bringing more than 10 billion dollars annually and growing. Tour buses chart our landscape from all over the country, and international groups visit us as well.

Nick Mosby - President of the Baltimore City Counsel and James Hamlin. The Avenue Bakery often sets the stage for community and political activism

Not long ago, a local group received a grant to do mural tours in West Baltimore and hosted fifteen tourists from Arizona. Well, the group had to start someplace, and it chose to begin at The Bakery. I was happy to engage them, serve them, and enlighten them about our history

and culture. One of the couples, a White couple, shared how they came to find out about The Bakery. "When one of my friends found out that I was going to Baltimore," the man commented, "he said I must visit this bakery, and he described the bakery."

I was blown away by how The Bakery's reputation had journeyed to Arizona. But I wholly confess that I was not surprised. Among our many highlights, we have been categorized as a mini museum in a book published in 2019 titled *The 111 Places You Must Not Miss in Baltimore* By Allison Robicelli and John Dean (Photographer). We're number ten on its list.

Amy Davis, staff photographer at *The Baltimore Sun*, included The Avenue Bakery in her book, highlighting Baltimore's rich history of theaters and architecture. It's titled *Flickering Treasures:* Rediscovering Baltimore's *Forgotten Movie Theaters* (Johns Hopkins Press, 2017). It's described as "a revelatory chronicle of Baltimore's movie theaters over the past century, eloquently told through extraordinary photographs and poignant reminiscences." Naturally, The Royal Theater, coupled with The Avenue Bakery and my nonprofit, The Royal Theater & Community Heritage Corporation's (TRTCHC) passion to rebuild The Royal, came to mind. We're grateful that she included us in her book.

Amy's work soon grew into a history and visual arts exhibit at the Smithsonian's National Building Museum (November 17, 2018–December 1, 2019) called *Flickering Treasures: Rediscovering Baltimore's Forgotten Movie Theaters.* At the exhibit's end, Amy graciously donated the entire exhibit to The Bakery. We unveiled it, mounted on the walls of our conference room, in front of friends, family, and the community during a dedication ceremony. Every piece of artwork or photomontage (our murals) that we've had, we've had an unveiling ceremony. And we've done that every year since 2012.

Later in 2020, we received an invitation to be included in an exhibit at The Baltimore Museum of

2017 Thurgood Marshall mural small

Industry. It was an exhibit on Baltimore bakeries. We heartily accepted the invitation. The museum visited us to take pictures and conduct interviews.

Our latest murals (to date 2023), highlighting the legacy and history of the community, garnish the front of The Bakery. It consists of two photomontages that depict The Battle of Fort Belgur, showcasing Baltimore's timeline during the Civil War. Folks don't know that there was a fort on North and Madison avenues. Frederick Douglass had a meeting with President Abraham Lincoln, urging him to allow Baltimore's Black regiments to fight for their freedom. On The Avenue, we're sharing that story. Our dedication ceremony held on Juneteenth even included a reenactment address.

Pennsylvania Ave. Mural at The Avenue Bakery

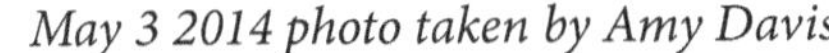

May 3 2014 photo taken by Amy Davis

Getting back to the Arizona tour group, on the day of its visit, it was nearly closing time at The Bakery. I welcomed our out-of-town guests but didn't rush them. We had a meaty conversation and we snapped pictures. And before they left, they expressed their sentiments in my current Legacy Logbook edition.

But at the time of our beginnings, thoughts of tourism were neither here nor there. We wanted to blast, above the volume of naysayers, that business could thrive on The Avenue. Accomplishing, right out the gate, a healthy stream of foot traffic, largely due to our signature staple of Poppay's Rolls—born from my mother's recipe, I quickly discovered the need for and importance of customer feedback. It was customer relations 101, a skill I acquired and refined during my foot-traffic days at the United Parcel Service (UPS). I clocked thirty-five and a half years at UPS before retiring in 2003. One of my many assignments, from which I learned much, was Account Executive. It quickly graduated to Major Accounts Manager.

BALTIMORE
Watch Now
LOCAL NEWS
New mural commemorates Baltimore City's hip-hop legacy

Without even realizing it, for years and years, I've always been open to learning new things. Lucky for me, UPS had a nasty habit of assigning you to an operation and as soon as you mastered the job, it would reassign you to another challenge, and so on. The bottom line is that it made me super conscious of people and relationships and it sharpened my business acumen—my thirst to manage and conquer operational details.

That first year in The Bakery, we learned from word-of-mouth that while our pastries were good, sometimes the customers found them hard. From that, we learned to protect our full trays of goodies with sturdy plastic wrap to keep them succulent and soft. It was a valuable tidbit that I'm sure we would have discovered. But getting it from the customer's mouth enabled us to get to it sooner rather than later.

Working as a sales manager for UPS, one of my many assignments, one of the things that I quickly learned was that you need to know how people feel about your business. Sometimes people will tell you, sometimes they won't. Sometimes they'll tell you and you don't remember what they said. Or you don't know who said it. Then you have those customers who just don't come back.

When we opened The Bakery, three things were essential because we wanted to make sure that when customers came to The Avenue Bakery: number one, it smelled good; number two, a customer was leaving out with something that tasted fantastic; and number three, our customers could get an education as well. The idea was to feed one's body and feed their mind. But how could we know without a doubt that we were accomplishing that?

Such a quest is also imbedded in my ongoing commitment to the community,

which, for me, is key to running a successful business. How important it is to know and figure out a plan to know how your customers feel about your business? How can one use that knowledge as a motivator? How can such knowledge drive change/innovation in your business? How such an engine become an asset to you—not only knowing how customers feel but also being able to respond quickly when customers have an expressed positive or negative piece of information? Feedback.

We needed to access those factors and receive our ongoing report cards in real time.

Hence The Avenue Bakery Legacy Logbook. And we put a fresh one out every time one fills up.

Instantly, folks were moved to either state their claim of having been at The Bakery; or tell us how they liked our baked goods, or comment on service, or simply share their stories— and sometimes artwork—expressing they're acquired inspiration after entering our doors.

Venture beyond our threshold and one can study The Avenue Bakery's running video on culture, history and entertainment birthed from the Pennsylvania Avenue Corridor's glory days, peruse our merchandise, posters and brochures (always possessing a message of positivity), enjoy our courtyard and concerts, and enjoy our visual arts' display—our colorful, informative, ever-changing murals that can be seen from blocks away.

Early on, gleaned from our Logbooks, was a comical customer's take on our customer service. On any given day, especially during our first year, customers could expect to be served by one of my loving and supportive family members. My son's mother-in-law, Susie Dezurn, often manned the front counter. She's warm and friendly, and her cheerful, charismatic personality is booming. We all laughed but made changes, too, when a customer wrote in our logbook, "I would have been able to get in and out quicker if the lady at the counter wasn't so talkative."

Oh yeah, that was real-time knowledge that we needed to know and improve upon immediately. And you'll be happy to know that welcoming, thoughtful customer service still abounds. But the lines now move expeditiously.

THE AVENUE BAKERY'S

LOGBOOK #1
(2011-2012)

movement starts

A→ 2011

with one★

Jim, Brenda + Family.
15 Aug. 2011

a flicker
turns into a flame...

endings
make space
to fill with hope
for new beginnings

dreams morph
from love, thought
inspiration
into reality
with determination,
preseverence and
the constructive
application of faith
and pure will.

Godspeed +
continued Blessings-- !!
[illegible]

P.S. Y'all got this...
and I got yo back

The Avenue Bakery
GUEST BOOK
15 Aug 2011 Est. 2011

Best of Luck -
Bertram Bailey Edmondson '68

Hardware Plus

Hope you well
CW HARRIS Edmondson "69"
Anthony T. Pressley, Customer #1
MARSHALL Collins Good Luck
Charles Tilghman JR
Wyatt Arrington "UPS"
Barbara Blount Armstrong - All the Best to You!
[illegible] - Ken North - Congrats
[illegible] Brown
[illegible]
Best Wishes [illegible]
Wonderful - So very happy for you...

Hallelujah to God through JESUS Christ who Revives us 2022

As-Salaam Alaikum!
Rasul A. Aquil

Great yummy stuff :)

Carl & Vicki Pendleton "Best to you"
Herb & Bob we wish you all the Luck
VICTOR CLARK, JR / DBED - "WELCOME HOME Jim"
Laura Collins (GOD Bless)
Mary Jones (Welcome Home!)
My Brother, Congrat! To you and the family

Best Luck Jim Brenda

JOE HENRY (SOUNDCHECK SOLUTIONS.COM) BEST WISHES!
DAVID BROWN NEW FAYETTE STREET MARKET AND DELI, INC OWNER 1956 W. FAYETTE ST (GOD CONTINUE TO BLESS YOUR BUSINESS)

May U Grow with the Community MT Brown

Congratulations, Jim -- and Best Wishes.
So proud of your achievement!
MJ (Gay) Brodie

I Love you + God Loves you Best - Much Joy Doug McFadden

Leslie A Saunders, MOED - 443-984-3014
John E. Kyle Bolton Hill Best wishes!
Jim Peiffer MDOT Good Luck!
KELLY LITTLE DRUID HEIGHTS CDC GREAT JOB!
Cynthia Harris Good Job
Renee Jenson - DHCDC - Best Wishes for a successful business
Richard Fradkin - Grubb & Ellis Co. - Congratulations and Best of Luck!!
Blaize Connelli Dygm Great move! Best of luck!!
Dionne Pratt - Thank you for bringing this alive!
Chelita Thomas Thank you God
Brenda Brown It's much needed. Good Luck Thanks God Bless
Murcena Bean - Waters Best wishes and God Bless!!!

What A Blessing?
Wm & Verel Jackson
3811 W. Harrison Ave.
Balto. Md. 21215
Edward W. Harcum
3011 Woodlawn Dr. Apt. F
Woodlawn Md. 21207
Margaret Makell
4930 Evans Chapel Rd. 21211
Mashaye Barr
HB Royalty Circle
Charlestown Community
1722 A Carlton St
Jay & Judy Williams
Charlie Dixon
723 Wicklow Rd
God just a blessing
Jacqueline White 2819 Edgecombe Circle North 21215

Good Luck
this Neighborhood
needs the black
stores to take back
this area

Thanks for bringing
something New in the
community
#BlackOwned

I am glad that a black bakery has come to this community. This has not been one here since Lafayette Corner Shop.

Zack Dermody - Jix - Way to go!
Susie Dezurn - Congratulations
Randy & Andrea Anderson - Congrats & Welcome
KATHLEEN SHERRILL - CONGRATS!
Kajarna Alston - Congrats and God Bless!
Lisa & Colleen Coutess Blessings and much success
Barbara Mason & Blessings to all, we need this
Cindy Chiulli Best Wishes to a Successful business
Mae Mosteller 415 Morris Hill Ave. Glen Burnie 21061
Annette Jackson 4202 Berger Avenue Gardenville
Mae Alston 3704 Walbrook 21216
Maureen Nichols 100 Chesapeake 21060
Tower = 413 Charter Oak Ave #21212
Carolyn Ar'Lena & Smilly - 515 Sanford Pl 21217
(Mann) Business last long and prosper.
James Sherman - May God Bless 4 Guys for ever + ever
The Future
Nikita Bell Keep God First, He will be your success Grace & Peace

Verdetta & Dan Wilson
Peace & Blessings with new venture!

Ms Dee Smith
503 Cumberland St. 21217

Delia Cross may God bless
2204 Penn. Ave. 21217

Alicia Aydlett
BCHD/STD Clinic
1515 W. North Ave

CARLTON MAYO
MADISON AVE
BALTIMORE, MD 21217

Jim Dow
4010 FERNhill Ave 21215

Alonza A. Boyd
4803 Tamarind Rd.
Baltimore Md. 21209

"LeLe" Edison
1821 W. Mount St.
21217-1706

DIONNE BUR
108 S Payson St
21223
THANKING GOD FOR YOUR BLESSINGS

Troy Jones Peace & Blessings

James Dean
3504 St. [illegible] Rd
Wilson Mill, MD 212444
Congrats!!

Inna Mae Becker
3710 Rennie Rd
21218
Good Luck!

Tiffany Hayes
2236 Pennsylvania Ave.

Monica McIntosh

[illegible] Savage
[illegible] Reading Ave
Balt., Md 21212

HERMAN & DORIS SMITH
3108 ELBERT ST - 21229

GEORGINE BOWEN
2603 LODGE FARM Rd 21219

Jackie Winkey
2475 Woodbrook Ave 21217
May you continue to be a blessing to this community as God has so richly blessed you.

Beatrice Chase
1903 Edgewood St. 21216

Karen Ireland

Brad Kidd
I'm so proud of what you have accomplished for this community! Keep up the good work and those rolls baking

Ramona (Mona) & Tyrone Morley's Children
From Sandtown Area
Welcome to the Area Wish you the Best

Welcome! Welcome! Thanks!
To Our Neighborhood
[illegible]

God Bless you! Bringing Up The Neighborhood!
C. A. P. PRICE WHATCOAT St.

[illegible] Bush 2418 Pennsylvania Ave Merchants Assoc
God Speed!

Impressive, great job and good luck - Patrick (owner across)

God Blessing on your new bakery
Jacqueline Johnson
Emmie Rice
Agape Church
[illegible]
[illegible] Shalom Community, Inc. [illegible]
[illegible] - 410-[illegible]
[illegible]
[illegible]
[illegible]

God Bless you and thank you for coming to us
2115 Arunah St 21217

Good luck
723 Dolphin St.

Welcome to THE Neighborhood Keep The Good work up

Welcome Store we need
[illegible] Vonnie

May God Bless you for bringing something positive to the community —

Your rolls are excellent keep up the good cooking God Bless You
2011
(Linda Customer)

Congratulations on your endeavor! May this be the right start to the revitalization of the neighborhood!
Robert Goodwyn, JoAnne Goodwyn
22 Tomber Ct. Gwynn Oak, Md. 21207

Hello.
So very glad to have you here.
Best of luck - [illegible] family.

Much Luck & Longevity
The Ridgelys

Peace love and light
Great Baking
Tho McKee's

May God Bless You
May Your Business be "5" Star

God Bless Yall
Keep them Coming Out the Oven!

God Bless you &
Good Luck
Joyce & George (Freddie)

God Bless You and Your Business
From business owner to Another!
Will Anderson

Best of The Best
Floyd Wright

Wish You The Best heard you on PR 88.1
Daryl Augustus

I wish you the best in the time you are around
Love: Intia

Good luck on your new business -
Prayers are with you
[illegible]

Wonderful and wishing you well with your new business
Lu Branch Ingles & family

God's blessing
Helen Boardley

Woodlawn in the House
M. Thompson

Best Wishes

For new hires contact Glynnis Bladden CFUF / STRIVE "A Dream Come True!"

May God continue to bless your life with Success. Keith Anderson Chain Saw Man

Thank You, Thank you, Thank you A Real Bakery in a Real Neighborhood Flo Jo

God Bless You & Yours! R. N. Miller

Wonderful! Wonderful Welcome

Balt, Md 21239

Welcome To Sandtown Cynthia

May God Bless you! Fam Derrick

Much Success! S. Brown

Best of Luck! C Thomas

Some "real food" being served on The Ave. God Bless Your Success! R. Woodland St. Peter Claver & St. Pius V Faith Community 1546 N. Fremont Ave

Help bring Pennsylvania Ave back to its glory! Thank you! The Purdie Family

Good Luck Ella Sanders

We needed something great On Avenue

Congratulations Best Wishes for Success

The Very Best!

Good Luck Mike Marrow

Good Luck Hope you enjoy a life long stay 8/24/11

Good Luck May you have much Success

Good luck

GOD Bless you
+ YOUR Bus.

Aurelia Barnett
Good luck

Good Luck

The Avenue Bakery
May God Give
You Grace & Mercy
The Avenue Family
August 2011

God Bless you
Best wish to come
and more you will make it
God got your Back!!! - K.W

GOOD LUCK!!

SJ

- MAY ALLAH GRANT YOU BLESSING
- AND SUCCESS...

- Earl Vandiver and friends

It's good to see a black owned and operated business, May God Bless You & family

A. Holly

Keep up the good work and may God
bless this business

To the Best!

May God Bless and Keep up the good work - Rena Golder

God Had supper, he break the bread and Drink the wine, at the last Supper, in his remembrance. May this house Be a Blessing to our Community. V.Burrow 8/26/11
Bless Your Family and may you Flourish

All our best

Good Luck

Good luck
you guys keep it.

Very Very Very
Very (Good)

Hammer Time
Name

Good Luck
God Be With You
You will be alright
A. Green

We can
make a different
I had a dream
go for your dreams.
Good Luck
Diane Smith.

Let's Keep the feeling of "Peace"
& Respect!!

Bless God
for your
vision
Zelda (Mt. Sinai Temple)

This is wonderful.
We need all the business we can
get. Bless You
Yvette Shipley

TO GOD BE THE GLORY!!
John W.

Best Wishes for
much Success
Pat R!

Best Wishes
Best of All
Stay Good!
J.R.D.

Enjoying the Pastry
Stay at it
Russell

We give thanks
for the Lord's
Blessings
Be Blessed!
St. John AME Church
2.12.17

Good Luck 8-25-2012
To you And
the Business
Neighbor Hood (Terry & Jewel)

May God Bless this Place
Shirly Smith

It is "wonderful" to have "businesses" in our community again!
Pamela Shields

May God bless you! Be successful!!
Love,
Roderick & Delores Johnson 08/27/2011

God/Allah be pleased with your endeavor. Derek 8/27/11

God bless and may your organization increase
8/27/11 The Nelson + Harrison Family

God Bless This Shop
Very Good

St. Peter Claver - Nefaladam
Great Day

May your oven never run cold
Daniel the Friday Night Bunch 8/27

May God Bless your business, we were truly overdue for a bakery in this area. Preston St.

God bless you and bakery
bring back that Good old Baking.

Thank God for you!!
hope you have the best of
Luck on the shop! God Bless.

I PRAY that you Be very Blessed!
may GOD Blessed you
and may you have A long stay!

May Allaah bless your efforts!

MAY GOD CONTINUE TO BLESS AND KEEP YOU IN ALL YOUR VISIONS AND ENDEAVORS

Bless you real good
Sadie Gooch

GOD BLESS YALL REAL GOOD!
TYRONE GAINES

"God Bless" "Thank you"

MAY GOD Be With you
ICE 8-27-2011

Good Luck
Sheila

May God Bless your Sherry

"Best Wishes in all your endeavors."

Thank God for the New Bakery

TAY God Bless You

Good Fortune + God Bless!

Good Luck
JeffB

Ditto - Martha

Best Wishes and Good Luck!!

Roy Muhammad

"Uncle Mae's Snack Shop 1313 ... St"

"Welcome and Thank You for Bringing Warmth to the community! Blessings Bridgette"

God Bless You
To God Be Glory
B. Counter

James you did it my man
David Hendricks
"Luv U"
God Bless You

God Bless This Endeavor; There hasn't been a Bakery around here in 35 yrs. - Perishers - they use to be on the corner where Northeastern Supply is (we use to steal their bread; we will be buying yours)
Alvin J. Bellamy aka "Reds"

James Hamlin, Jr., Brenda Hamlin, Brandon Sorrell, James Hamlin, Belinda Hamlin, Daughter-in-law Etoy Hamlin

Brenda Hamlin and Football Hall of Famer Ed Reed

May God
continue to prosper
you!

Thanks for your service

"Absolutely Delicious"

Praying for you
your will be
Alright

Lois Jamison
Edward Oates

Good Luck

Leon Speight

Leon P.G. Perr

Best Wishes
and good
eating (yes)
TROY

Best Wishes
Kelly Kelley for a great new
Cunningham Community
"2011"

Best wishes in your
NEW ADVENTURE
George H. Knight (Joe)

Best Cinnamon Apple
Twists on This Side
of Town → Good
Luck
Mana
2011

Very Good
God Bless
Mille

Best Wishes
& Good Luck
This is what
we needed
an old
Sandtown
resident
V. Jordan

God's
Blessings
and Best Wishes
Doris Finley
9.2.11

Best Wishes
9.2.11

Dear Eddy, It looks Great & smells even better! Good luck to you & your family. Love Ya, Rita

Best wishes to you, your family and this wonderful establishment! Congrats Damon

Congratulations to you & your family on the business. May God continue to be with you.

Linda Keep up the good work

The Joseph H. Brown Jr. Funeral Home Wishes you much success!

Duane

May God Continue to Bless you! A spirit that knows peace A life that knows love A heart that knows God! This is my prayer for you.

KEEP THEM BUNS COMING (MOUSE)

thankyou for being Here :)

WElcome To The NeighborHood, We are so Glad To Have You Here!! Roger & Sylvia Cromwell

James Williams Jr AKA AS SPANKY Think you for Some good old Home made BUN'S! much Love!

SElly OF LBS! I LOVE BAKERY

I really enjoy the muffins. We need something like this in the community. Wish you continue success Quintin

GOD BLESS this place for Success

DENEY & AMARIN DAIEL

"There must be Love in your Bakery - God Bless You" Jackie

Thank You for Adding Breakfast to the ... all. Come Here on 9/3/11 ... Just like you & your family

We love your bakery Thank You for bringing life to the Community

Love Stephanie :)) <3

Kenny good luck

OMG! ...

Thank God for your Vision and breathing new life on the Avenue. The Best is yet to Come!!!

Much Success in this new venture 9/6/2011 Gail

Melvin Eley Good Luck 9/6/2011

God Bless In all you do
Helen Morgan
Greater Mt. ... Church
529 ...
Pastor ...
9/5/2011

CHARLES Smith
Good Luck 9/6/2011

To God Be The Glory
9.6.11
May he shed his grace & mercy continuously upon this establishment
Carole & John
"Amen"

Good Luck
May God Continue to Bless this establishment in every way!! Hats off to the Chef
D. Harris
Mervo H.S.

God moves IN a way we don't understand!!

The Best I've ever had. God Bless you! 9/6/11

It's wonderful to have a family business in our community.
[illegible signature]

10/11/11
God Blessing on your New work
Smith

Get more Pastries & Donuts
Sept. 8 '11
[illegible signature]

Wishing you Gods Blessings
The Marshalls

God orders our steps I pray He continue's to keep you Bless you and your business
Michelle

Best Wishes
[illegible signature]

Good Luck & Best Wishes
from the Bailey's Beckwith & Patterson's

To Always
Trying to improve
and bring business to
The Avenue. Now we can
say- without a doubt the best
business on Ave is yours. Something
Sweet + good.
Darrell Cutt

May God Keep and prosper the
Bakery and all who come
through your doors

Praying God's Blessings
on you, as you go
forth Rev Nelson
Anna Lane

Good luck
Dolores [illegible]

May God
Keep you in his
Prayers Victoria

Ladies,
It says a lot (to me)
when entreprenuers are
humble enough to respect the
love of, and the love that
goes in baking. Good Luck
and God bless.
Moja Huba
Amani Moto

[illegible]
Victoria

God Bless
your business"
Marsha

(N)

Best Wishes
Such a Place
Beautiful Place you do well
[illegible]

Thanks for the Rolls + Buns
Karin

Good Luck
B. Bucy

Hope you
Do Well
Red!

Dear
Mr. Jame
I'm glad you, Did somethy
Very Good to this property.
you're a good Friend & I can
to me
Eren Lee
your
part time
Handy man

BEST
WISHES
GOD BLESS
YOU with much SUCCES

Alfred Phillips
Ithaca NY
You have a very good shop!!!

Good
Luck
from
the [illegible]
Family

11/4/10
Much Success
Edward + Liberman
Mullenkon

Just Right Maintenance
Home Repairs 443 250 8535
Good Test

Best of Luck & Success
2012

Best wishes & Good luck
the Name of Sloppy White
8/2013

THE Best every time
1600 Bruceet.

C. Cavalier
Wishes you the
Very best of success
8/19/20

God bless and
keep you is my
prayer

God Bless You
R. Hill

Congratulation on your new Bakery May God continue to bless your Business
Nicole Pearl Hair Spa LLC

Thank you for being Here!!

Thanks for Showing our ppl Dreams DO Come True!!
Much Success

GOD is Good
From Bro WILE
Eugene Scott

Best Wishes.
Thank for adding Good taste to Penn Ave and the Rest of Baltimore.
David Skinner
Purple Honey Music & Entertainment Group.
purplehoneymusic.com

Rolls look like my Grandmother
had to have some!!!
God Bless B.B. Wells

Great, Stay focused regardless — you'll do fine — Doc Wells

Best Wishes
To you on your
New Bakery
From a old school
From around way
Hattie Jr
Flemming
Betty BDD
One Love

Best wishes to the new business. I will spread the word to all of my Correctional Officer family.

Lt. Hamick Chase
MCTU

Best Wishes. Much success!

Peace
Calvin V Dotson Jr
9.9.2011

Kudo's & Best Wishes
Pat & Bob Rhodes 9/10/2011
Historic Frederick Douglass High School Alumni Association

Good Luck and Best Wishes
I wish you much success
Sgt Jones

Best Wishes (Thoughts)
Bro. Lorenzo Caraway Jr.
You Have my Support 100% 9/9/11
Emanuel Moore
Richard W. Whitington
Mary Johnson
Richard Johnson
Derick L Jones

Good Luck
May God Bless You
Cathryn Octavia Washington
Much Luck with your success
Your the Best!! Sandtown

Good Luck 9/10/11 Ms. Sug

May God Bless and carry You
Your presentation is worth a return
Jesline Ortiz 9-10-11

May God Keep and Bless You + Your Business
Richardson 9/10/11

Good Luck all the Best
Wishing you Great Success Sept 10, 2011 D.M.H.

Keep up the Good Work Ms Debbie

Keep up the great Work!
Historic Marble Hill Community Assoc, Inc.
www.historicmarblehill@hotmail.com

Best wishes
Burke family

Welcome!!
What A Joyous Site
With Love Please
Continue to Make this (Baltimore)
A happy place once again
Old School M. Owens

Scott

Wonderful!
India Ortiz
9.10.11

Please to have
a Neighborhood Bakery
God Bless And
Much Success
Ms. Ballenger

Best Wishes from Tangia! Kiahanna

Best wishes and good luck to your bakery from Loren Todd + Judith Jasper of Baltimore. We hope to make this one of our favorite spots!!!

Best Wishes to this Block

Meet My family Wishes U & Your family Good luck + Susses Johnson family 2234

The Buns are hitting every time. Great!!! (K. Hopkins)

Good Luck Sept 11 2011

Hi! Made to see a Bakery Back in town Nothing But The Best of wishes N Good luck!

Blessings be upon you keep doing What you are doing!

Hello I am very glad to see a bakery back in town. That's really what I love

Me Don't Like It

Welcome to the neighborhood! Thank you for blessing us with baked goods! M. Tyler 9-12-11

"Hope you great success!!"
Paulette Barrington

Best Wishes
Betty!

Good Luck and Best
Wishes Phillip A.L. Green
MARCH-WEST Funeral Home.

Keep God first
in all you do and
the rest will follow!)
Get a website to expand exposure and
expand your social media presence
Best Wishes,
Robert Callup

BARBARA
MORRIS ♡

Good luck and
hope every one love
the avenue Bakery
XOXO. ♡

I have lived in this community
for over 36 years. I came to open
a mission, known as the U.R.C.
McCulloh St. Mission. 2112 McCulloh
we have out grown our place
and now are located as a
church at 1939 Walbrook
It is my desire to work
with all the community for the
progress of our people.
Thanks for being here
Truly I am glad to be saved.

Love Always
Bishop Wm E. Howard

Thank You 10/13/2011
For Opening
We Need A Bakery
J.M.

WHO NEEDS LUCK?
WHEN YOU GOT BLESSED
ROLLS AND BUNS
LIKE THESE!
MUCH SUCESS!
John J.

9/13/11
Thank you for resurrecting my Mom's Rolls. May God Bless all of your endeavors!
Love
[illegible]

Best Success from Sam Stackhouse 9/17/11

It's been a long time coming
Thank You,
God Bless
TEE & Family

9/17/11 May God Bless You with Success
Peace
[illegible]

Give me a wheat roll!!!! [illegible]

Great Success
Deborah & Patty

Bread pudding I got 3 in 1 day

EZ

Much Success
Welcome Home
[illegible]

Gods Blessings & Hope Pray you will succeed

With Congratulations and best wishes for much success.
[illegible] 9-18-11

The wheat rolls are so good keep up the good work please stay
thank you
Vaney Family

[illegible] Gibson
Fist Time
Thank You

Apple Cinnamon Bread pudding melts in your mouth, gotta try it ymmm ☺

Saw You on TV.
Best Wishes

God Bless you In your Business Success
Tera Atkinson
SandTown
9-17-2011

SmAPley / The Best
Bobby B.
2011

U Guys have my support "Peaches" "57"

Best Wishes
Charita Roque
2011

9/16th/11

WELCOME TO THE NEIGHBORHOOD. BUSINESSES SUCH AS THESE ARE MUCH NEEDED IN OUR COMMUNITIES

VERE EDWARDS

9/16

From Brian & Wendy Field ☺

Much Happiness with UR Business!!

9/17/11

God is still in the Blessing Business - You Are Blessed and your hands are blessed!

Continue to produce great & delicious pastries - The Best is Yet to Come

Apostle Zeldon

9/16/11

Thank God it's great to have a black owned business in our community

Much Sucess

9/16/11

"Much Luck"

I will continue to support "U"

S. Yates

Good luck hope ~~you~~ love to everyone

Heard about you thru friends Good Luck & Congratulations 9/17/2011

Ashleigh Cheek... Lean Well here !!

PP

The Best of Luck Mr Shivers

Pauline Linthicum
Rolls are like grandma's

"Great Place Keep the faith ☺"

David Martin

God Bless You.

Good Luck In Your Creative Indevor

Dana Franklin + Joan Campbell

God Bless Norman "Woodsie" Campbell + Dennis Brooks
Dennis Campbell + Charles "Buddy" Brooks
member of "the Cadalacs" (Speedo)

Kelvin Good Luck

Best Wishes

Good Luck From The Whittle Family ☺

Wonderful Addition to commitment to Upton!
Desiree ...

Tina - Good Luck in your buisness. If help is needed im willing to volunteer (443-253-4386)

09-21-11 (Wed)
A Business well needed in the area. I pray you will be supported & endeavor. YAH Bless You.
Augusta Jones-Stokes

Congratulations from PressXpress
God Bless ♡

Keep up the good work & bussiness
God Bless

Thank for coming Back home.
Andre Wilson
410-241-6925

I am graceful
Love
Sandra

Thanks for talking to the kids! We all loved it! Thanks for everything!!
Ms. Waddell

Thanks for the food
It was great
Uthman

Wishing y'all the Best
AND Hope y'all stay as long
as you can Congratulations
AND the Best of Luck
Keep up the good work!

Tony & Debby Ambush
Wishing you success from one business owner to another! 9/26/11

Keep it coming umm Good
Officer Baker CD

Nubia & Co. Jewelers
Wishing your abundance success.
Trying out the coffee & sweet potato muffin *for starters* See you again soon.
– Peace & Blessings
– Nubia & family

Wishing you all the luck
It is nice to have you
in this area of Pennsylvania Ave
God Bless you
From Ann C.
552 Gold St.

Congratulations & Good luck
From the family of Lena J. Boone
dcharlesdangme@gmail.com

Success comes from
Having the love and passion
For what you believe in doin
Good Luck

Congratalations
on
your
Dream!
M. Stokes

God Bless
You and your
family in all
of your endeavors.
Sylvia Gilchrist
and family

The very, very
Best of Luck!
I'm so proud
and impressed...
God Bless you,
Patricia from
Enterprise...

"Edward Coates
Good Luck"

Awesome Bookstore

What A Joy!

Chuck WAZ HERE!!!

To fans + Family:

The Community needs positive change and economic development that encourages Africans-(African American) to know that they can do great things. This business is a great thing. A great thing in the hood. It is monumental that you have established a community room.

Our people will give back to those that we can recognize as being leaders in our community not just by words but through positive action

"Thought without action is empty AND Action without thought is blind"

Keep Up The Good Work AND Greater Things will Happen Because You have seeded a powerful seed. Peace

[illegible]

9/28/11 Wishing you well with the store. Good luck in your adventure. KB

9-29-11 God Bless you Welcome to neighborhood

9/30/11 My family and I really enjoy your [illegible]

[illegible] & the Best

2011

Wishing you & yours the best of luck! This is a small world. Brandon's former teacher! [illegible] 9/30/11

KEEP ON KEEPING ON [illegible]

Good luck [illegible]

10-3-11 Hey Guys Welcome to the Ave. N the Name of Jesus, I wish U all success & love. May all of U're dreams b complete right here on the Ave. Keep the faith + U'll stay here. Love The Lucas's

God Bless You!!! Mr. and Mrs. Charles [illegible]

God Bless Good Luck Ed [illegible] 10/5/2011

What a nice surprise find today - Thanks be to God! Good Luck. Peace & Blessings Cindy!

So Glad you Brought it Back to the Hood! God Bless You! D. Lynch

God's Blessings and Stay Strong! Michael L. [illegible]

May the Good LORD Continue to Bless this establishment [illegible]

From a friend of the "Avenue" & former member of the Gold Street Boy's Police Club football team - Matthew "Billy" Wright

[illegible] in the World - [illegible] Blessings on this [illegible] enterprise [illegible] city - Keep up the Excellent Work [illegible] family

Continued Success Mr. Lee
Zion Towers
1100 Penna. Ave Apt 1307 Balto. Md 21201

Happy you are here [illegible] [illegible] God [illegible]

The Avenue Bakery Rocks
I Love coming here to get great sweets + rolls

Myra

Thank God A Real Bakery is in the city [illegible] Tony Harkin

48 [illegible] champ [illegible]

I'm truly Blessed & Appreciative the Ave Bakery has Come to Penn Ave Respectfully [illegible]

Blessings + Greetings to your beautiful establishment. May you go far above + beyond. Thank You!

The Birth of The Avenue Bakery

Even before it was in my head to build a business that the community in which I was conceived could be proud of; it was in my heart to feed its inhabitants—in some way—especially its youth—on the rich, cultural, and cohesive nourishment I had known so well during my formative years.

So, when the scorn of outsiders boisterously branded a death sentence upon the historic Pennsylvania Avenue Corridor, declaring that neither commerce nor community could thrive there—instinctively, I went to work. What really struck me was how folks would make the point that The Royal Theater should have never been torn down. My philosophy has been, why cry over spilled milk; let's figure out the options, make a choice, and proceed.

2016 Bakery Before/After

The building I purchased in 2004 was the Old Baker's Hardware, which was a dilapidated eyesore of a property on Pennsylvania Avenue that had big, ugly trees, a nasty, ugly building garnished with a telephone booth in front that served as central headquarters for prostitutes and drug dealers to market their goods and services. Crowning it all, high on a side adjacent wall, was a huge billboard that advertised death, destruction, and, at its least, addictive anesthetics in the form of nicotine and alcoholic products. I vowed that one day, that sign had to go.

Initially, I envisioned a business center. It would be an administrative hub for community organizations, serving the community and

James Hamlin and Stuart Hudgins, men on a mission

providing jobs, including summer jobs and job training for youth. My hope was that the State Center's project would mean the need for office space for a state agency as well. Those plans, which included business and architectural plans, took a few hits. And a challenged U.S. economy, around 2005 to about 2008, didn't help matters either. However, also during that time, I had been busy and happily delighting family and friends with my rolls and the special recipe I came up with since I never got my mom's.

It's often said that God's timing is indeed everything. Because that's when a Danny Henson simply said to me, "You've got to put something on The Avenue that people can't get from anywhere else." Knowing that one of my major goals was to right the wrong, perpetrated on this community—demolishing The Royal Theater. My (then) acquaintance and muse, who would later become a member of our project team for my nonprofit, The Royal Theater & Community Heritage Corporation's (TRTCHC) Development Project, knew that I wanted to prove that enough interest in the area could be built to make a case for rebuilding our landmark. Danny, a developer and a previous housing commissioner for Baltimore City, added, "If you want to get them to come back and rebuild The Royal …," he advised that I should supply a strong incentive right at the starting gate. My rolls, with a few tweaks, became that thing!

The Avenue Bakery Drawings, rendered by Kathleen Sherrill for James Hamlin

What a wonderful establisment!! Congrats on your success & I wish you years of more
- Kelly Nash
owner of Little Cherubs Daycare

10-17-11
Congratulations!!! We NEED you in the neighborhood. Thank God, you will be open on Sundays (beginning in November). You'll be continuing a long time tradition in our community.
An old-time resident (over 50 years on Druid Hill Ave) 2128
Mrs. Ellen T. Dutton

I'm so proud of this establishment. I grew up in the 1400-1500 blocks of Druid Hill Ave. in the 50's & 60's. Blessings to you all!
Pastor Glenda McCullough

May GOD bless you with prosperity!
- Tywanna Chrisp of NPBC

Congratulations on your Business. Everything so wonderful. God my family with you. many more years to come. We come from Loch Raven but Northern Parkway to get your wills. Keep up the good work. Good luck family

~~It would~~

It would be a blessing to be able to receive employment at this store. Thank you!
Theresa Robinson
I'll check back later!

God Bless You
Thank you For Comeing To The Avenue
The Moore's

Much Success with your Business & may God continue to Bless you, your family & this forgotten neighborhood
Mr. & Mrs. Cason

Hold the Vision...
Manage the Facts...
Know the Truth...
[illegible] 10/20/11
Naturecurehealth@Aol.com

"The Best of Luck."
Frances Staton

Good Eating

Congratulations. I am inspired by the information & renewed and proud of your success as a Black business highlighting our heritage.
Brown & Dorothy

Be Encouraged
C. White
Psalm 50

Good Luck
Vicki

Good Luck
Hilda Ellison

Congrats on your new establishment! We wish you longevity and prosperity. Arce (MSC) + Rob (School #130)

Congrats God Luck Frances P. Mendel 10/22/11

God Bless You May everyday He keeps a hedge of protection around you. 10.22.11 Ifura Cate Family

To the Hamden Family - 10.22.11 You have a wonderful Business model. God Bless You and much success. Olmer + Yvonne Phillips

God Bless Thank You For Your Service Roxanna

May you Enjoy all of Gods riches blessings! Thank you for excellent service. Peace & Blessings Pastor J. Kanley

Best Wishes From Catonsville MD R Howell

Peace & Blessings! From Johnnie an original and South African resident on 41 ... my History!!! One Love!!

May God Bless you R. Duckett

Peace Love & Blessings

11-4-11

Minister Wayne Lee God Bless!!

May you have continued success in business + in life May God's blessings be upon you Ahsad Wilkerson (Randallstown)

God Bless + Good Luck! Tony O. Dixon

Congrats!! Ms. Maybelle was here and I am hungry Tell E A Shush

GREAT NEW BUSINESS! KEEP DOING WHAT YOUR DOING!
Tim Bennett
Good looking out
Welcome
Yummy
The best
Nice people
Courte■uios and kind
Delicious
Clean
T.Williams
this bakery is one of my favorite
Best Bread Pudding in town. Taste like Grandma's!
T. Kelly
good stuff having a Flat screen T.V.
S.Williams
Peace & Prosperity
11/5/11
good business keep it up. your doing a good Job.
S.Williams
good Success Be successful
D.Muse
Congratulations
Best of luck on your new establishment. May God continue to bless you w/ peace, joy, happiness, & Prosperity!
11/5/2011
God be with You!!!
James
2012
Only God and Determination
To Jim
Great

Glad you're Here

Jammie M. Lyell

Many Successes

Thanks

BEST WISHES DOUG

ALL THE BEST Rodney Dennis

Great Job!!!

Buzz Shaw

Susquehanna Bank

Wendy Powell

Good Luck

Best of Luck

God Bless

Congratulations: Continue to Make One Step & God will Make two!!!

ALL THE BEST BRO. JAMES - MILES (BRO)

Much Success Jay Carty

Finally Made It Jim Glad you're Here! Much Success

Congradulations on this beautiful Establishment May God BLESS you all

Just on time caterers Evans

Mrs. Sharon R. Coulson Evans

May God Bless your business!

Good Luck

I luv the great customer Service and the great clean and good tasting items you have

Kim Guins

GREAT Buns NEVER TASTED SO GREAT

Congrats and God Bless

Best cinnamon Rolls Ever

Betty and family

And I thought my husband had great buns.... Martina

vantourist Lyles

Loretta Harrison

God Blessing 2 U all Larry Newton Sr.

"This Bakery Is Good Stuff!!!"

Khandi Harrison

Catherine Lyles

Glad you're open on Sunday now!

Good Luck God Bless 11-12-11

I wish the bakery many blessings and future progress. The best of luck. Evelyn

Love + Sammy Williams
2 Cinnamon Man
Good Luck

Thanks for Sunday's it truely a Blessing
Roxanna

Great Vision
Awesome Bakery
Beautiful Business
Great Success
Ms R I/II

God Bless You!

God Bless your efforts
Prime Minister Elect of Judah - Israel
Jenny m. Blackwell ... 2011
"Timmy"
Knights Templar [illegible]
5334 Maple Ave
Baltimore, Md 21215

Good Luck & Pass the Bread!

Shalom
Baruch HaShem.

yall have the Best cinnamonrolls ever
Destinee & Shona
Tee ♡

Congrats to your may God keep you open forever
Jessie Barnes

Keep it delicious!

Best Wishes & Much Success!!!

God Bless You Guys

Much Success!

Always. May God Bless this business.

LeRoy May God Bless You

Luck and Success

May God bless you in all you do.
Evangelist L. White

Much Success + Great treats!

Congrats to your may God keep you open forever
Jessie Barnes

Keep it delicious!

Best Wishes & Much Success!!!

God Bless You Guys

Much Success!

Always. May God Bless this business.

LeRoy May God Bless You

Luck and Success

May God bless you in all you do.
Evangelist L. White

Much Success + Great treats!

Peace and Blessings
To Your New Business
Thanks for Coming to the Hood!
Mr. + Mrs. Cook
Salon Blush wishes you much success!
Sierra
God is Good.
Good Luck & God's Blessing to you all
Cindy Howard Family of Windsor Mill 21244
Conney Family wishes much success!
Congrats! and well wishes
Best of Luck
Good Luck with your new business.
Betty D.
Gilmor St
Best wishes
Cincinnati OHIO

Yeah!
May God to continue to Bless YOU!!
Awesome so glad to see you and the Neighborhood Best Wishes Good luck
Thanks For Coming!
Best of Luck Kareem & Briasette
HAPPY NEW Years
The best bakery in the City Rolls Rock
Best of LUCK God Bless
Sister Joanne
Chika
Good luck
Faith
Good LUCK
Yum! thank you!!!
Hello!! Thanks & the Buns!!
Good Luck & God Bless
Best Wishes and Happy Holidays
Pearl's Place 2578 Hollins St.
Thanks for EVERYTHING!
Thanks for EVERYTHING
Wish you All Success Always
Arnold Jackson
Awesome!! & Stay Blessed
Your Wheat Rolls Are Off the!!
May God Bless You & Keep you!!
Really great

Good Luck in Your Success May God Bless Jackie & Our Church Family in the Neighborhood 32 11 Division St where Rev. Leslie Davis

Leah

"Wishing you the very best" Beverly Alleyne of Howarde Grace, MD. & Battle City Circuit Ct.

Good Luck Doris This is a wonderful addition to the neighborhood

From: Gabrielle

good job!

I'll be signing your book 20 years from now. friend 2 friend wo.

Congratulation May our Lord Continue to Bless you!

Rev. Holly

Hoping That God blesses you with business abundantly! Lord Irvin

Good Luck

11/23/2011

Really Good
Bread Puddin
Yum
Tony Matthews
&
Family

Saw you
on TV
Keep up the
great work

11/26/2011

Keisha Elliott
Veolia Transportation
2nd time in and
enjoyed my cinnamon roll
and back again

Keisha Elliott

May God Bless your Business

Pastor
Kenny Johnson
was
here

"Lets Just Support People"

It's our first visit, we are trying an assortment of baked goods and hope to be frequent customers! We've heard great things.
Brian & Jocelyn

"Where there is purpose there is life" Mika

First Time
Great Rolls

Bread Pudding
is The Best in
Sandtown 1600
Bruce Ct.
Life
Boogy
2012

Thank you and welcome to the community

Pastor Julian Rivera

Joyce Reed

Blessings & Welcome to the community

Thanks

Thank you

Wee needed this around

Congrats

To God Be All his Glory Welcome

Mr. Sykes St. James Apts

God Bless Your Journey

Nann Mitchell

Best Wishes

Vickie Lee

Dr. Charles Johnson of Palm Springs Calif

"Just stopping thru"

Best of Luck in your Business

It smells Good, Many Comments

Love, Angie Butler

Best of Business

Much success

Welcome to the Neighborhood

May God bless your Business!

DARNELL AND SHERRY 11-26-11

I Love your BreaD!

Love Gabrielle

Good JOB Avenue Bakery

Luscious Sweet Potato Muffins
Mmmmm mmm! Good!
Jennifer Coates
Sandtown

Such A Blessing
to have a Good
and Sweet Bakery
in our community
J. A. Foster

Best of luck
Good wishes
+ God Bless

Leah

Leah

Love it!
Keep up the good work

Keep up the
Good Work

EXCELLENT WORK
LET'S WORK TOGETHER
PHOTO DESIGN
AMIR MOHAMMED
410-366-6713

Eric Brown
Support Black Business!

Cathy Grant
God Bless!!

God made apples and grapes to eat The Ave. put them together to make a sweet treat
God Bless
Leon P.

To the great ones whom create the greatest tasting homemade with Love yeast Rolls... I Love them Keep up the awesomeness
Mongie
McCulloh Homes Resident Council

It's good to see a good clean honest Black business. I will support you all the way
Timothy Dean
Plus the food is good

Saw commercial on T.V. The Bakery is all that it said it would be! Blessings

1600 Bruce Ct
Bread Pudding
The Bom!

"2004 Madison, St. Marc & Rhonda
"Mini Pies & Bread Pudd'n & Sause"
The Real Deal yep!

Awesome
-Luv-Laya

Wyatt Arrington, Curly Brown, James Hamlin

2023
NEIGHBORHOOD
SPOTLIGHT
AWARDS
CEREMONY

1st Time Coming
I pray God will
Bless you and your
staff. May prosperity
cover you today and for
many years to come

Rev M. G. Wood
Providence Bapt Church
Jan 20th 2012
God bless you.

1/27/12
About time a black
owned bakery with class!!
Keep up the good job & remember quality
and good customer service.

First time here
Service looks splendid
... Business on the
Avenue 1/27/12

Jimi
Keep Bakering

Good Food
God Bless we must
Before we Ate
Min M. Merritt
Zoe Miracle Church

12/04/2011
God Bless
Cherry Hill
Shipley Family

12/4-2011
God's Blessing always
Spriggs and Watkins family

12/7/11
Kim Clary Thomas
Rosa Ryors cousin
God Bless You

12-8-11
God Bless
You & yours and
keep up the good baking
Stanley

12-7-11
Love the
Rolls!!!

M.M.SMA was here god Bless

M.BSMA was here god Bless 12/9/11

Thank you for the good cookie

Good Stuff

Aleatha may GOD Keep U

Aleen L Leake was here to GOD Bless And Keep you

Keep up the good work great job! ☺ Kemmy

May God Blessing your Mary Stanley 11-11-11

BIG UPS Love, HJ-5's

I Have Heard so much About your Bakery God Bless!! 12/11/11

A pleasant and delicious Bakery! May God Bless!! 12.14.2011

God Bless 12-14-11

May Allah (God) continue to Bless You & Yours Raymond Kamm

Thank God for Your Shop

Great Spot!

Best Wishes Rick Barth

God bless you

Many Happy prosperous Years to the Avenue Bakery

May God Bless you

I Love this Shop! The Avenue needed something Classy!

Thank you God for putting a nice beautiful Store here!

Thank you Jesus! Keep Coming!

Blessings to Your New Business May Angels Surround you!! Prosperity
P.J.
Machelle & Acree

Keep God First and the rest is History
~ B Ademiluyi

Keep up The Great work
Marcel Umphrey
www.[illegible].com

Jenn: Good Luck to you with this fabulous establishment
Fred "A[illegible]" supports you
[illegible] Archer
God Bless You

Congrats & It smells really nice in here I can't wait to try it.
Floyd

This is my first visit
Congratulations on your new business
Keep it in the neighborhood!
Blessings Angela Jennings

Congratulation on Success!!

This is my first visit and I will be back
Chris Pierce

God Bless your Company.
Yours truly
Leonardo
tv HBO
tv Series
the wire

Thanks,
R C

Many Days of Success!

From Marshall & Patricia Spence
May Our Heavenly Father Continue to Bless Your Establishment
Much success, And your serve this Community.
Keep on keeping on.
"God Bless you All"
Be [illegible] Always
Happy Blessed [illegible]

Good Stuff :) !!!

THE AVENUE BAKERY'S

LOGBOOK #2
(2012-2013)

Love Your Products
Wish you were open
more
Mary D. 1-7-12

Keep up the Goods.
McRohan Laurens St. Apts.
1-7-12

My name is author Randy Johnson I thank you for your convenience and Service... hope to see you a many more years from now... Appreciate the fact You bring it all from a vision.
1/8/12
2012

1st Visit
Keep On Pushing
on God
Got You
Remember Customer
Service First
Blessing Will
Flow

The Stokes
1/11/12

Macko Price 1/11/12
Price's Variety Str

Thank you so much for taking the time to meet w/my daughter + I on how to get started on our own business. You are an inspiration!
Valerie + Kristen Reid (1/11/12)

From the daughter,
I really appreciate you taking the time to speak with me. I learned so much & I hope in the next few years you will be able to come to Atlanta because you have heard of My Sweet Addictions & just have to have a cupcake.

The Smell is Lovely.
Its a pleasure to have
this Bakery here.
God Bless You.
Marlene Browne Apt
1613 Eutaw Pl. #203

God Bless you and Keep you, and may your business prosper
B.J. Horton

Cedonia Betts / Benny's Snowballs
1555 N. Gilmore St
Reginald Locks
1611 Vincent Court
Priscilla Smothers
3554 Duffield Av
Balto, Md 21215
Richard D. Smothers
1415 Kingsway
Balto, Md 21218
Ingrid Davis
1529 Shields Place, 21217

I Have Two Daddies: An Earthly Daddy and A Heavenly Daddy - Author Lynn Calvin
e-mail: twodaddies earthly — heavenly@hotmail.com
James Robinson - Riley Rd
Michael Stukes Sr. & Michael Stukes Jr.
David Shuster
Smells great. Keep up good work. Neighborhood needs this 2012. Wishing you much success!!!

Guest Book

Caldwell Jackson 2804 Parkwood Ave, 21217
Antoinette Powell, Mark Cottman - Mark Cottman Gallery 1014 S. Charles St. Baltimore, MD 21230
Darlene Wallace 9031 Amber Oaks Way Owings Mills Md 21117
Russell Sands 806 Radnor Ave Balto 21212
Kevin McDowell - 1234 W Lafayette Ave, 21217
Christopher Lawrence - 2714 W. Lafayette Ave. Balto Md, 21216
Lee family 2566 W [illegible] 21216
Rosalie Dandridge 2719 N Lafayette Ave 21216
I WAS LAST WEEK 7 Ellisfamil 4500 Wakefield Rd. 21216
Ashley & Makenzee Williams
[illegible] Wow!!!! The Great
Mr + Mrs Derrick Thompson - God Is Good!!!!
Richard Johnson and Corina Amato
729 N Fremont Ave Baltimore Md 21217
Vernon Carter
3813 [illegible] Rd Balto Md 21215
Mozelle E. Johnson 1161 N. Mount St.

Very Nice! Weensie

LOVE IT
MR. Rick
1316 Woodbourne
21239

All Was Well
Percy Spears

Congratulations!
Sandra Dobson

Very good Yummy :) Niat

The best buns in the World Niat

1600 Bruce Ct 4 life!!
Bobby
2012

Best Bread Pudding in town Hands down!

Marlene Arthur 1004 Stamford Rd #29
Rebecca Johnson 1616 Westwood Ave #21217
Shirley + Shantae - [illegible] Ave 21216
Nancy Fields 2858A Linden Ave 21217
[illegible] PO Box 3833 21217
Trudy Watson 5402 Jonquil Ave 21215
Winona Matthews 3716A White Pine Road 21220
Odell Reaves 8554 Hayshed Lane Columbia Md 21045
Messe Evans 2100 N Eutaw PL 21217
Tychelle y Costley 2100 Eutaw St. 21217
Naomi Wilkens 135 North Bend Rd #3C 21229
Carol Juarez 1367 N. Gilmor St
James-Dinette Posey - 7516 Haystack, 21244
Mr Richard Johnson
Mrs Mary Johnson
Vivian Barksdale 1717 N. Carey St. 21217
Michelle Aumond
Alicia Nesbitt 1701 Eutaw Pl. 422
Darrell Washington 1538 Mountmor Ct
Dorothy Hopkins 18 Lapman Ct 21228
Dee Darby 1421 Walker Ave 21239
SM Smith 531 Sanford Pl.

Smell good as soon as you open doors.
1st time here
Will return & comments.
Passed this place 2 to 3X's
had to ask someone for directions
Barbara Pickett 4/21/12
Be Blessed to meet the owner today
Cashier very friendly, pleasant.
Love to you all
God bless the business!

Thomas Glad
To have you

Kevin Brown
@ 4-BLOCK
1600

Wonderful Concept!
love the openness of your kitchen!
Be Blessed in all Y'all do!
Chef Lamont P.

MIKE
AND
TERRY
4-25-12

Iva White (legal para@yahoo.com) 4 ur website and specials
Lisa & Leslie Bundy 1513 Argyle Ave

Keep up the Good + Excellent Job!

Artis-Brian Alston
1601 Retreat St
Balto. MD. 21217
Very Good and Clean
Food is Excellent!!!

I like what you do Abdulhakil 700 Cumberland

Love your business! D Hammond (thammby@Gmail.com)

the smell is wonderfull — Rev. Roberta Miller Holy Temple Church at 594 Pressman St

Please Sell Donut
Etha
Chitnita

Barbara Robinson Love your Bus.

nellekinney98@gmail.com
Zachary Scott 700 pennsylvania apt 212
Rachelle Gibbs
Charles Jackson

I came all the way from Morgan Park because I heard these rolls were best. They are the bomb! D Jordan

Welcome — First Time Customer
OTanya Brown
Fatimah Smith 2/12/12 May Allah bless you
Cynthia Lee Evans — Holla!
Talea, Tytiona, Tyrone — DELICIOUS
Reginald Looks
AME church

WE ARE SO PROUD OF YOU AND YOUR BAKERY. GOD BLESS. AND LOTS OF SUCCESS
THE SELLONS

Good Luck!
Jones

Please Sell Donuts
Paulette

You Guys are GREAT!!! :)
Good Luck. God Bless You.
Keep up the good work. It will pay off at the end of the day. SB
Very wonderful service and delicious pastries.
"God Bless for all that store has done around the community. God bless you all."
Just what this AREA NEEDS something sweet. Good Luck.
"love From U.Y.I.P. Black owned Black love!!! Bro. Herc (443) 257-2491 let's connect"
I LOVE ALL YOUR baking 2/18/12 Gloria Cowan
Leon Henderson of west Balto. Good Job.
THANKS For Being here Love + Blessings

2/18/12
Love the rolls!
Cheryl Wms.
God Bless The Bakers. The Raisin Buns are Great. Thanks. I let you know about the Rolls. Keep up the Great Work. Monica Ross
This is our first time here and we love it!
Enjoyed the rolls — Kim Moik 2/19/2012
Excellent Mango Smoothie- Kamaron M
Loved the colors of the store, the smell (yum) the taste! Deborah M.
THANKS
GOD Bless, love all your Baked Goods Continue to bless this community. Have a great day. Purnell

Taj Briscoe was here 2-24-12 Awesome
From: Geraldine
Keep up the good work. Keep the Faith you have a very Nice Store. you Roll them Rolls

Milroy B Harried Was Here!
Jaime A. Carrington
Thanks for having me!! 822
Ronald Rawles Thanks for Having me ON 2-24-12
Class # 822 Dyshawn Sprye I Had a great time
Alonzo Lockshop of Baltimore
Derrick Cobb was here

Al Helena was here

Glad I came through today! So glad you were open!! Jill

Nice to have you as part of our up and coming neighborhood Nadine 2012

* If you Love God you will be Bless so have a nice day and Bless. God love you x D.T

God Bless your Business Amen

Good to know your business brings life to Pennsylvania Ave much success Audrey

Harvey's ate Del Best Sho Smell's Good Mikey

God Bless your Business with Love & prosperity

Best time we got a coffee shop on this street.

CAN Not Help my self I Love u Guys iN NO Body else

Love The Sherman's EAst SiDe + west SiDe

William Taylor - All I Can Say is Great Rolls Good Luck and Long Life

God Always look over the Good!!

Thanks for the cinnamon rolls they are the best! Nikki & Nasir

The food is delicious. We love the rolls.

Bringing the Avenue back to life thank you for baking + cooking it up! Mark Steiner

Support Black Businesses!!! W. Holmes

3/2/12

"I really enjoy the pastry from this shop. It takes me back to Grandma baking. God Bless to All"

OMG!! 3/2/12
Your fresh Buns R awesome!
Ms. LaKeisha DeLoatch

Pastor Terry G. Thornton
Sweet Hope Free Will Baptist Church

This is the spot for all your sweets and goodies!

"KEEP up the Good BAKINS.."

Sure smells good in here, this is my first time here. Now to see how good the taste is. Philip 2-2-12

Ricky & Jackie Sheer

March 7, 2012
We finally got here!
Fran, Dodi and Betty

March 9, 2012
I thank you Mr. Hamlin for giving back to us the community. May God continue to Bless you! Tangy Thomas

Peace is with us all, Thanks for your serving A. Wall

BUDDY was Here...

Mr. Hamlin
I am so proud of you! I stopped to experience the vision! Greatness at its BEST :)
Thanks for being an inspiration.
Dr. Evan Gudes
Principal, Booker T. Washington MS
3/9/2012

and Here.

Come on down to the "Avenue Bakery" the food is Delicious
03/15/12
Bless you
Mmm mmm mmm goooood!!
This is the best place to get your bread and sweets from, black sweet people keep on cookin'!
Best cinnamon buns
Best cinnamon rolls!!! god bless you!
I Love it!!!
Can't Wait
Can't Wait
Hmmmm
For Another bite
Delicious
I love the chocolate cookies
Nothing But The Very Best
DASSIT!

It's All in the Family—and Valued Friends

The Avenue Bakery has been about family ever since its conception. When the idea came to me, I gathered members of my immediate family in my family room to bounce the idea off them. My lovely wife, Brenda; our son and daughter, James, II and Belinda "Lin"; and my niece, Ashley Crawford, who was attending Morgan State University at the time, were receptive to the idea and willing to put their elbow grease to the test. My grands affectionately call me Poppay, so hence the star of the show at The Avenue Bakery became Poppay's Rolls.

Son,James Hamlin, Jr., Mrs. Brenda Hamlin, grandson Brandon Sorrell, James Hamlin, his daughter Belinda Hamlin, and Daughter-in-law Etoy Hamlin

Brad Redd, whom I had met when I was the second Vice President of the Baltimore City branch of NAACP and chair of the Economic Development committee, helped me put together the pro forma and business plan for The Bakery. Also, at the time, Brad worked for NAACP's national arm and was in charge of the NAACP/ Bank of America Home Buying Program. A mutual associate, NAACP Baltimore President GI Johnson, asked me to coordinate the program for the branch. Brad and I worked together there,

Son, James Hamlin, Jr., James Hamlin, Sr, wife Brenda Hamlin, Daughter Belinda Hamlin, and her son, Brandon Sorrell

James Hamlin surrounded by Family and Friends

and he was also on the Business Breakfast committee that I chaired at the Branch. Brad's help was invaluable.

Also, during the time when The Bakery was coming into being, I was friends with Omar Muhammad, who was the director of the Morgan State Earl Graves School of Business. He came up with the idea of getting his students involved from a marketing perspective. They produced conceptualized marketing plans, and my niece Ashley, whose eventual degree was in Hospitality from Morgan, became invaluable when it came to important matters of food service and was the architect of our *Hazard Analysis Critical Control Point* (HAACP) Plan which the health department requires.

My wife, in-laws, and siblings were trained and took turns manning the counter. My daughter, Lin, a.k.a. my Bakery right-hand, helped me with recipes and basic kitchen operation ideas. It was Lin, who came up with adding bread pudding to our menu of items. One day, she came to me and said, "Dad, I know what we can do with the rolls we don't sell." The idea was a hit. And soon, we were selling out raisin, apple, and peach bread pudding squares.

Also, in due time, my grandsons, Brandon and James, III, were working customer service, becoming patient pros at it, too. Our menu of items grew and grew and gained steady popularity—especially during the holidays.

And I can't forget about my UPS buddy Wyatt Arrington, and his sister, Jane, who now live in Jacksonville, Florida. They were in there, pitching in just like family, during the bakery's opening week. And they did the same for years during its Thanksgiving peak season. I still have that marble rolling pen that Wyatt gave me as a token of love and admiration. Although, to this day, I haven't told him that it rolled off the table one day and cracked in half. I still have and cherish it, though!

Today, my family and cherished supporters remain invested with their blood, sweat, tears, and contributions to ensure that The Avenue Bakery thrives.

[illegible]

Yall Hurt me by
taking off for that
week yall was Close
M Johnson
4/4/2012

Peace be still. With Patience we all grow!
Randy Johnson 3/23/2012

Elayne Young
Lived in
community 40 yrs
1st visit
Heard nothing
but good things!

Back again
got my children
Hooked on Cin Buns
Love u very
much

yeah yo!
Amen 2 that pimp!

Mr Clarence Bond
once lived at 2012 Brunt in
~~the 50's 60's 7-74~~

Thank
you for choosing
our community.
[illegible] :)

Im trying
for the first time
if it's good as it smells
I will be back
I guarantee
again/again

Thanks and
good luck
DMF.

Herb the 3rd
of
G.A.G.
Get All Gettables

Your Buns Rock!
L.W.G.T.
[illegible]

The Lee
Family

1614 Bruce Ct

+Christ

Best of Luck
much Success
for years ahead
Bert Hopewell
4-21-12

Smells
GREAT!
Jean Longo Jr.

Deacon: Archie Lee 4/13/2012
may God Bless this
Business to the fullest Peace!

To Tammy
N Freddie
N John N
4/7/2012

Best
rolls
in town
6/1/13
Nile
Tony
Yvonne

Veronica Hopewell
April 13 2012
Excellent Experience!

04.13.12
Louise Lewis, leading Lady
May God Bless you Always!!!
New Life Fellowship Church of Christ
559 Robert St
Balto. Md 21217

4/14/12
I LIVED IN THIS NEIGHBORHOOD 60 YEARS AGO. THIS BAKERY SEEMS TO BE WHAT IS NEEDED TO GET THINGS STARTED ON THE RIGHT TRACK FOR A RENAISSANCE.
THANK YOU. THIS IS GREAT.
MUCH SUCCESS!!!

"BreadPudding's"
Fantastic ONE LOVE
Bobby
2012

Got To Start
Coming 4-14-12

I Love
Summit AKP Cup

As Always
Fantastic

As You Reward Us
...May God Reward You
Us 1st & Together with
Almighty God (Allah-U-Akbar)
El Razul El Saladin El Shabazz
& Family

The Rolls are
Excellent

It's good to be back for 4/20/12
the best cookies in B-More.

1st Time B'more
Smells Great A.C.
Gimme Mine
Can't wait Bronx

Loring Cornish
Sampled your wares
at Nick Mosby's
100th Celebration
Pretty Tasty. Stopped by

1st time here

SLB

You have inspired our
neighborhood for all of
the right reasons.

4:20-4LIFE
A.W.B.

Nuke & Fruity Loop
4/26/12

"DRShake"
Whitelock City

Sandtown
Fam.

Jones Farm Future
"Uptown
Community Garden" 10 13 12
CMR

Fremont
Horse stable

Sarah
Rockville, MD

Good Luck
and may your biz
Grow Grow and Grow
to demonstrate that
if you try you can
Succeed!
God bless

Much success.
A blessing to the
neighborhood.

Hey! I heard the food
is off the chain
here. I can't wait
to sink my teeth
into the food
Much Luck
God Bless

Best in town
Bread Pudding
Bobby B.
1600 Bruce St
For Life

Best Sweet Potato Pie!
2006 Brunt St

Good luck
in the short + long term -
Sharon

God Bless you, Jesus Love you
+
Holy Spirit protect, provide, + Comfort
+ guide you
Welcome to Sandtown

God
Bless
Barbara
Richardson

Good Luck and God Bless!
Perez Family

Bree Ross love the smell good luck!!

Bless you with good business
Thanks for
Bringing History Back to The Ave

Keep up the Good
Work, God Bless you with
the amazing talent now!
Keep People Smiling

Keep up the good
work
Love them rolls

God Bless EACH and Everyone
who works Here and please stay
on Pennsylvania Ave

Nice LAYED BACK FEELING!

Great Place

Great Place!! 7/26/12
Phlunda Peel

Great Food
Mom White
Bakery + Pop's
Snowballs
The Best!!

Nom Nom Nom Nom
Cinnamon Rolls

God Bless you and your Business I love
the Sweet potato mini pies.

Nice Bakery Good feeling
Here All Items Are Made
with Love
John DeMartino
Crescent Processing

Just what Baltimore has needed! Many years of continued SUCCESS! Betsy Gardner

Be Blessed! Awesome atmosphere, product and vision! continue to prosper and progress for our community! Dawn Fitzpatrick Metro Sisters Network Balto

Bro Kirk Sutton SR. thank you

Best wishes + great success ... Family

Anastos, Amaror and the Jay Blessed

2 Jun. 2012 Wishing you much success in your dream. Keep the faith.

I love your store

Robert C was here again! Wishing you double luck!

May God Bless You with much Success Rhonda Scott

Best in town up & down & all around !!! 1600 Brucell & wife 2012

From Patterson Asbury AME Zion We thank you for you bring a sweet smell to the community!!

Best Wishes to this Place God's Blessings!

Kee Roberts, CEO Kee Roberts and Assoc. Inc gives The Avenue Bakery 6 stars!!! XXXXXX

Thanks for such lovely service May God continue to Bless you along your journey

Mark Sicilia

The Best Excellent Asset to the community!!!

CONGRATULATIONS, WELCOME TO
THE NEIGHBORHOOD
THE GORHAMS

thanks for the
Bakery - My Family

O MY
BOBA
Very GOOD
OMG
O MY GOSH

Congrats to your
Bakery
Jonah, Tonya, Chris

Thanks for those goooood
cookies they are delicious

Super good!

Wonderful, wonderful!
(Just like my mother's pudding!)

Linne

Mark Clark
keep up the good work
Thanks
2012

"Good Luck
Tee Jenkins ~~& Husband~~ Joe
Customer Counter
"UPS"
GOD Bless!!

Very, Very Good
Pastry, May GOD Bless
You & Your Staff
as well as Your Family!
Thanks Again!!!
"Mr. Haile"

good luck: 2012
from: James Thomas &
Much continued success
& hopefully a Branch
could be set up on
Bulloch County Liberty Road Area
Jandy Lloyd

Simply The
Very best
1600 Bruce Ct.
2012

Pies
go
together
Keep on Keeping on
Mike B

God Bless You
in your new Endeavor
My Mom enjoyed the rolls
Eula

So Glad You're Here
your Sunday Crew!! (always your first customers)
The White Family! :)

May God Continue to Bless
you. Sis Helen Dixon
St John A.M.
810 Carolton dr

I'm here every week getting your
delicious rolls, sometimes raisin buns
Good Luck and God Bless you and
your Bakery. J. Powell
2012

God must have touch
The Bread Pudding
God bless
1600 Bruce Ct

Peace & Blessings
the best of everything
Sis Delores
St. John A.M.E. Church

The wheat rolls are
the BOMB. I went
to bed last night
thinking about them.
To God Be the Glory
Alexis MORTON

Bless The Hands
That Prepare
And all of those that
come to Buy.
Bless You
always.
8/15/2012

Nice Clean
Bakery
much Success In The
future
7/1/2012

Good Fortune & Great Success to You + Your Family Blessings

J. Bell.

Congrats.
May God Bless
C. Milton Tucker
AΦΑ (2012)

may God Bless you forever you prosper in all you do, you & your families.
Cindy

THIS PLACE IS AWESOME!
JUST AS YOU ENVISIONED IT....
CONGRADULATIONS, JAMES!

LOVE YOU,
ANTOINE

GREAT
VERY GOOD PLACE
LOVE IT
Thank You!!

God Bless y'all
from Kings Deliverance
Holiness Church 1200 N.
Fulton ave. 410-728-8040
Bishop John Jones

Glad I have You! The food is Good.
-A.K. Scott

I AM going to Truly miss y'all
Love the Latte's
thank you sooooo much
you guys ARE the Best. Tanya (NC)
2232 Pennsylvania Ave

K. Scott
Anew customer and a good customer Soon to come Back continue The good service
Thanks

May your business continue to be a blessing for your family & the community from The Wonderful [illegible]!

Bey!

God bless This BAKERY
1600 Bruce ct.

Simply The Very Best 1600 Bruce ct

Kenya
Lil Troy
Tricia
2012

8

GOD Blest Darroll Cribb + Family

I ♡ this Bakery

Michael Tisdale
3500 Carsdale Ave
May God be the 21207
Glory!

God Bless
This Bakery

Robin A Adams
1814 Walbrook Ave (21217)
410 733-1953

Emily Anderson + Pam Miller
1703 N. Calvert St

ROBERTA L. McKinney
2949 W. LAFAYETTE AVE.
21216
Very good.

ON A RAINING day
its NOTHING like Bread
Pudding to Put A smile
ON YOUR FACE 1600 Bruce
4 life

Good Eating!
Stay in business.

Stay in business

The Rolls Here
Are *THE BEST*
Twitter: @BonnBossBaby
FB: Nadito Ledie

I heard about you from a gentleman who was a paramedic in West Baltimore for many years. ~~Best~~ Best wishes for long-term success.
Debra Lacy
Columbia, MD
debralacy@comcast.net

This is what success is all about
Denise Chapman
Baltimore, MD

Bread Pudding is delicious and sweet. Peggy ♡

Delicious Apple Cinnamon Rolls
Best on the Planet

Love the Rolls
Mrs. [illegible]

What can i say that havent already been said!
1600
Bruce Ct

It was a Honor to Visit your store
God Bless all. Pauline [illegible]
R.A.C.
B. More Leaders

To: [illegible]
You have a Nice spot

Your Bread Pudding are the Best
Mrs [illegible]

God Bless!!
[illegible]

Thank.

James & Team —
What a great place!
Congratulations!
Linda & Steven Rivers

[illegible] Success [illegible]

Wishes The Best
[illegible]

BEST OF LUCK
Pierre Stewart

Carrie Jackson
Happiness

Congratulations!!
Great Work & Dessert
Al Collins

I'm back again
Roberta McKinney
Everything is Very good!!!!

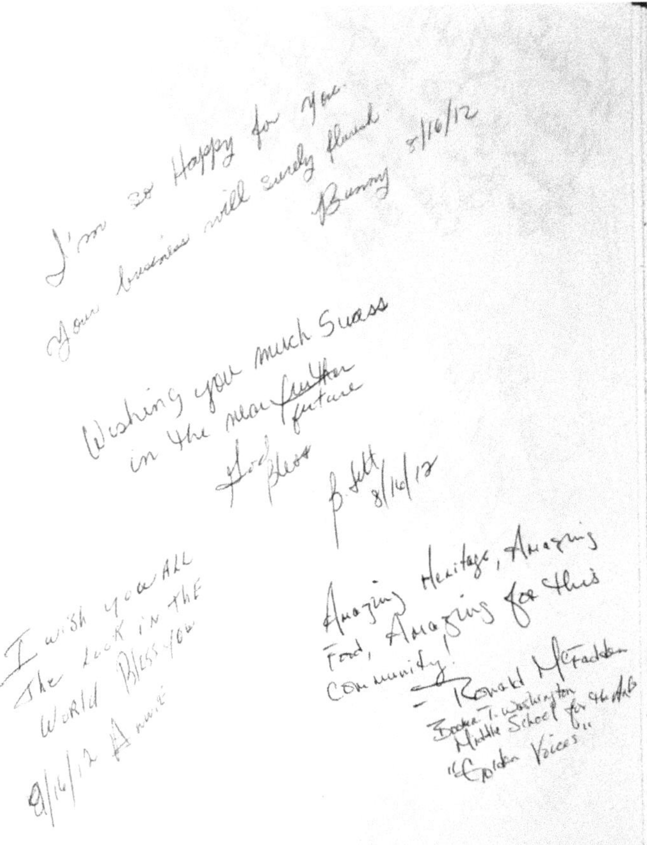

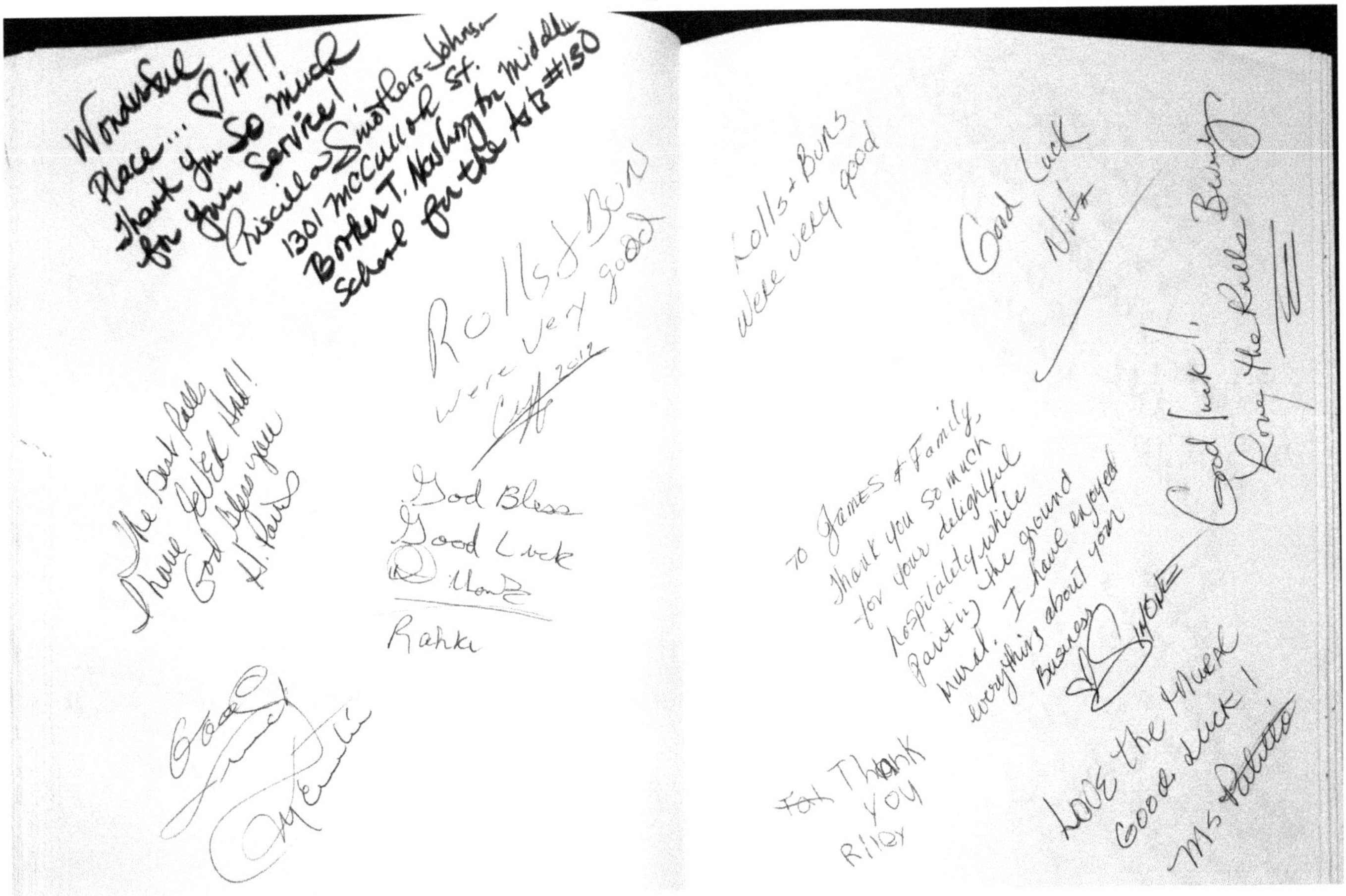

Wonderful Place... ♡ it!! Thank you so much for your service! Priscilla Smothers-Johnson 1301 McCulloh St. Booker T. Washington Middle School for the Arts #130

Rolls + Buns were very good

Rolls + Buns were very good

The best rolls I have ever had! God Bless you

God Bless
Good Luck

Good Luck

Good Luck Nita

Good luck!

Love the Rolls

To James + Family thank you so much for your delightful hospitality while painting the ground mural. I have enjoyed everything about your business

Thank you

Love the mural Good Luck! Ms

Rick Sones
Good Luck
Plumber Local 486

8/23/12 Diamond & Kelly
Nanada stumble into this hidden jewel from Philly

Yolanda Moore

Paul [illegible]

Lena & Ron Were here

God does everything well! He commands us to love and treat everyone as we would want others to treat us. As long as you let Him rule and abide, you will be victorious!
"Connie" Ross & Family

Glad to see you open! Been trying to get some of your good sweets! Came a long ways!
Gloria Hodge 8/18/12

8/18/12 Finally!! A Black-Owned Business in this Area Worth Having!! God Bless and Good Fortune!!
M.R.J.

Good Luck!
Clarence & Audino

LUV LYDIA JAMES

Alright Ya'll
Congratulations
Deborah Foster

Peace & Blessings
Christine [illegible]

You so sir!
from Ella

Good Luck always
Pat & Joe

Congratulations
Mary Parker

The best is yet to come
[illegible]

9/2012
Congra!!
God bless you and yours

9/2012
Dear Jim!
Thanks for setting the bar of excellence! This is awesome.
God Bless
Sharon [illegible]
TOP 100+

James Thomas was here
good luck

9/1/12
What a jewel to find. Everything looks wonderful. Best of luck!

Always a pleasure. You are admired by many for your hard work + vision. All the best.
Bill Henrich ("GHETTO MEDIC")

May God continue to flourish your business. Be Blessed for all that you Doin' this Community

Keep up the good work let's keep it going for another year!!
1600 Bruce Ct

The Gilyard's
Traveled far to taste a little heaven. Grew up on Pennsylvania Ave + Layotte many years ago. Great service good eats.

Best of luck in your business!! (Love the purple - my favorite color.) Looking forward to enjoying the rolls and sweet potato pies.
Norma

Shameka & michael was here 2012

My first visit here
I saw the news coverage
and from that I planned
to stop by, especially
since I live in the neighborhood
of my church Macedonia Baptist
Church of Balt. City. I hope
to visit again soon.
Best Wishes for a successful
business. Wendy Gordon

09/14/12
Best Luck
April Byrd & Barbara Bentley

As-Salaam-Alaikum
Rasul A. Aquil

DONALD HALEY
LOVE This Thank FOR
BEING HERE
Johnson family ♡

My friend Preston
got me out of bed
early to come here
I sure hope this stuff
is good! Elaine

8·30·2012
HANNAH ABRAHAM-REID
ANTHONY ABRAHAM
ALWAYS PROUD
TO SEE OUR
BUSINESSES DO
WELL!!
THE ROLLS ARE
TRUELY
DELICIOUS!!
MUCH SUCCESS!

Congradulation
A.L.P
Harlem New York

8/29/12 @10:14A
WoW! Finally
made it! I've heard
nothing but good things
about the bakery. Good Luck
Congradulations — P. Bey

Best in town ☺
Just That good
1600
Bruce Ct

Life & Co.

Congrats.
B Lou

Timothy Johnson
Born & Raise on Pen [illegible] Luck
And Bless Hope Everything
goes well

James Hamlin, Football Hall of Famer Ed Reed, and Hamlin's grandson, Brandon Sorrell

Happy Mommy's Day from Fugitive Task Force

First Time Here and Absolutely Love It! Di.

Congradulation From Simmons Memorial Baptist Church, Senior Usher board

P.S. wishing you nothing But Success

Sherry /sec

Harmon W and Jennie H Was here and we loved it!

The smell is so inviting thanks for bringing black back to the neiborhood Good luck and god bless

Denise S.

Thank for bring old fashion cakes

Damon

Looks like my mother used to make

9/14/12

Thank You for The Cakes and Pies

Amos Church Rev Hudson

May God
continue to bless
your business. Congratulations
Rev. Marguerite Campbell-Brantley
The rolls are awesome
THANKS FOR
FINDING MY
SAXAPHONE
TONY MATTHEWS
I'm
Hooked!!!
Keep it up
Love it
Kim & Rick
Jamal
&
The Boys
Welcome U to the
Ave.

11/14/12
The Avenue Rocks!!
Thank you for your commitment to the community ~
Carla Hayden, CEO
Pratt Library

11/13/12
Gayle Watkins
Window Seat Publishing
BAKENCOURAGED!

11/16/12
Jim
Thank you so much for giving yourself to the community by sharing your gifts and talents. Poppy's rolls are simply divine!
Rhonda Edwards

Lady Bree Bake

11/16/12
This is wonderful.
The best friends are made through baked goods.
Betty Stemley

11/16/12
Jim Such a blessing you are — to the avenue, the past & the future. Your dream is so close to becoming a reality.
Love ya Sunshine
Mary Welcome

11-2-2012

Thank you for bringing life to life. The bakery is awesome!
Best wishes,
Elijah E Cummings
Member of U.S Congress
(7th-Md)

We voted for you, Elijah — go go go!
Jon M Lynn say so.

This was the best Idea so for
Shirly
Thank You 4 reminding us of us...
Morton Moden Moves

Just the very Best in town no ups & downs about it
"1600 Bruce Ct."

Tevin McPinky & The Powell Family

Very Good and Delicious Raison Buns
The Shop in the world. Nice & Fresh never stale.

I finally got in.
I miss it every week
It was definitely worth the wait
J.B.

I ♥ U Guys!
See J.

I finally got to visit your bakery!
love always
The Wilson family
Sept. 16, 2012

LET THE GOOD TIME ROLLS.

CONGRAT's ON THE BAKERY
Peels
Sept 16 2012

Keep Up The Good Work
9.16.2012

God Is Good
Praise the Lord.

11/28
The
Wm C Brown
Comm. Funeral Homes
Love the Avenue Bakery!

GOD Bless
you guy, hope
you succeed! ☺

James Suggs
God bless you.

The
Branton's
Finally
Tried
The Bakery

Good
EATEN
Larry Reaves

Ray Arrington Sr.
Chloie love you
Thanks for the Memories!

"KEEP Doing THE Right Thing
GREG Gilmore Shogun's KARATE
School..

Bless the
Lord!
May God continue
to prosper in the
Business! Deac. Lowe

Eloise & Rufus appreciate the "wedding rolls"
Thanks!
Big Martin!
Little Bud
The Bakery is Smoking!
Keep Rocking & Rolling
Dogs Pound
"Thank you all!!
I Love Our History"
Best of Luck w/ Bakery on the Great Penn Ave.
"Wishing you all the best" E. Wills 9/27/12
Thanks
good luck
JOY Lewis and Dianne Lewis
May God Bless and Keep You and Your business and Family and Love one's all The days of Your Life!
Peace & Blessings
Barbara

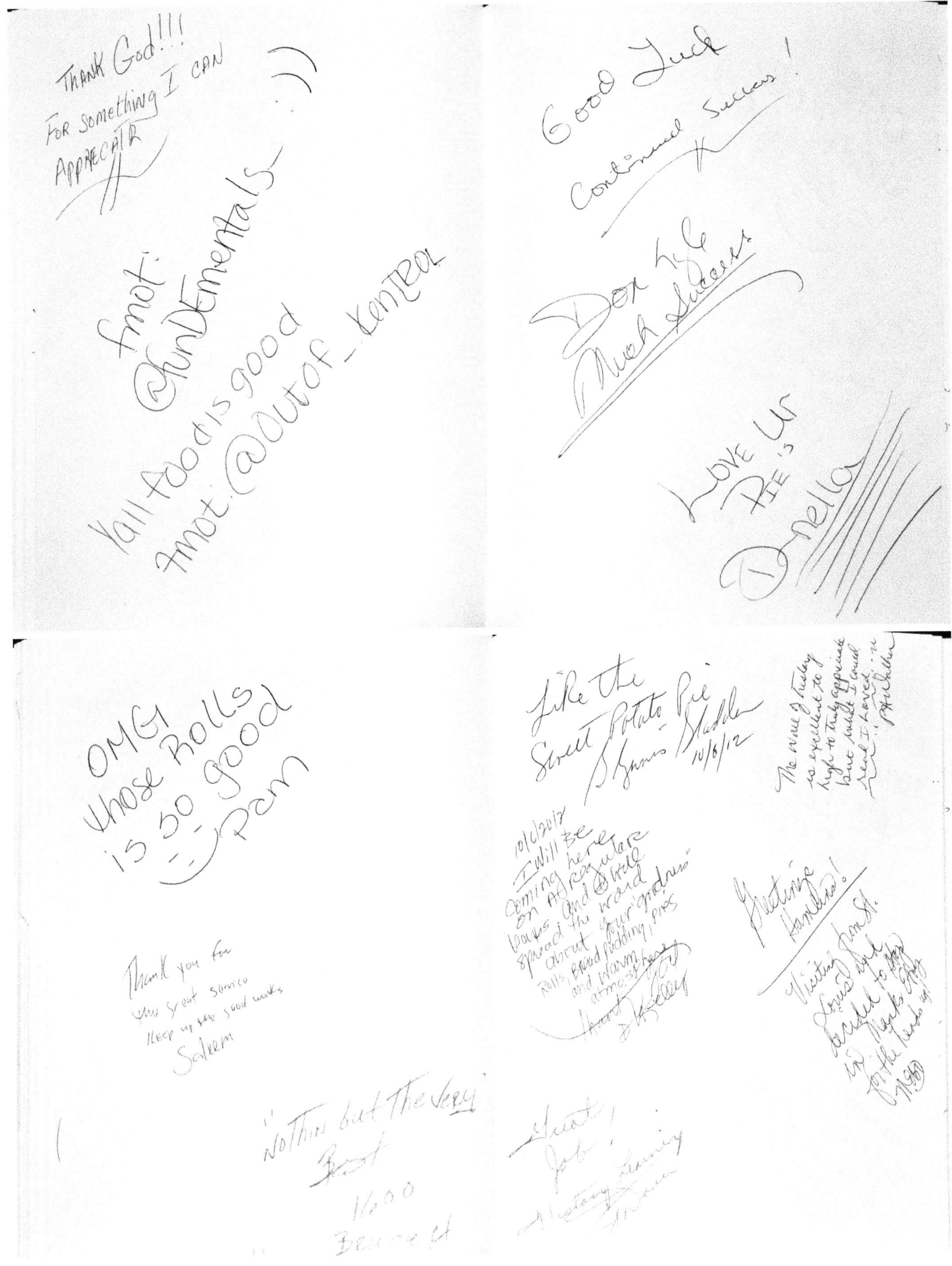
THANK God!!!
FOR Something I CAN APPRECATR
Good Luck
Continued Success!
fmot: @funDementals
Yall food is good
fmot @Outof_Kontrol
Much Success
Love Ur Pie's
OMG
Those Rolls
is so good
Pam
Like the
Sweet Potato Pie
10/6/12
10/6/2012
I will be coming here on a regular basis and will spread the word about your goodness rolls, bread pudding, pies and warm atmosphere
Greetings Hamlins!
Thank you for
your great service
keep up the good work
Saleem
Nothin but the very
Best
Great
Job!

OMG
Everything I had
was good but those
Rolls will keep
me coming Back!!!

Tijan Davis Jr
I love your
rolls!!!

Thank you
for everything you
do for our community.
Wisdom Spring
(Booker T. Teacher)

Long Time
Coming

Roll with it. Anita Fulson
Cherry Hill
Sandtown Windsor Hills
Big up - Mr. Carter Lakeland St.
Love you!

I tried the Sweet Potatoe muffin
on 9/30/12 in my Bishop Elliott office.
Spoke with my Elder Bailey to get
information about your bakery and I
am here today 10/1/12 to get my
Sweet Potatoe Muffins & Rolls.
Be Blessed
Lisa + Heaven

10-10-12
I was driving by and saw your store
I thank God that I stop in
your Sweet Potato muffin is wonderful
many blessing to your busniss
Timothy Scurry
Overlea MD

Jim,
Much Success!
[illegible]

You are great
i love your
cookieas
from, Ben
Lewis

It smells
lovely in
here
10-12-12

This Bakery is the best Bakery !!! [illegible]

Its About time
thank God

Barbara

May God Bless You

Keep the Good
Work up
Sylvester

thank godness for
having this place

By Dara
I love this
place it has
the best rolls

Me and husbands
first time here
I will let you
no next time I
come back
Shaquita M.
Jermaine J.

I love it !!

P4G
- Deonay S.

Good Day Sir
[illegible]

HOT AND GOOD
THANK YOU LORD
Theresa

Keep on keeping on n
Rock

Great taste! Just like
mom use to make!
Ivy

"Nothing but the
very best 1600
Bruceet.
L

Awesome keep up the Good
Job Tageri
God Bless
you & your
Business

Oustanding!!!!
Thomas

Awesome! first timer will
return!
Fran

I Think ALLAH
For the Good Taste you
have Here.

First Time Visitor
Everything looks great.
I want to buy everything!
Best Wishes for a great
Successful Business!

Thank You
Brent

Enjoyed the bread
and pies.
Jenaya
&
Paige

The bakery
is my everyday
stop!

10/19/2012
Very Impressive!!!
Much Success and
Keep up the Excellent
good cooking!
Yvonne + Olivier Phillips

10/20/12
Great Food!
Best Bakery - Continue
Blessings

Great Job,
Good products!
Rolls are a little light!

My Apple Pie
is The bomb
Larry Newton
God Bless U All
Keep it coming

Excellent! 10-19-12
V. Jeffries

Oct, 20, 2012
My First Impression
is A very open and well
organized atmosphere!!!
Much Success!!!

20 Oct. 2012
Very much impressed
with products, service and
the wealth of "Historical
Artifacts" provided for
our viewing
Donald Morris
1957 H.S. graduate
Lots of memories
Keep up the good
work!

My first time Here

Good to see you as always
my first time —
Wishing you the Best

Peach Cake
Smells
GREAT !!!
MUST TRY
altho
we didn't
get ONE!

November 10, 2012

I Like their
warm Rolls
Buttery,
So moist &
Yummie

November 11, 2012

I just received a grand tour of the "Avenue Market" by the owner/operator, "Jim Hamlin". I'm thoroughly impressed with his passion to keep alive the rich history of Pennsylvania Avenue, its businesses and cultural attractions.

Thanks, Jim for keeping the Avenue alive.

— Harold D. Young

11/4/12 I love the bread pudding
Michael Brown
Senator Mikulski

12/01/12
Thank You Guys.
Bless You
The Best Bakery in Town
Keep up the good work
U have Good Smoothies
12/2/12
#1 BAKERY
PEACE & LOVE
12/8/12
All the way from D.C. to try some of you goodies
Wonderful!!!
Barbara Billy Johnson
12/8/12
The place & program are awesome!
Keep up the good work!
12-8-2012
Awesome Beans!
Awesome People
Awesome Purpose.
Keep up the good work.
12/8/12
The smells grab you first!
Thank you for all you do for the community
MA, 2012
Awesome!! Thank You for the Experience. You do great work!
Yummy
Thank you for enriching the community!
Best of Luck
I love the concept and wish you much success.

Serendipity is Sweetest When Served Up with Healthy Habits

As I mentioned early on, I thought that the building and land I purchased would become a business center hub, so I sought out Kathleen Sherrill, an accomplished architect in Baltimore, to turn my vision into a viable plan. She did. However, fast forward to nearly four years later (about 2008), I found myself asking Kathleen to translate my revised vision into a viable blueprint—for a bakery.

And here's another one of those examples of God laying His foundation for one's life and passions, brick-and-mortar by brick-and-mortar. Ask anyone who knows me, how especially when it comes to business, I like to arrive early—not just on time—for meetings and events. In fact, if I expect you to accompany me to an event or meeting, you already know that I'm going to give you a time that's at least a half-hour earlier than the start time. Most folks who love me concede to roll with the punches rather than protest.

Graphic Artist/Designer Stuart Hudgins

Sometime around 2002, well before I had purchased the building and space that would become The Avenue Bakery, and before my retirement from UPS, I was invited to an event at The Center Club, located on Light Street, in Baltimore's World Trade Center. To tell you the truth, I've forgotten the exact nature of that swanky occasion. But I do remember that the invitation came due to my growing reputation as the Community Relations Manager for UPS. I also know that I arrived early to conduct my usual recon mission: discerning the layout, the attitudes of the other guests, and the general feel of the event.

It's always good to be early to get an opportunity to see who's coming in, who's feeling comfortable, who's not feeling comfortable, to assess the crowd, and everything like that. Kathleen Sherrill arrived early as well.

Just as I had with several other attendees, I walked over to Kathleen and introduced myself as, "the District Community Relations Manager for United Parcel Service."

Kathleen's face broke into an immediate smile when she responded, "Oh, my dad worked for UPS for years."

Now, *my* smile was widening when I asked, "What's his name?"

"Clarence Stargill." Kathleen answered.

"Oh my gosh, you're kidding me," I said happily because her dad and I had often worked together.

Clarence and I would sit down and counsel on different things during his time, working as one of the Loss Prevention Managers and during my tenure in human resources. He was a great guy, owning a toothy easy smile and personality. Sadly, Kathleen's father had long since passed away by the time we met. But before long, Kathleen and I grew to share stories about her father. There were some stories I didn't know about Clarence's home life. And I shared a few stories, she hadn't heard about the big, 6'2" tall man, who could have easily been a formidable lineman on anybody's pro-football team, if he hadn't chosen a career path at UPS. Everyone at UPS was fond of the man who could palm a basketball or a package in his huge hand. And, over the years, Kathleen; well, she's become like a second daughter to Brenda and me.

Business-wise, Kathleen remains our architect-in-residence, so to speak. She believes in and supports the work of my nonprofit, TRTCHC. Down through the years, whenever she's needed, Kathleen jumps in with her expertise to further its mission and foster the revitalization of The Pennsylvania Avenue Corridor.

Wyatt Arrington and Curly Brown with James Hamin, all Retired UPS Partners

Just got here it's right
12-7-12

I loved it

GOD Bless you and your family
GOD Bless your business - it is
truly a blessing to the neighborhood
Everything is delicious and you can
truly taste the Love in every item.

RAVENS
SUNDAY
12/something/12

Steelers
for
Life

TRAVIS WINDER
INSPIRED
BY
EDUCATION

SMELLS
GOOD!!

P.S. Hope
it taste better

May the Lord
Bless this Bakery
and all of the
people who make it
Outstanding. God Bless,
Madonna + Al

To GOD B the Glory
4 the MARVELOUS things
he has DONE. (Thanks)
12-12-2012

Steelers

LOVE the bread pudding.
12-12-12

Fantastic
God is Surely Good & Worthy to Be Praised!
These goods are GREAT!!
Bishop Andrew & Bishop Ronald Howard

Jesus Blessings 12-12-12
You're the Best
Steelers

Today is a great Day
Share your gratitude with
Someone!!
12-12-12

Keep on Keeping on
Rocky
12/15/12
God Bless You all!
Anthony
Steelers

Sat 12/15/12
It's nice to come to a welcome atmosphere with wonderful people.
Keep the welcome Spirit alive
Amelia 1st timer

12/15
In a wonderful mood and space.
Got my peach cake, rolls, and pie!! Rob
Staff is great!!!

12/28/2012
So proud of this place. Wonderful, wonderful pastries & rolls. Love comes to my people to help!

Best of luck
Thanks for being here

BLACK POWER!
ROCK 12-21-12
You are so nice & your food smells and tastes delicious!!
9 years old
I agree with Chelsea!

I Love Coming here
everything is wonderful
are the Staff is excellent
12/16/12

I love this bakery!

Cash [illegible]
It's smell great in here

Keep up the good WORK!!
God Bless you!
Ray Poulson

Best Wishes for the Holiday
Glenn Lyles

Thank You for my danish & pie! Happy Holidays.
God Bless! :)
[illegible]

Thank You for being taking the intention to be here
Thanks

Great addition to the "avenue" since I left Baltimore! Congratulations, good luck, and happy holidays! :)
Rhonda C. Pinkney
Charlotte, NC

12-21-12
Shirley Summerville
you have good cake, Roll + Merry Christmas!
have a Lovely Day
shirley

"Best to you"
Edward & Ruth Brown 12/21/2013

12/23/12
Hey Avenue Bakery
Just wanted to ~~share~~ that when people visit you for the 1st time they dream of their return!
The stories about you are Always packed with "goodness" — Thanks for everything!
Jackie Cooper [illegible]

12/29/12
Keith Waters
May you continue serving such goodness!

Good-n-High
My New Bakery

Augustus Roberts :)

Will
~~Was~~ Unique

this is the best place ever
Janet

1/10/13
Tasty good & Homemade Rolls
Teresa

Make more muffins
M

Valri Addin was here 1/11/13
WALTER COLLINS 1/12/13 Great Spot GOD BLESS YOUR BUSINESS!!!
A Taste of History 1-19-13

LaShaun

1/20/13 Love from Chicago! –K. Moir

01/20/2013 I hungry Open up let me in
Ronnie Hunter was here 1-25-13

MYRON L. JOHNSON P.O. BOX BALTO MD 21215

Support your own

GOD Bless you! MVA

Anthony Cook

Good Luck to you all Tony Jackson

Big Will Babylove 2/1/13 GOD Bless you!!

"Worth the wait" L.R. Lou FREDRICK Thanks A Mil

Melvin Cooley Love it! Keep up the good work 2/2/13 God Bless

The best of luck and success to you always Pat Thompson & Family

Love this Place Mary Simpson

Ms Della here again can't stop coming 2-2-13 Love this place

You ARE making me fat — but AT 60 who CARES — Love your Baked Goods J.Fisher

Good Stuff Kreative Katz Barber Shop Billy Tarrant Love THIS Place!!

Great Service

Your Cinnamon Raisin Buns are the best! ☺ The Wonsion Family

If I love nothin else about Bmore - I LOVE the Avenue Bakery 2/13

ITS SO SO SO GOOD

It's So Good

Tasty Tasty Tasty

Your Rolls Rock

Your Wheat Rolls are the best! Can't Get Enough. You have a beautiful establishment; Keep up the good work 2.6.13

Love The Cinnamon Rolls etc. Keep up Good work & I will Keep coming back

"KEEP ON KEEPING ON" "BLACK POWER"

Rock

Congratulations!

BEST OF THE BEST OF LUCK

Great experience. Information is power, We all must stand together. Adrienne

This is a very nice place! Keep up the good work!

Good Luck in all your endeavors

Think you for all the good desserts you have sold us God bless you Feb. 28.13

Keep up the Good work

Your Rolls are "sinfully" delicious! I Hope you are here for a Long Time Mr. C

31-13

JMillz

Dawn P

Gwen was here From ova East

The Best ever!

Walbrook Warrior

Debbie Jones 3-14-2013

Valerie Mooney was here

Shout out from Twon

"Continued Success" William C. Brown Funeral Home Family and Staff

Congratulations for helping to bring [illegible] back to life!

1504 Penn Ave

Brandy was Here

True Avenue Legend!

50 Sweet!

Eggie Ross Sandtown I Wish You Well

Today I visited [illegible] [illegible] will be scrumptious. Varnell

Good to be here at last!

Good Luck

Continue Success B Mason

Nice work you guys are doing Keep it flowing

Nancy Harrison

Very Colorful Very Wonderful

Jane & Naeem 4-23-2013

Wonderful

"Keep on Keeping on" "Black Power"

Rocky

Keep Up The Good Work!

Corder Corner Photography

Photos By Corder

Thanks! For Being Here! God Bless! D Barnes

Thanks for the delicious Hot Rolls, and Excellent Service Chris [illegible]

Thanks it remind me of mama rolls sitting in the back of the stove rising on Sunday Morning Thanks Yvonne Crane

Hot Rolls Thank you

It smells absolutely delicious in here. First time stopping in. Annette

Still THe Best Bread
Pudding in Town 1600
Bruce ct 4/1...

God Bless
All the Best

Rolls were the
Best
Robert West
F. Jones

We just Love this
Place.

4/3/13
This place has such a cozy atmosphere, the reminder of history makes me proud of my heritage. The sample bread was awesome. I love the history + bake shop collaboration. My dad's your friend Mr. Jimmy!
From The Barnes Family! Jessica/Lee/Jerald
Keep doing your thing + helping the community

I try to bring a steady of friends to this wonderful establishment. We appreciate this place. Thanks
A.R. McCutchen

4/6/13
I love this place!
Congratulations!!! you've saved my morning appetite.
Maria Aldana

Mariah

Love this Place
Much Black owned and Proud
God Bless y'all

Hi! Thanks for opening this place! I love getting the poppy seed buns on my way to the library to study Korean! I love the ~~taste~~ taste and the hospitality!

정말 감사합니다!

(thank you very much)

^^

4/20/13

-Tammy

Hi!!! Thank you for the pound cake and poppy seed buns

4/21/13

~~[illegible]~~

-Tyroin

Hi!!! Thank you for the choclate cake I love the taste of

[illegible] April/13

My name is [illegible] and I absolutely love love love the lemon pound cake (bread puddin sauce) its delicious. Wishes you much luck! Continued Success

Best Coffee in town and ahhh the Dinner rolls

Norma G

I JUST TRIED THE PEACH UPSIDE DOWN CAKE. IT'S PEACHY!!!

JOEL

KEEP UP THE GREAT BAKING.

I was looking 4 Coffee and here you are. THANK YOU.

4/21/13

I really enjoyed reading the wall. For over 30 years I lived in the Community. Now, I feel good. Creations are. Signed [illegible]

I LOVE THE BREAD PUDDING JUST LIKE GRANDMA USED TO MAKE

MARTIN [illegible]

"2013"

Part 1

My first time! The sweet potatoe pie looks Yummy. Will get back to let you know next time. Same place Part 2

Its my first time IN the New store I tried the apple pi's its AMERICAS Best

Jon

I'll Be BACK

This is my 1st time coming here I think I'll come back soon

-[illegible]

I love the Apple Crumb Pie, I cant discrib the taste

Artie

Aaron Brooks

To God Be The Glory
James

Jill Bailey 5/1/13
Keep up the good work

2 May 2013
What a beautiful spot. Keep up the good work!
Matthew, Maggie, Kirk & Margot

Thank You
Stacie Peeert

Mr Mychael Jackson Was Here

Tim Dimpley Black

"Please Bake Some Red Velvet Cake"

To Whom Blessings The Elders Blessings were Dreamt and Became a "REALITY." For Home and Community.
Stan Myers
Carlos 20

"GOD is Great
his love everlasting
be blessed in his Glory"

Let's keep this bakery open + successful
C. De Ford, ABCPSR

This place is great! I would live in here & live from old school B-more. I love it.

Great food!

Best wishes from the Wonson Family

"The Best Rolls"

I'm so glad that we have a bakery in our community! Keep doing what you're doing!
The Thompson Family

To God Be The Glory
The Very Best To The Business
Employees, Community; Families
Delegate Melvin L. Stukes
Dist #44 Sat May 11, 2013

Coach Nate Edmundson

To the "Blessed"
You, The Owner is Truly Blessed. GOD saw and he heard what you asked For. He said, "Knock & The Door will open!" Ask and he will deliver. May GOD bless your new business.

I Luv everything that comes from this Bakery
Annie Bond

I love the Manner's and politeness of this Bakery
Fast Eddie O.

Praise God from whom all blessings flow. Excellent food. Pleasant disposition of staff. Clean facility. The increase came from God
Blessings, Vickie Coates

Love the revamping of the history. Had an educational moment. Love the cleanliness of the place.
Tracey Adams-Watson 5/23/13

The food is wonderful and great service provided
[illegible] 5/24/13

I love the Service, Smell, professionalism, and the Great look of this Bakery!! :-) I Thank God she is a wonderful women in God. We pray 100 % anointing on this business.

I Love your Place
Keep up good music
it is very nice good
for the young people
[illegible]

1:25pm 5/25/13

Keep on Keeping On! Dear Paul.

Visiting from Miami
Great Service :-) !
Kevin W. & Family

Very good Service - Josiah Age 11½ Wade

I Luv everything that comes from this Bakery
Annie Bond

I love the Manner's and politeness of this Bakery
Fast Eddie O.

Praise God from whom all blessings flow. Excellent food. Pleasant disposition of staff. Clean facility. The increase came from God
Blessings, Vickie Coates

Love the revamping of the history. Had an educational moment. Love the cleanliness of the place.
Tracey Adams-Watson 5/23/13

The food is wonderful and great service provided
[illegible] 5/24/13

I love the Service, Smell, professionalism, and the Great look of this Bakery!! :-) I Thank God she is a wonderful women in God. We pray 100 % anointing on this business.

I Love your Place
Keep up good music
it is very nice good
for the young people
[illegible]

1:25pm 5/25/13

Keep on Keeping On! Dear Paul.

Visiting from Miami
Great Service :-) !
Kevin W. & Family

Very good Service - Josiah Age 11½ Wade

THE AVENUE BAKERY'S

LOGBOOK #3
(2013-2015)

5/25/13

Anthony, Lisa, Rashad

Heaven

Tony Smith, John Doe

We were blessed to get some good food to eat. What a Wonderful thing

Love Yall

5/25/13

Thank you Mr. Poppay for the Buns!

5/26/13

Good Cookies

Ahmed Nevek

June 1/13

Shahaadah

was here!!!

6/1/2013 Awesome cookies!!!

Awesome!!!

S.F.

Awesome!!!

6-13-2013

Shaquita Matthews

Daron Matthews

Jermaine James

Jackie Haynes

Best fresh everything

I could be here all day! Faye Powell DC/MD

Excellent Bakery Goods

Kim Wilson - Love this Bakery 6/15/13

Marsha Sutton Delicious!! :) 6/15/13

THE PIES ARE GREAT! Tre

My family loves your pies! - Tanea

The Sweet Potato Muffins are off The CHAIN

Delegate Melvin L. Stukes

Sat 6/15/20

HAPPY Father's Day

6/2013

Welcome To The Avenue Bakery Home of Poppay's Rolls

Katrina Brown

Tori Brown

Devin Adams

Christine F. Brooks

Patricia A. Edwards

Mr & Mrs. Mays

Lakiah Pittman

Jewel Crum

Mr. Hamlin,
Please call me about a fundation dedicated to reaching the children in the community. pls call Jewell [illegible]
443 739 3529
[illegible]@yahoo.com

Glad to see that things are going well.
Sorry I missed you...
Miss you, Antoine

I travel the north of Randallstown to be in this part of downtown. I appreciate the ambiance & your presentation. Love your rolls. Keep [illegible]
[illegible]

Mr. Hamlin,
Thank you for welcoming us to the Avenue Bakery and for all you do to build strong neighborhoods and communities in our City. Be [illegible]
[illegible] 7/1/13

Wow!! First time here. Brought a lot brother-in-love caught me. I will be back!! Thank you! God Bless
Valerie Wilkerson

I just love this place!!!
7/9/13

Mr. Hamlin,
Thank for all you do for our community!
Keller 7/1/13

Thanks for a wonderful establishment. Reminds me of old times 7/13/13

[illegible] 7/13/13
[illegible] of [illegible] Associates
God Bless

Keep the Jazz Alive
R.S. [illegible] Jr

Please stay open for the people of color
Ben Burns

James, Keep it coming!!!
[illegible]

The Best Bakery Ever
Em Em good
[illegible]
7-7-2013

Love your poppy rolls
Thanks [illegible]

Love your food
Keep up the good work. It's my 1st time love it!!!!!
God Bless
Kemp[illegible]
2013

My first time but it smells delicious in here and ppl are very pleasant
[illegible] 13

I have NOT EATEN Rolls this Good
SINCE PERKINS SQUARE Baptist
1982

First time here
Just to see what you are about
Maria 7/19/13

Kevin
?

First time in.... and I Love the vibe: small place but big vibes. Love realness – keep it REAL!
David Ross

Loved the Sweet Potato Pie
delicious
Carter

(WINNER)
Rodney K. Martin
What A TREAT
Doing it good
in the HOOD.
7/21/13

Heard about you
Now I too, are
Ready to spread
the word!!!
Kenny
7-21-13

Congrats great site and location Phinehe Orp

Way to go! B Happy

George Chair

I LOVE the BREAD PUDDING TRY IT YOU'LL LOVE IT. MARTIN. H

God bless

Listen to Him

Shermca Bushard you don't know but only him

THANKS Tony White

Thanks for hosting us! TFA Baltimore

Congrats Debbie on your Happy Business Lee

My son loves the Smalls pies he calls them secret pies

I love your Rolls!! 가게 정말 감사합니다!

OMIOM GOOD!

TASTY!

IT'S ABOUT CHANGE!

I love your cookies coffee and everything

Jermaine

Can't wait to try my lemon pound cake

Jim,

Great Food

Great Atmosphere!

Thank you for investing in our PA Avenue, West Baltimore, our City!

I'm so proud of you!

Anthony McCarthy

27 JULY 2013

GLAD TO SEE AND WISH YOU NOTHING BUT THE BEST

Melvin Lucas

Peronica Fleming

Love This Bakery

You guys are The Best

God Bless you ALL

Pastor Ron Edmonds was here! several Times

redmonds21@hotmail.com

The baked Goods are Delicious!! ☺

I Tell everyone I Know about you.

~~Customer Service~~

The Best!

You remind me of some place I've been back in Time ☺

TO Mad is on EOIwu FOOD

Good Job

Hello nice bakery

8/15/13

THIS IS MY SECOND VISIT AND THE FOOD HERE IS DEL——OUS AND I WILL RETURN AGAIN!! I WILL TRY A DIFFERENT FOOD EACH TIME THAT I VISIT.

V. Halsey

8/15/2013

Celestine Howard Columbia, Maryland
Carol Howard Atlanta, Georgia
Clara White St. Petersburg, Florida

Excellent Bakery Goods
Excellent Coffee
Excellent Service
Friendly Atmosphere !!!

Beatrice Wiggins of East Baltimore
have yam pies & buns.

Pauline Linthicum

8/16/13
Praise God I finally made it here when they were opened... it smells Heavenly can't wait to order and enjoy. Amen
Mary A. Whalley

Ummm Ummm good!!!

8/16/13
Rue Wright
God Bless

To God Be the Glory

Please Stay.

Robert Roslyn Turner

Jim: I finally get to not only eat some of poppy's rolls again, but this time I get to sing for my dinner. Thanks John Milton Mosley 8/17/13

8/17/13
Awesome - Dr. Dennis Stokes

08/17/13
Thanks for keeping our history alive.
Wonderful event ~ Gail Robinson-Brown

8/21/13
Thank You For the Love
R. Hunter

Cherrylle C Burge
August 17, 2013
Wonderful place to be!

8/19/13
Was so lucky to be here on a Monday!
I feel so special that he opened!
just for me! HaHa For Booker T. Washington
Thank You! This is a Middle School
Special Place! Teachers!
Priscilla Smothers-Johnson ☺

Loves
D. Rolf

August 25, 2013

Love, glacia!

I Love the chocolate chip
cookies and strawberry cheesecake
roll!!
yummy!

8/29/13

Thanks be to God for
the blessing of a good
bakery near by.

Trusty
Taste so good.

8/29/13

It's wonderful to have a nice
black owned clean business on
the avenue - we'll be back. Yea!!!

Robert The Smith Sisters
From Towson, MD

Thank Jesus!!!
for these beautiful
tasty deliciouse treats
please you don't
let them leave!!

Vint Hart

August 30, 2013 at 9:57
Annette & Mr Walter
was handing out. A good
older friend whom I run came
for decide to try out our New
Bakery on the mall. Peach Cake
Pineapple upside C
and Oatmeal Cookie
I will let you know how good it was
next time. Thats what it about
support each other especially of the
food good

Best Wishes
IN All YOUR ENDEVORS
George H. Knight (Joe)

Good Job Keep on pushing
Anthony Williams

Thank God FOR This Good
BLESSING Here
Bishop William A. Thomas
St. Matthew's Church

Robert
Best pie
Robert

TABANSI OBIALO 9-1-13
PITTSBURGH PA
EVERYBODY EATS WHEN THEY COME
TO MY HOUSE

What a place. Love YA!

KAKA BRUCE
Pittsburgh, PA 9-1-13

Christine F Brooks 9-1-13
Thank God for the Bakery
Chris

Nichelle Hicks

Good & Enjoy the Rolls
BVS

9/7/13
Best bakery
in Baltimore!!

The God is GREAT!
May you continue to
enjoy His Blessings
Bro Khaleea Muhammad
9/7/2013

Love This place
Please Keep it open!

The Best
Pies On the
West Side!!

God Bless
& Keep up the Good Works
9-7-2013

Best Wishes
Wendy Gordon
Macedonia Baptist
Church

MS Maybelle
loves Yall!!

GREAT PLACE! LOVE IT INDEED

Silver Spring MD.

Love the Look

Love the restaurant style

Haven't tasted yet, but when I return I'll share

Louis & Elizabeth

Rolls just like my grandmother used to bake

Yummy Yummy these sure are good

Elizabeth

Keep up the Good Work

These are the BEST, BEST, BEST BUNS EVER!!!

Arlene W.

Everything is wonderful

It Looks Special

I really love it

GOOD LUCK

9/15/13

The wheat rolls were delicious. Reminds me of my grandmother's rolls. Wishing you the best for your business!!

Michelle

9/15/13

I have not tasted the rolls yet. However, the atmosphere is very positive from the customers. The church ladies are the best.

Marsha Moore, Dallas Texas

they are absolutely delicious

19 Sept 2013

Wonderful treats to eat!

Gerri Kennedy

GREG GILMORE

GREAT TREATS

Keep up the Good Work God Bless You

Love the Place

Keep up the great work

Love the cake

Clifton Mayo

9.20.13

10-31-13
GREAT DAY
GREAT BAKERY
G.E.G.

Grabbed some menus!
Love My City!
-Miss Lisa Holly

TyRone & Veronica Ross
From Seattle, WA
Thanks good Bakery.

Best Sweet Potatoe Pie! 9-21-2013

Best chocolate chip cookies!!!

After eating your pies and buns its a taste that u share with everyone

I Love this place!!!

Thank you for allowing us to come visit.
Little Flowers ECDC

Best butter pound cake I ever had
D. Allen

2013/9 First Visit

Ditto on the
• Coffee
• Rolls
• Pound Cake
• Sweet Potatoe Pie
J. Givens

Best Coffee in town
Texas

Madis Freeman

Best Rolls in town (Taste like Grandma's)
The Gatewoods

BW Love your Butter Cake Signed Dianna Marlow & AJ

Butter Cake Signed [illegible]

Perfect Butter Cake

first time!

will keep comming back

Joe!

Brooke Price — I Love Sweet Things

Congrats [illegible]

10/19/2013

Eliffah Richardson

Ummmmm Good!! Lee

We wish you the Best, It's good to see you here. God Bless ☺

"The Best" Lomay Fonville

Eastside Good Luck

Very Nice & I'm telling everyone ♡ Tayia Walker

Good Sweets Reminds me of Grandmom's Cooking

I Love Your Sweet Potato Pies They are Great Debbie

Best Baker ever!

Peace & Blessings!
Keep Penn Ave Alive!
JKJ

Keith Lucas
Good Luck
Blessings Day

You are greatly missed, when you are not open. ☺

Nov 2, 2013
What a great place! It fills me with pride. We wish you much success and we will definitely be back
Dwight & Sheila Williams

Nov. 2, 2013
A wonderful place, amazing, & great happenings, success for the future.
Keith Henderson

First time!!

Jackie & Larry
1st Time

Madisyn

My Brother + Sister-N Law
I am so proud of
Love
Sandra

Nov 3, 2013
Peace and Blessings to you and your family always. May the Lord keep you in Business for as long as long
Love,
Jeannie Williams

Nov. 3, 2013
Love, Peace, Health, Happiness & Prosperity!!
We are so glad that you are continuing our "History". We have such a rich heritage!!
"Harambe" — Let's all pull together!
Bea Williams
Mia Pluim
Charlotte McCulloch

Rev. Minister ... Nov. 1, 2013 — To God be the Glory

My Start at UPS—Hey Brother, Sure I Can Give You a Lift?

Retiring in 2003, I had had a great thirty-five and one-half-year career at United Parcel Service. It had its ups and downs, like any career would have, but that's to be expected. I started working there on November 13, 1968. The year 1968 was a big year for me. It was also the year I graduated high school and got married. But the weird thing was, I was not looking for a job at the time. I was working for *The Baltimore Sun* in an apprenticeship program to become a printer. Like most jobs of this type, the new guys work at night. Working at night was not an issue for me because I worked nights at Mount Vernon Textile Mills during my three years of high school at Baltimore's Edmondson High. Prior to that, as a child, I spent many nights changing diapers and feeding my infant brothers and sisters; that's another story.

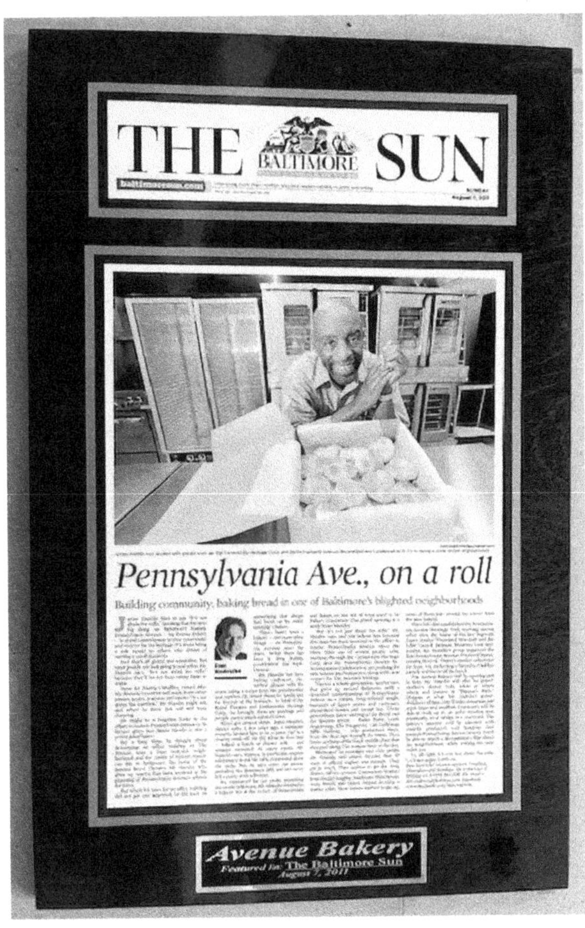

However, while working at *The Baltimore Sun*, my best friend, Thomas Lewis, who lived across the street from me on McCulloh Street, stopped by the house to tell me there was a job that paid $3.45 an hour. He wanted me to give him a lift over there so that he could apply.

"I need a ride out to the place," Lewis said, "If you have the time."

Sounds strange now, but back then, the minimum wage was $1.25 an hour. And I was making a decent wage at $2.25. So, I wasn't looking for a job. At that time, Lewis didn't have a car, but I did. We were both nineteen.

I took him out to Moravia Park Drive to apply for a package handler job. Well, I got bored waiting for him and decided to fill out an application. This meant I would be interviewed, too. I will never forget that experience because that was the first time an African American interviewed me. And I'll never forget the interviewer: Willie Mann. Willie was a young guy, about in his twenties, weighing around 170-175 pounds and stretching upward, past six feet tall or so. He was dressed in a suit and tie. But the biggest thing I noticed was that he wasn't, as we used to say, "light and bright." Sometimes for African Americans who moved forward in corporate America, looking closer to White was a factor. But Willie Mann was my complexion. In addition to how he was dressed, also impressive was the way he spoke, moving about in a company that had African Americans in management.

Again, the year was 1968. Rev. Dr. Martin Luther King Jr. was assassinated just months before my encounter with Willie Mann, and a lot of companies were not hiring Blacks. The next thing that impacted me was his assurance that there were advancement opportunities as well. And I had always wanted to have a job where I could wear a suit and tie.

This suit-and-tie thing came as a result of looking out the window of our second-floor apartment on Argyle Avenue, watching for my mom and stepfather, James Crawford, to come home from work. At the age of ten, it was my responsibility to babysit my brothers and sisters: Tony, Ricky, Eldora, and Sandra, and to have dinner on the stove by the time they got home. While looking out the window, I used to see people coming from work in construction-job attire; many of them had other labor jobs as well. But what most impressed me were those who came home looking sharp in suits and ties. And they weren't preachers. Keep in mind that I was living in a segregated community, so whether or not a person I observed was a doctor, lawyer, or a ditch digger, the major point to highlight is that we all lived in the same community. Of course, it's not like today.

While you've heard of white-flight, there's also upper-affluent flight. As families of color began to do better financially, coupled with the end of (or supposed end of) segregation, it was only natural for families to seek better places to live.

Sadly, such a natural phenomenon means that the wealth of positive images vanishes before the eyes of those who are left without options.

But as for the youth of yesteryear, we had plenty of positive images and examples to emulate. They were working folks we could aspire to be like.

The night after we completed our application and were interviewed, I received a call to start work. However, Lewis had not gotten a call at all. I felt pretty bad about that but decided that I would take the job. I gave my notice to *The Sun* and started my journey at UPS. I felt better about the whole thing when Lewis later landed a job at the McCormick Spice Company. McCormick Spice paid well and had benefits. As a true friend, he had encouraged me to take the UPS job, and it did not affect our friendship. However, I tend to discourage young job seekers, including my kids, from taking their friends to job interviews.

When I reported to work the first night, I became even more impressed with the company because my supervisor, Eddie McClurkin, was also African American. Having only his name, I had assumed otherwise. At the time, I had not heard of any African Americans named McClurkin.

My first night on the job was exciting. I was given safety instructions and training methods on how to unload trailers. This was not the suit-and-tie position, but I felt that one day, it could happen for me here. Making $3.45 an hour was like hitting the lottery. Mr. McClurkin, Ed, as he preferred to be called, was delighted with my work from Day One. It seemed I could unload trailers faster than what was required. As a matter of fact, in some cases, they had to tell me to slow down so that the workers sorting the packages could have time to read the labels. The pace of my work was derived from the experience I had gained in my very first job.

In 1961, my family lived at 2000 Druid Hill Avenue on the third floor. The three-story rowhouse was across the street from Archie Laden's corner grocery store. Mr. Laden was a short, round Jewish man who always seemed to be gnawing on a big worn cigar that stuck out of the corner of his mouth, twenty-four/seven. He was heavyset and bald with a layer of hair around the sides of his head.

One day, at the age of thirteen, I asked him if he had a job I could do. At first, I was a little concerned because he had a big Boxer that I would often see him feed in the store's backyard. Although the dog didn't seem vicious, and I normally did well with animals, I cautiously decided not to let that deter me. I inquired, and he said, yes, he had a job for me.

"Report to Henry in the backroom," Mr. Laden said, chewing on his cigar and pointing the way.

Henry was an African American young man in his early twenties. Henry taught me how to clean fish, quarter chickens, and how to wrap products up for customers. Sweeping the floor and cleaning the place as well as occasionally helping the little old ladies in the community carry their groceries home was also a part of my job. Besides learning a strong sense of responsibility and a strong work ethic, Henry also taught me a sense of urgency. Whenever I had to cut up chickens or clean fish to fill a customer's order, Henry would always be there to say, "Hurry up, hurry up." Because of this, I got so good at cleaning fish; I could scale a fish, and throw him up in the air, cut off his head, and filet him before he hit the table. Well, okay, I'm exaggerating a bit—but not by much.

Well, needless to say, I've held on to that sense of urgency ever since, and it served me well at UPS, eventually operating The Bakery, and in my mission-drive to do whatever I could to lift up West Baltimore. While I was working at UPS, I allowed myself to feel like I was finally accomplishing a firm financial footing of things. It really allowed me to take care of my young family and move my family forward. Today, that same sense of urgency and passion fuels my desire to see the revitalization of a community I love.

The Awardees

James Hamlin & The Avenue Bakery

DRUID HEIGHTS

www.theavenuebakery.com

James Hamlin owns The Avenue Bakery on historic Pennsylvania Avenue in West Baltimore and founded The Royal Theater & Community Heritage Corporation, which is dedicated to reviving and rebuilding the historic Royal Theatre. The Royal Theatre was one of dozens that made the Avenue a thriving hub for Black businesses, and world-class arts and entertainment. James is passionate about preserving Pennsylvania Avenue's legacy and has hosted a jazz concert series in the bakery's courtyard, gathering renowned musicians and the community to celebrate Black artistic excellence. The Bakery is also home to books, murals and signage that tell the story of Pennsylvania Avenue and James regularly gives tours and talks to visitors—who have come from across the country and as far away as Canada, Sweden and France. Pennsylvania Avenue was designated as a Black Arts and Entertainment District in 2019 after many years of organizing, demonstrating the power of James's vision.

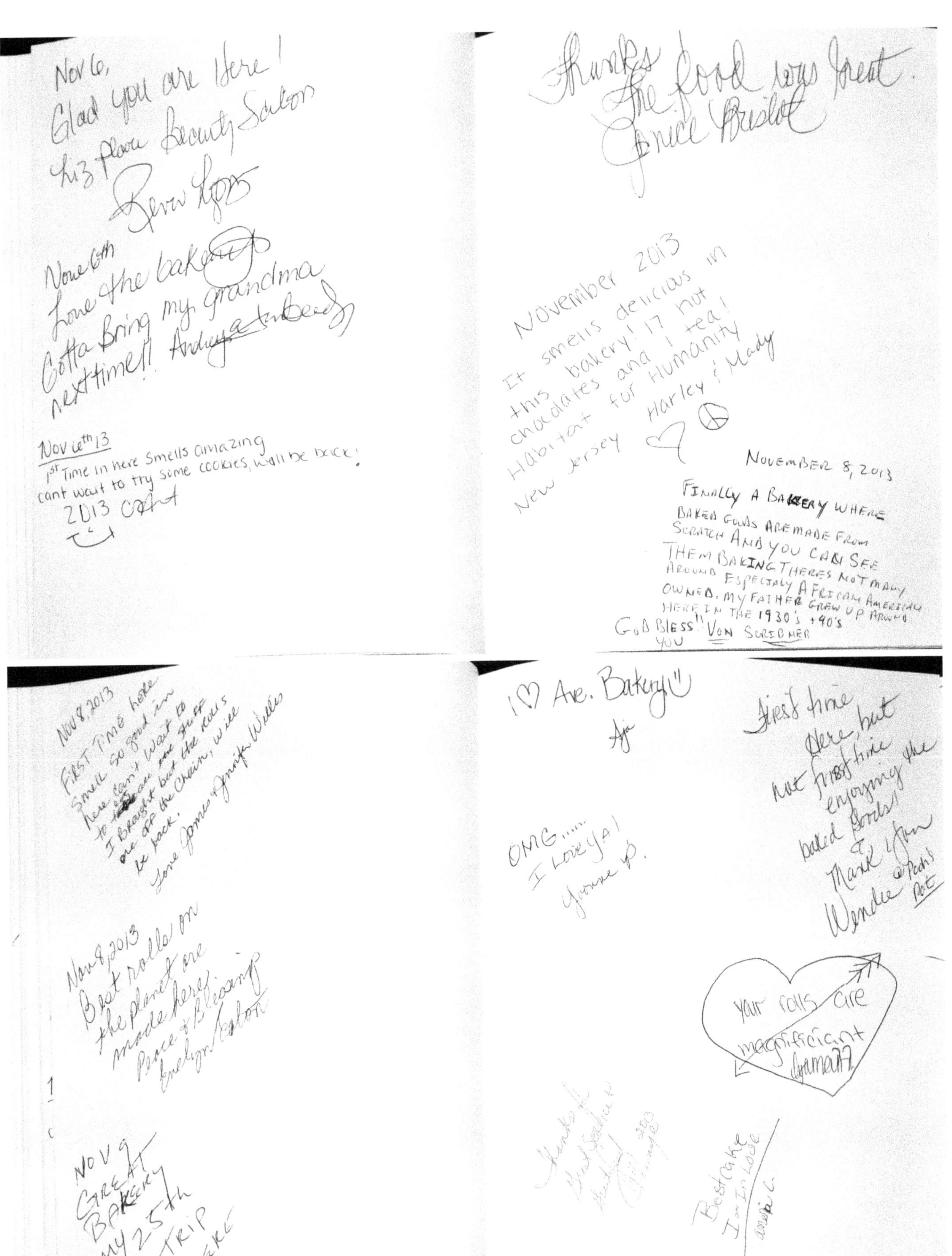
Nov 6,
Glad you are Here!
Liz place Beauty Salon
Nov 6th
Love the bakery
Gotta Bring my grandma
next time!!
Nov 6th 13
1st Time in here Smells amazing
cant wait to try some cookies, will be back!
2013
November 2013
It smells delicious in
this bakery! 17 hot
chocolates and 1 tea!
Habitat for Humanity
New Jersey
Harley & Mady
NOVEMBER 8, 2013
FINALLY A BAKERY WHERE
BAKED GOODS ARE MADE FROM
SCRATCH AND YOU CAN SEE
THEM BAKING. THERES NOT MANY
AROUND ESPECIALY AFRICAN AMERICAN
OWNED. MY FATHER GREW UP AROUND
HERE IN THE 1930's + 40's
GOD BLESS!! VON SCRIBNER
YOU
Nov 8, 2013
First time here
Smells so good in
here
I ♡ Ave. Bakery!
First time
Here, but
not first time
enjoying the
baked goods!
OMG.....
I LOVE YA!
Nov 8, 2013
Best rolls on
the planet are
made here
Peace & Blessings
your rolls are
magnificent
NOV 9
GREAT
BAKERY
MY 25th
TRIP
HERE
Best cake
I am in love

Smallory can't get enough of the rolls, bread pudding and pound cakes. S.W.C.

9/29/13

Johnson Jones 15 and Tony

Serena Campbell Very first visit. Such a delight 11/14/2013

Vicky + Mike Got a taste of the new Bakery. 8 mile

OHH!! SO Good

Tina

Best Food in town

Crystal + Joelle was here first time visit but well not be the last. Thank you Thank you and Thank you

Yummy rolls!!!

Peace & Much Love

It's GOOD

God willing Best Holes

Larry NYC

THE SWEET IT AND good BAKERY in B'MORE

Welcome 2 the New Avenue

Best Bakery!

With All Respect "2013" God Bless

Wonderful! CMB 11/20/13

The Best Bakery yet!! Chantelle Dett 12/7/13

A dress so sweet in love!!! Blessings to all

Great Wonderful Thanks R. Henderson 11-23-13

Great Bakery

Friendly Service

Thanks for Being in the Hood! Rox (Wilmington, DE) Roxw1962@gmail.com

Best rolls in Town Anthony

Thank you for the wonderful rolls!! my mother was taken back to the "Day"

Ewy Elvis

The rolls are so good we are taking them back to Michigan to share with the family. I do not get home now

The Prestons

One of the Best Bakery's Ever. Thank You! Harvey Brownell 12/2013

WELCOME 2 the Avenue

The Best Charles Owens

1709 Baker st

MSBrown 9563

Jim & Brenda — love the Rolls & all you do... you are Awesome! :)

Brenda McKenzie

A lovely place, smells like home was all the wonderful baked goods

Just marvelous Shell share & return

Peachie's Sandtown

Wonderful Bakery, The Royal will stand again yeee Normalee Young 12/11/13

The staff were very customer service friendly

Paul BRASWELL AFRICAN AMERICAN ART Collector

PW BRASWELL

Love you Every thing

Delicious Rolls! Great Service! Beautiful Art and History!

Thomas Coplin

Much success Pat Jones

Best Wishes and continued success with your wonderful business! You are an asset to this community!

12/11/13

I pray the Lord's blessing on your business & brand.

Thank for this bakery this is the best. Laquinda ... Tony Lucas

Thanks to bringing this bakery here to us Auntie

Customer Service Excellent

Aunt Andy these pound cakes good

I love your rolls they have the taste where just can't get enough of them!!! My bestfriend amefia loves your cocanut cake!!!

I jus Luv those Sweet Potato Pies Big ups to the Avenue Bakery One! Desiree Montgomery

Happy Baking to all of you

I love your Goodies

Thanks a bunch Great Success Olita

gabrielle

Merry Christmas to you all, and have a Happy New Year love + Blessings 2013 Ms. Lisa

Happy Holidays Love the food!!

Happy Holidays From the Forest Park Senior Center

Merry Christmas my first visit & you're awesome

May God Bless You with Much Success

Merry Christmas to the best bakery in town!

Happy Holidays Audrey Ms. Valerie

Merry Xmas

Merry Xmas Love you good food Bettye Buckley

Merry Christmas!! My first visit & you're ...

Wishing You All A Very Merry Christmas and Happy New Year! Much success in 2014

Happy Holidays!! Love your Sweet Rolls

HAPPY NEW YEARS
Benny & The Boys
Mike's HVAC
Rescue

Hello Bakery!
Love your
Rolls, Ice Tea
Cakes, Pies
Everything
HLFCOC

Keep the Bakery going!
Be forever Blessed!!!

Lovely Bakery
2014

Your sweets taste like they are from Heaven 2014

THE BEST BAKERY EVER

Beautiful
DELORES COX

©1/23/14

Prosperity Unending!
Deborah Lee 1/25/2014

1.30.14
First time here!
It smells so wonderful.
The Smiles are Great & Pleasant!
And I'll come again.
Thank you – Mama Nura

May God
forever continue to
Bless and keep you
strong and successful
Love Everything!
Sterling
2014

Best wishes
much success
your sale are
awesome
C. ...

Starting My Clean Day
1-31-14 Anthony ...

Thank you
for being here
Brenda

Best Wishes
Audrey 2014

Best pies ever mikes
Shanka HVAC
Rescue

Worth the trip from Minnesota!
Bill Woodson 2/8/14

Thank You for Excellent Service
It's Good to see Black Owned Business

Your little pies
are wonderful.
Best Wishes,
Sallie 2014

Great Success
& Long Jevity
Big NARD

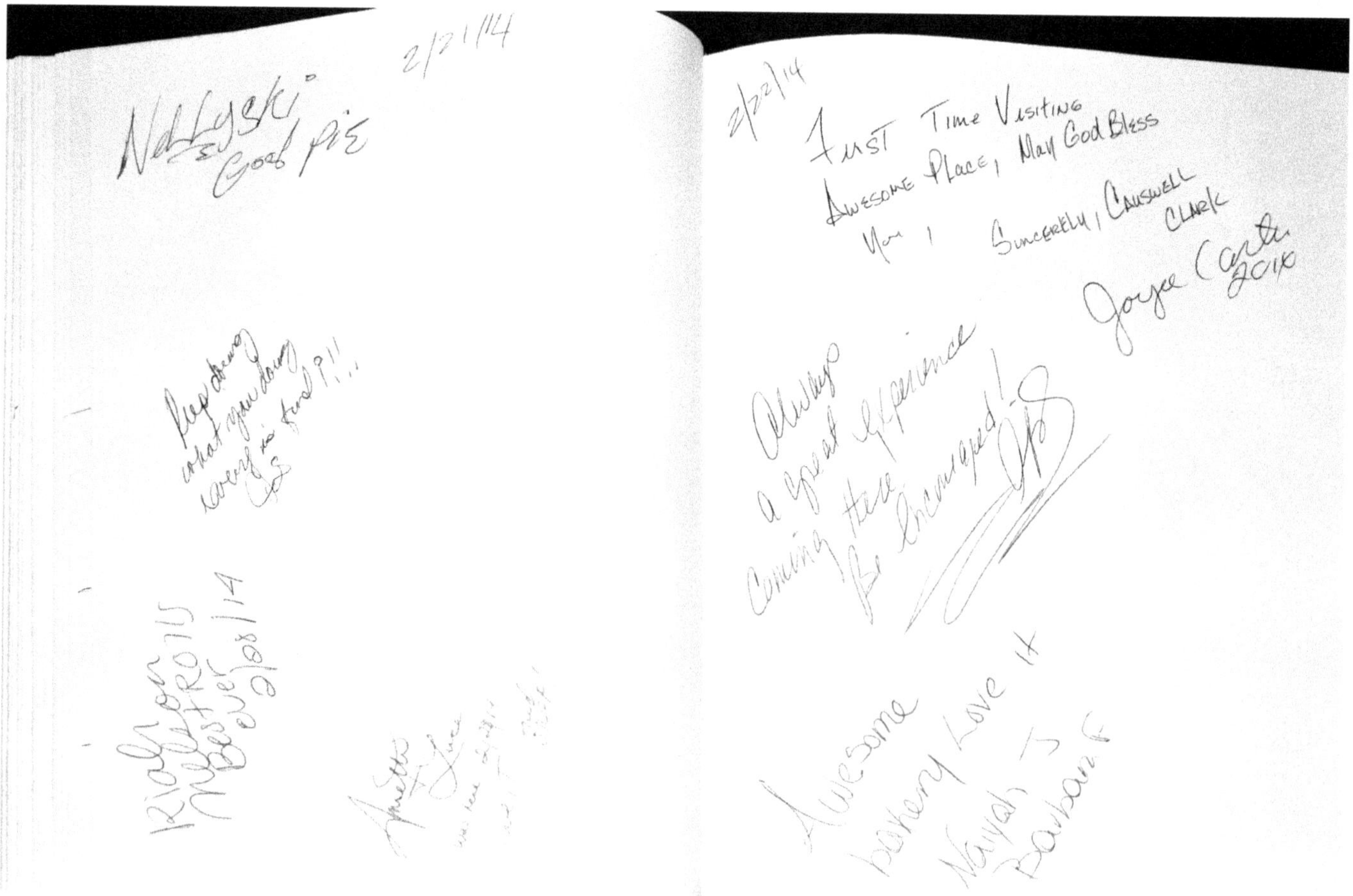

2/21/14

Nellyski
Good Pie

2/22/14
First Time Visiting
Awesome Place, May God Bless
You! Sincerely, Causwell
Clark

Joyce Carter
2014

Keep doing
what you doing
...

Always
a great experience
coming here
Be Encouraged!

Rialhon
Nelstrom's
Best ever
2/28/14

Awesome
bakery Love it
Naviah J.
Barbara F.

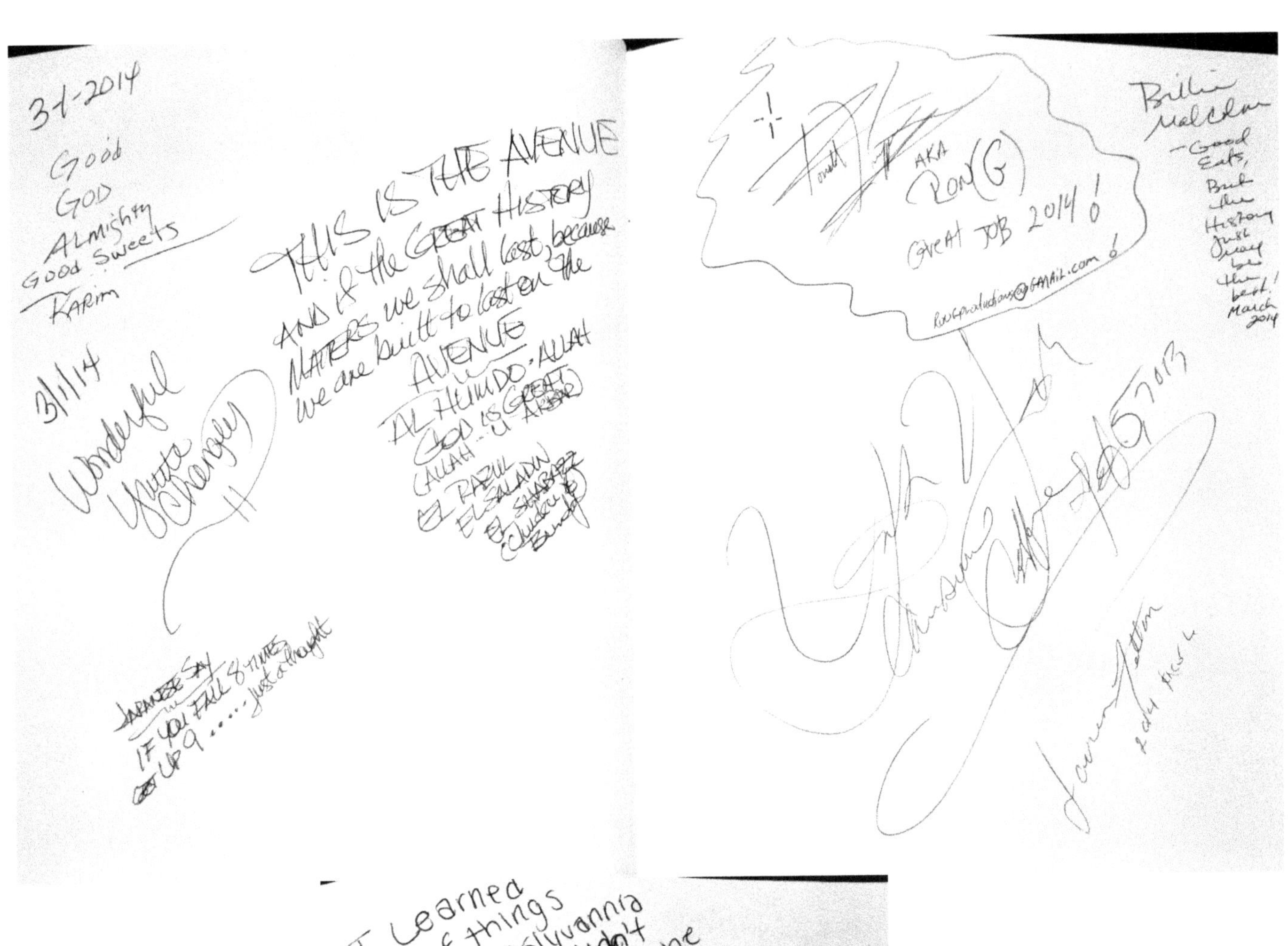

I Learned alot of things about Pennslyvannia Avenue that I didn't know. Thanks for the History lesson.

— Ayanna Coleman
(7th grade student)

Thank for your service.
to the History lesson.
Thanfor your kind heart.
Anna Jeffries

I am so very pleased that you decided to revive so much history. It is so important to have an establishment such as your where you can be educated as well as eats out of this world eats

God Bless you Kim W.

Wish you the best in your Business

Great Eats. Love the Treats! Thanks for making a difference. Ms. Patricia Edwards 21207

Great Service! Great Coffee! ♡ Baltimore Dusie Max

There are only Buns better!

HOWARDU Alternative Spring Break (ASB) has been serving ~~North~~ & East West B-more for a week! Thanks for keeping a few of us warm in the cold! Spring 14' "Truth and Service."

Great Team Thanks for serving us! God Bless! From: Howard University ASB 2014

3/15/2014 Thanks for Services

March 21, 2014 A Pleasure Visiting the Lobby of your Bakery. Brings back fond memories of yesteryears. Bake Goods Are Great!! Sewatto

March 20, 14 75yrs

God Bless You & Family Bro. Jesse Mellar & Family

Keep up the good work! Jenkins & family

Good Luck

God Bless You!

Dakio was in the House for The Apple Cinnamon Rolls

This Business is helping to return a standard to our community of the relationship between residents and the businesses in our community!! Keep up the good work!
Christopher Ervin

If you fall 9 times get up 8 and carry-on the Ave is forever....
Chuckie B

Thanks! For bringing Pennsylvania Avenue Back to life! Much Success!
Maria

GOD IS GREAT
HE IS WAITIN FOR YOUR PRAYERS
EL-RAZUL EL SALADIN EL

Best Desserts Ever

Thank you
Clara Maureen

and the Price is right!!

ROCKY

Best wishes!! thank you
Polly

Keep on keeping on!!
Looking good

The Avenue Bakery

The Bomb.Com

We love you'll out here
Keep up the good work!

Great store with a lot of history
Mooney

Darryl Harris

The Best Rolls
Thanks
Zack

Love Your Sticky Buns!!
Anthony

Thanks

Delicious, Delicious, Delicious, Delicious.

Dontrell Jones
"Baltimore 4 Life"

Saw your place on line by accident, glad we found you.

"Excellent Food!"
Community Love
Greater Balt. Urban League
The Avenue Bakery
4/2014

The Rock was Here

Mr. Russell Young

MAY GOD BRING PEACE & BLESSING

KUDO'S TO AVE. BAKERY A TRUE BLESSING TO THIS COMMUNITY

BEST BAKERY IN TOWN BY FAR GREG GILLMORE '14

My Bakery On the Ball

The Avenue Bakery "Good Luck" Anthony White 2014

We had a wonderful time at the art mural unveiling The Johnsons Helen Ryan Varese

To the Avenue Bakery The Blueberry Muffin was Truly Heavenly. Also Thank You for the Great Work in the Community

I PRAY MUCH SUCCESS FOR THIS PLACE IN "JESUS CHRIST 'NAME'" MR. ALSTON

To the avenue Bakery May you have a long life here in this Community. Be blessed Mr. "C"

Derrick Ryce says this place is Nice

Good Luck

mama!

The Best Cakes ever! - Charon!

- Reagan

- Tysheena

Let God nurture your Spirit While the bakery nurtures your tummy

"This IS A DREAM Come True"
Best Rolls in town
Jonette Sitta
2014
Emmanuel C. Moore
2014

WATCHING YOU GROW
FROM BRICK TO BUN
FROM FRAME TO FOAM
HAS BEEN AN HONOR.
HM

God Blesses In the Sweetest Ways

Blessings:
Not only are your goods Sweet;
but so is your spirit!
Be blessed
Cindy Willis
Ms MD Plus America 2007

This is my first time being here!

Shay was here
on June 26, 2014

New York
So Nice They named it twice
New York
Brence
New York

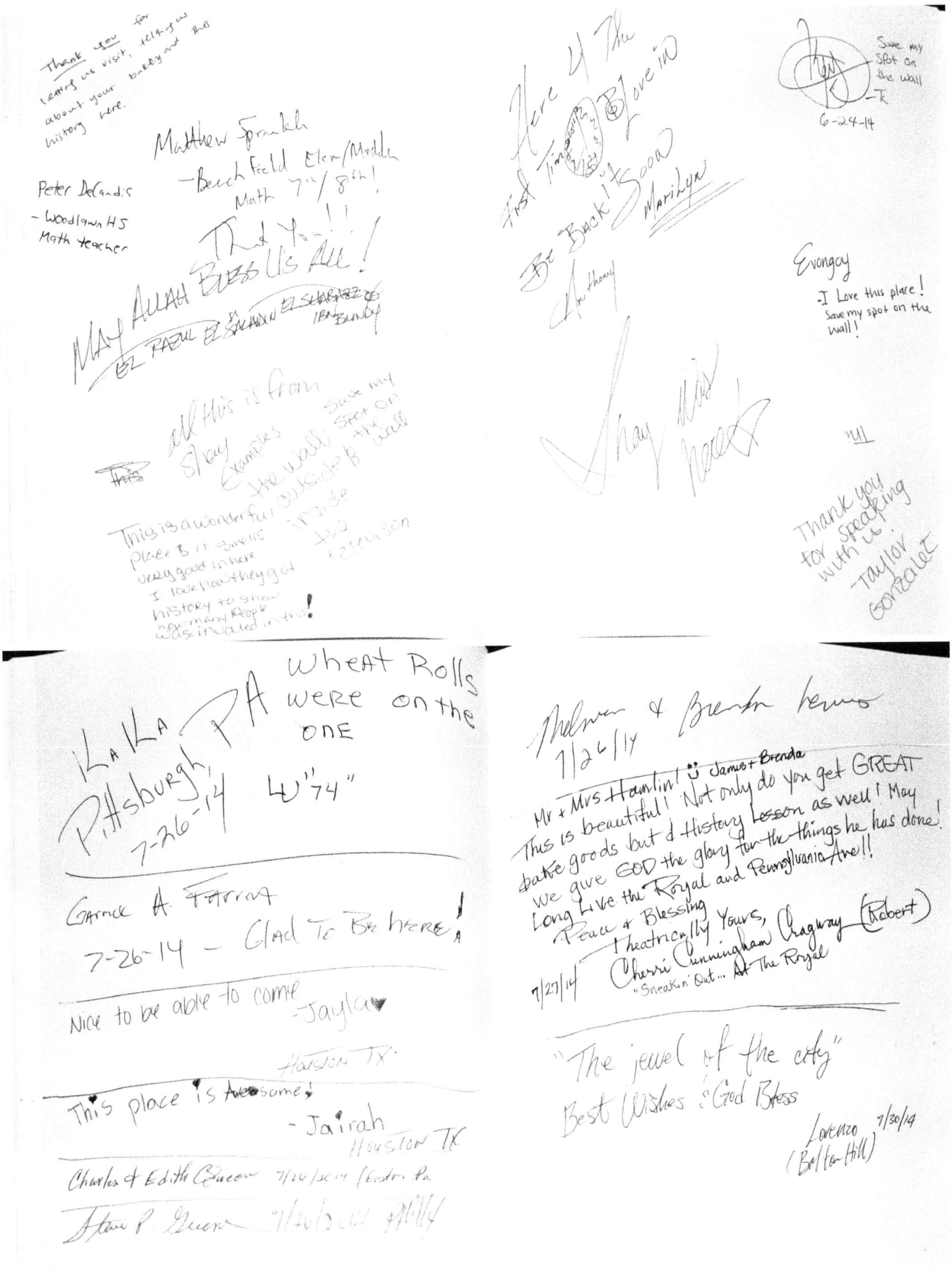

Thank you for letting us visit, telling us about your bakery and this history here.

Matthew Sprankle
-Beechfield Elem/Middle
Math 7th/8th!

Peter DeCandis
-Woodlawn HS
Math teacher

Thank You!!

May Allah Bless Us All!
El Razul El Salahin El Shabazz
Ibn Bundy

All this is from
Examples
Save my spot on the wall
the wall outside B inside
the television

This is a wonderful place & it smells very good in here
I love how they got history to show how many people was involved in this!

Here 4 The First time 7/21
Love it!
Be Back! Soon
Marilyn

Anthony

Save my spot on the wall
-TK
6-24-14

Evongay
-I Love this place! Save my spot on the wall!

Thank you for speaking with us.
-Taylor Gonzalez

Wheat Rolls were on the one

LaLa
Pittsburgh, PA
7-26-14
4'' 74''

Garrick A. Farrar
7-26-14 - Glad To Be Here!

Nice to be able to come
-Jayla♥
Houston TX.

This place is Awesome!
-Jairah
Houston TX

Charles & Edith Queen 7/26/2014 Easton Pa

Steve P. Queen 7/26/2014

Melvin & Brenda Lewis
7/26/14

Mr + Mrs Hamlin! James + Brenda
This is beautiful! Not only do you get GREAT bake goods but a History Lesson as well! May we give GOD the glory for the things he has done! Long Live the Royal and Pennsylvania Ave!!
Peace + Blessing

Theatrically Yours,
Cherri Cunningham Chagway (Robert)
7/27/14 "Sneakin' Out... At The Royal"

"The jewel of the city"
Best Wishes & God Bless
Lorenzo 7/30/14
(Bolton Hill)

Icon Patti LaBelle and James Hamlin

THE BALTIMORE SUN

baltimoresun.com

Pennsylvania Ave., on a roll

Building community, baking bread in one of Baltimore's blighted neighborhoods

Fullbright Family Reunion
6/27/14 The Kennedy Family
Mr & Mrs. Frederick M. Kennedy
6/27-14 Cleveland, Ohio 44128

Barbara Bonhomme 7/5/14
PoetsSpirit@me.com
&
Rahn V. Barnes
rahnv54@comcast.net

The Smith Family

7/15/14 Thank you for keeping our heritage, history, our story alive!
Jean Allen
selfdevelopment.success@gmail.com

Peter Franchot
comptroller
State of Maryland
7/14/14

Thanks for greatness
The Davis Family

Best Wishes
James.
May God Bless You
In All Your Endeavors.
Leonard & Eugene
7/25/2014

Lots of Blessings
Flo!!

The Best Sweet Potato Pie in Baltimore
Janice Bristol
East Baltimore
jnbbristol@aol.com

Thomas & Keisha Terry

Anthony
B.D.K.A
AntMoe
From Sandtown
I
lOVE
THIS
PlACE!

James,
So glad to see the Bakery progressing to become a staple of the community. And to witness a vizualized dream become a Reality!!!...
Love you,
Antoine
7/20/14

Wonderful Establishment, Truly a delight to my palate
Woe Woe "2014"
& Roc

I Like this Place 6/13/2014
Carroll Young

Thanks for Blessing ... Love.
"Mayo" Family Reunion 8/9/14

My First Visit from DC
Shirley Dillahunt
Mayo Family Reunion 2014

D.C. Homegrown Entertainment 8/9/14

Tyler xo Cotton

The Ward Family 2014

As A World Traveler This Bakery (Panaderia) is on A Internation Level
God's Bless this Great Place.... Leslie

AS A WORLD TRAVELLER THIS BAKERY (PANDORA) IS EQUAL TO THE BEST...

Kim Brandon

This place is water to my soul. XOX

I finally made it! I am impressed! Great Customer Service

Sarah Matthews 8/1/2014

Wonderful business that is preserving and continuing the rich history of West Baltimore! The Mitchell Family – Katreen Mitchell

Jade Newhouse two thumbs up!

Dave was hot enough!!! I am back again!!!! (410-325-0217) Coach J.J. (email me everytime you have CHEESE Cake arnold.harper410@yahoo.com) Thanks

Come here all the time! Nia

Nia Hargrove

Maria Colon

Anthony A. Colon 7-7-14 good food!

Beautiful Concept Great Food Friendly } Lots of Love

Barb & Jackie Blake

THANK YOU SISTERS PEACE & BLESSINGS. LOOK FORWARD TO NEXT VISIT. Mal

The Crawford Family of Williamsburg Great Place

8-6-14 Cinnamon crushers sweet tea Donna and Pat Giles

The Crosby Family of Sandtown 2014

LA-LA

Best Rolls I've had Since Grandma's
Bettie Boo South Carolina "2015"
Made by Kennedy Banks
Maya Angelou
Kennedy B.
8/8/14
God Bless You
Cindy P
CP LOVE Continous Praise n Love
Everything Smells good
May God Bless you with much success.
Much Love & Continued Blessings Always Yolanda Parker CTA
Good Luck
THANK GOD I FOUND U GUYS! Best Rolls Ever. Love VAL

Tracie Taylor

BLACK FACE!!!

Shakima Griese

Shama Ray

Ray's Temple

Ronald S Faulkes-Bey
Peace & Blessing 8-27-14

Jean & Marcello & Donna
Have a good Labor Day weekend

James
have a great
Holiday
Peace!!!

Ashley Williams
God Bless!!

Blessings to
such a wonderful
business

Great Rolls
Outstanding w/
JELLY/BUTTER
HOWARD

MAY God be
with you!

Smells
Great!!

Thank God the
snow is gone–
Now I can make my
way down here. As much
I hear about the good old
Rolls. Got my sweet pie

Love everything
God bless you!!

Love your
Food
Cake

I had
been here
100 times

Wesley

I Love
them too!

sup!

yummy!

cool!

Rolls
are great

This looks really
good but I dont have
any money :(

yahoo!

Chandler

March 19th
2016
Madison
McLean

Liam?

I Love
Your
rolls!

Yummy!

Yahoo!

Awesome

Thank god
for you guys

Nothing like nice
hot rolls
after church

Cheese
burgers
are
awesome!
#Random

Smells

Steven
Washen

Wolf
Haley

Thanks
Anthony & Diana
See you soon
Good Luck

Andrew & Gloria Reid
Randallstown, MD
Merry Christmas

Congrats
Annette!

Good Luck

Thank you
Merry Christmas

Congratulations
on your success

Congratulations on your beautiful new business.
May God Bless All you Do!
The VAI

Merry Xmas +
Best of Luck Ralph
#1307 Zion Towers

Congratulations
Seasons greetings. May God
bless you and your Bakery.
Ronnie & Christine

12-24-11
Best Wishes
To your New
Bakery! I
Love The Rolls
I travel all the
way from Morgan

Wishing you the
very best. I'm
so proud that
you have been
able to accom-
plish this!
B. Brazier

May your Business
Prosper

Oh Thank GOD with
for Blessing us with
this Bakery. Sooo GOOD!
Kat (2011)

Thank you for your Kindness
and for your great Rolls!
2011 Lynn
Great Cupcakes ♡

Love The Bakery family
- Marlene

Merry Christmas!! 12-24-11
What a Blessing to Be able
to purchase Home-made apple
pie for our Family Holiday Dinner.
We are So Happy to Have you
in our neighborhood!!
Sylvia Cromwell
&
Family

Back Again,
Loved your bread pudding
+ especially your Rolls
Timothy Dean
(Tim)

Congrats on your entrepreneurial journey & sparking economic development within the African American Community. Continue to IMPROVE & PROGRESS!

OMAR NATASHA IMANI

12-24-11

God is in the Blessing Business. Much Luck Leslie & Prissey

GOD Bless YOU!
US NAVY/Baltimore
Ed

Welcome, Love & Peace
[illegible] & [illegible]

Congrats on the establishment & going concern. Continued Blessing + good luck!
D. Owens

I hear the best joe is in here. Bootsy

I'VE BEEN DOING WORK AROUND THE CORNER AND SINCE I HAVE I'VE BEEN COMING IN THE AVENUE BAKERY AND IT REMINDS OF THE BALTIMORE I ALWAYS KNEW AND LOVED. KEEP IT UP AND I'LL SPREAD THE WORD "B-MORE IS BACK"
BRENT

"KEEP ON KEEPING ON"
BLACK POWER Rockett

May God bless u + yours
Martha + Julian

What a statement toward the revitalization of Penn Ave. [illegible]

The food is great. I love to see them bake the items so I know what they are fresh. Great job. Wishing you much success.
D. Carroll 1-5-12

Good Vibes, Good Family Business, wheat Rolls, Good Luck + I Love Food
[illegible] Hughes 1-7-11

Rock Steady & reach for the stars. If you miss the moon is good. Just Being Me
Bud

Joe
June

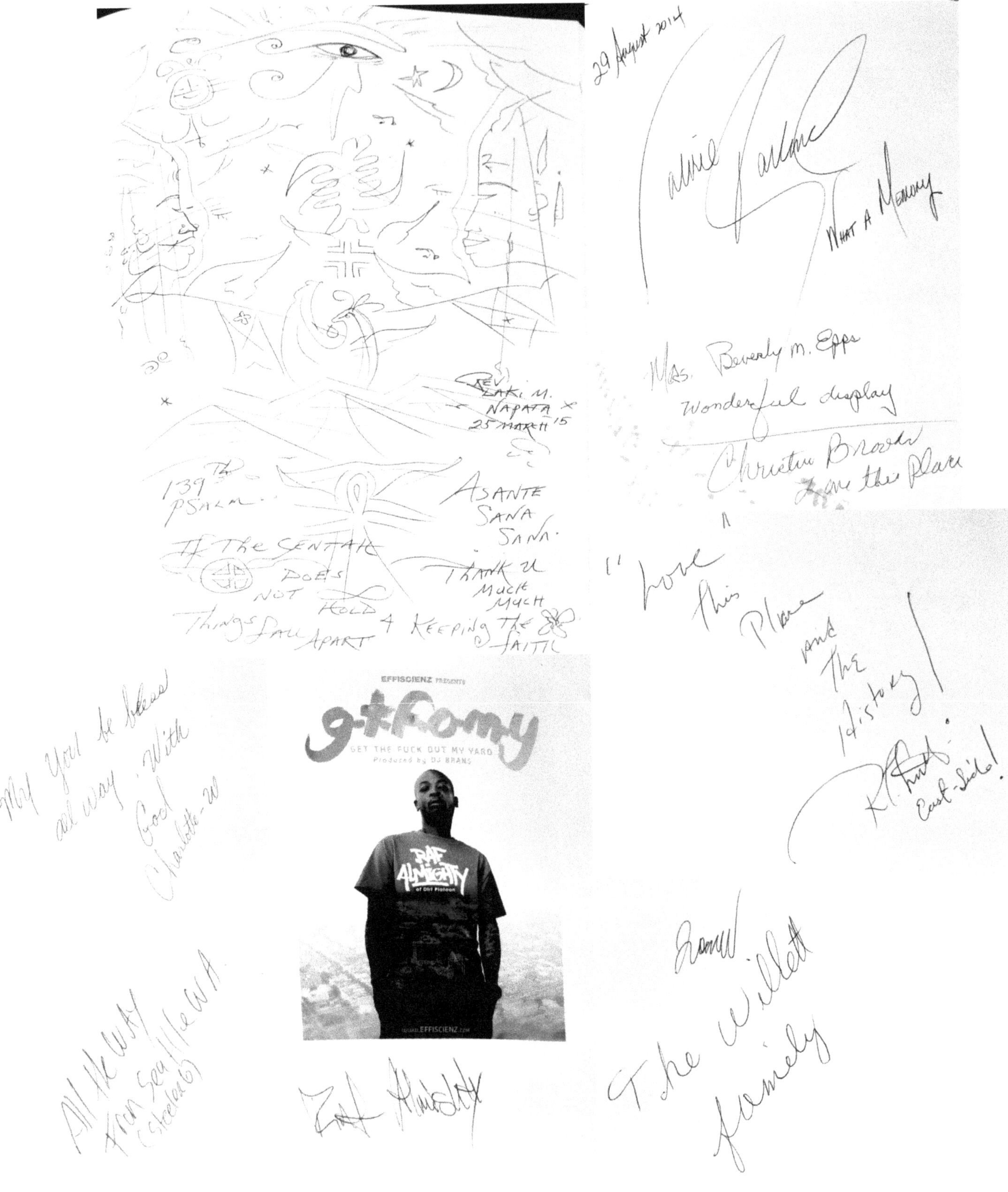
REV. ZAKI M. NAPATA 25 MARCH 15
139TH PSALM
IF THE CENTAR DOES NOT HOLD THINGS FALL APART
ASANTE SANA SANA
THANK U MUCH MUCH 4 KEEPING THE FAITH
29 August 2014
WHAT A MEMORY
Mrs. Beverly M. Epps
Wonderful display
"Love this Place and The History!
East-Side!
EFFISCIENZ PRESENTS
GET THE FUCK OUT MY YARD
Produced by DJ BRANS
RAF ALMIGHTY
www.EFFISCIENZ.com
The Willett family

Sincerely Mark Romeo
Sep 4, 2014
From the Dome
Came in and had
Some Good Cake

Thankyou from: 9/6/2014
Dr. Keiffer Mitchell (Baltimore City Council House)
son of Clarence Mitchell Jr.
and attorney Juanita Mitchell (FIRST BLACK WOMAN TO PRACTICE LAW IN MARYLAND)
nephew of Parren Mitchell (FIRST BLACK MARYLAND CONGRESSMAN)
grandson of Lillie Mae Jackson (PRESIDENT OF BALTIMORE BRANCH NAACP)
Brother of Senator Clarence Mitchell III
Brother of City Council member and Senator Michael Mitchell
Father of ~~Senator and~~ Councilman Keiffer Mitchell and State Delegate
Grandfather of Marques NewHouse, Jade NewHouse, Keiffer Mitchell III and Kenna Mitchell
Uncle of Clarence Mitchell IV "C4" Lisa Mitchell Senaur (FORMER HOUSE DELEGATES + SENATE OF MARYLAND)
"THE MITCHELLS OF MARYLAND
"WITH GOD ALL THINGS ARE POSSIBLE"

Nannette Mitchell 4304 St. Paul St. Balto. MD 21218

Q. B. S.
Great Job James!!!

I love this Place It is Cool.
AilAYAhK.

1st Time Here!
Love this place
Keep up the Good work
God Bless

Everything is
Sooooooo Good!!!
God Bless all

Sept. 30, 2014
God Bless the Avenue Bakery for continuing the "Dream of the Chitlin Circuit will never Die".
God Bless You James Hamlin - You are truly a crusader for keeping our hope & dream alive. Looking forward to Rebuilding the Royal Theater ... brick by brick.
Peace and Blessings,
Teresa Cunningham

Jim,
Poppa Rolls are better than my grandma's homemade rolls. Shhh! Do not tell her I said that!
Many Blessings,
James W. Harper III

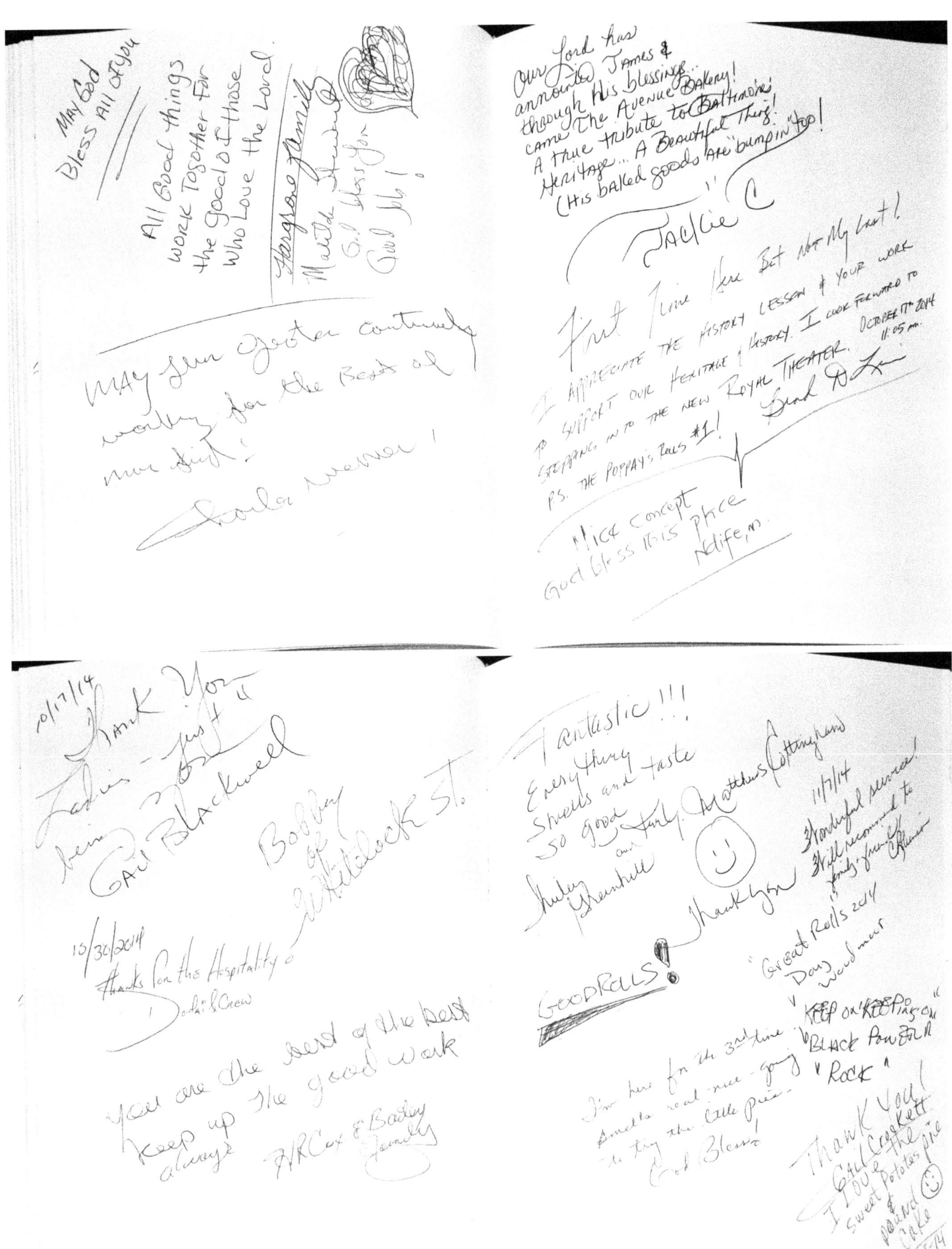
MAY God BLESS All of you
All Good things work together for the good of those who Love the Lord.
God bless you Good Job!
Our Lord has anointed James & through His blessings came the Avenue Bakery! A true tribute to Baltimore's Heritage... A Beautiful Thing! (His baked goods are bumpin' too!)
JACKIE C
First Time Here But Not My Last!
I APPRECIATE THE HISTORY LESSON & YOUR WORK TO SUPPORT OUR HERITAGE & HISTORY. I LOOK FORWARD TO STEPPING INTO THE NEW ROYAL THEATER. OCTOBER 17th 2014 11:05 am.
P.S. THE POPPAY'S ROLLS #1!
Nice concept God bless this place
10/17/14
Thank You Ladies
GAIL Blackwell
Bobby of Whitelock St.
10/30/2014 Thanks for the Hospitality
You are the best of the best Keep up the good work always
Fantastic!!! Every thing smells and taste so good
Matthews Cottingham
11/7/14
Thank You
GOOD ROLLS!
"Great Rolls 2014"
"KEEP ON KEEPING ON" "BLACK POWER" "ROCK"
I'm here for the 3rd time. Smells real nice - going to try the little pies. God Bless!
THANK YOU!
I love the sweet potatoe pie & pound cake
11-5-14

Laurel MD
Love your store with Black History!

Ray Williams
J&R Transportation Service
Curtural Heritage Tour
with Lou Fields 11/7/14

Wonderful Place!
Good food for the body
and the mind!
Inspiring!

Beautiful bakery
Thank you for
making Baltimore
beautiful 11/8/14

Fabulous Bakery!
1st time visitor
what an absolute delight!
May You Continue
To Be Blessed +
Highly Favored
Thanks!
Keisha 11/20/14

Beautiful People
Beautiful Bakery
Black Own
God Bless!!

First Timer! Great Place. Great Atmosphere!
Will Be Back!
12/9/14

Smelled it from the street... had to stop in! 12/7/14

First Timer,
Smells great will
be back soon!!
12/18/14
-Brenda-
-Breshia-
St Louis MO.

1st Time a great time!!! The
Baker was wonderful. Very
friendly Will Be Back!!
12/10/14

1st time here!!
Beautiful environment
Truly Blessed!
To God be the glory for a wonderful place!
Will be back
12/7/2014

12-20-14
Queeey Quee
From SA
A.V.E 1500!

Smell so good make you wanna
slap yo momma!!

How Passion Evolved into My Day Job at UPS

It was a habit at UPS to keep its employees on the move within its operations. For many of its loyal and enterprising workers as soon as one got comfortable at one task or position, it was time to move on to conquer a new one. While this sometimes presented its challenges, for me, I learned to roll with the punches (or transfers) because it enabled me to learn, apply new skills, and acquaint myself with a full picture of operations at UPS.

After many assignments, I had long since moved on from driving trucks and delivering packages in multiple UPS districts, I was now in Sales. Loving the community, it gave me just enough leeway to *lend* some of my time to volunteerism at my alma mater, Booker T. Washington Junior High School—always promoting the career opportunities of UPS and urging the company to get involved with the students, of course.

Since 1996, UPS had allowed me to transfer by request to different districts. Previously, one could only transfer from one location to another, according to the company's needs. Different assignments and transfers always presented something valuable for me to learn. For example, working in the Washington, DC, and Northern Virginia area District had given me time to witness the positive influences of the late former DC Mayor Marion Barry—setting up administrative office spaces that not only courted new businesses and commerce but also new jobs and youth summer jobs. All of

that was in my head when I first wanted to set up administrative offices in the new building I had purchased. I wanted to set myself up, or at least lay a foundation to flourish The Avenue with bustling commerce and choice for its residents. In 1996, I'd also figured that I would be retiring in the next ten years, availing myself right in the thick of things within the community.

I transferred back to the Atlantic District, encompassing Baltimore, most of Western Maryland (Frederick, Hagerstown, etc.) and even parts of Delaware. Things were going smoothly for me as a sales manager when my district manager, Mel Smith, called me in his office one day. "I got a job for you," was all Mel said.

My immediate thought was, *uh oh*. Here I was, thinking that I had done something wrong and wondered where I was going next to repent. Lo and behold, the district manager said, "You are now the district community relations manager." He further explained that while my new job was not exactly defined, "your core assignment is to make sure that we have a successful United Way campaign, and you need to represent UPS in the community."

Bam! That was it! From that, I got an opportunity to create a whole job assignment, and I just went at it—whole hog. I couldn't wait to escalate my activities encouraging the students at Booker T.

And time here two days in a row. May God Bless The Avenue Bakery 12/20/14

To Jazz
the love of a life time 1/15/2014
Lloyd W. ... Sr.

Rudy ... 1/17/2015

You are the Sweetest Sweet ... 1/17/15

Haven't been home in a while. This is a great surprise. Wishing you nothing but success
Patricia W. 1/17/15
Portland, OR

Good Home Cooked Baked Goods
1/24/15

Thank you for the opportunity to help our youth know who they are and where they belong.

DR WALTER GILL
the first African American to graduate from Baltimore City College High School in June, 1955
(AKA the Urban Professor; Sport; Wali Hakeem)

Thanks! You are wonderful!
Laura P. Byrd

Peace & Blessings!
CLEOPHUS BELL
Keep on, Keeping on
Perserve our history and culture.
Thank You! One Love.
Johnnie Jackson

More To Come for The Avenue ☺
Brian Stephenson

Thank you for what you do for US! Peace and Blessings

From the Gray to yours. Thank you for your service Peace + Blessings

Much Success God's Blessings

Things have changed since 1959. Good to see it's still around for us. B. Jones

Good Luck God Bless the brooks family. Annette, Edward and Dante' and Libby.

Much Success! 2/21/15

Jim, the time is NOW! Continue to DO that which is necessary and know that the revolution of the MIND has always required the word and action Peace + Congrats

Phi Beta Sigma supports the Avenue Bakery 3/21/2015

So Glad to be here after the Riot for good bakery foods 13 May 2015

Happy Mothers Day
[illegible] 13/May/15

very nice store
my Name is [illegible] Donaldson I live in Linden NJ 07036
[illegible] Donaldson 1609 South Wood Apt 5 Linden New Jersey 07036

"THE FIRST THING THAT I SAW WAS, THE YOUNG MAN WASHED HIS HANDS... GREAT EVERYTHING AFTER THAT WAS FANTASTIC!!! KEEP DOING WHATCHA DOING."

It is always good to see someone open a business in the black community. However when it is a black man that does it, well you cannot [illegible] heart. May GOD bless you and keep you. You will have a long-lasting customer in ME!

[illegible]

March 21, 2015
Praise God from all Whose Blessings Flow Praise Father Son and Holy Ghost. I prayed sincerely for a Black Owned Bakery, and here it is in Balto. MD 722 Pennsylvania A[illegible]

Hello.
We are friends of Bill and Rachel Hemmick.
It is great to come here.
We'll be back some other time with more people. Steve and [illegible]

May God continue to Bless and keep you all!!!
Minister Charlene Stafford
Mt Sinai Holy Church
5901 Joseph Ave
Dr. A. Moseley, Pastor

3/21/15
Glory be to God for the great things He has done and continue to do in the lives of His People
Sister [illegible]
May He continue to Bless You [illegible]

3/22/15
Love your bakery. [illegible]

"May God Bless you and your Bakery" Matt + Zelda

To Our Closest Friends!!!
Thanks JJ, Great Job
Love
JEFF + VAE MASH
Carroll County

Smells delicious

Robertson, R
Clark, L
Herbert, C
Edwards, L

Your rolls are delicious
-Chantell

Zoe Fisher
Daniel Leyva
Shamiya Artis
Keshawna Edwards
[illegible]
Big Rand-O
[illegible]

THE DESERTS ARE SO WONDERFUL THEY MELT INSIDE YOUR MOUTH!
[illegible]

Cameron Kellis
Shannon Beasley-EC
God Bless ♡
Bessie Brown
May God Bless This Business

May God Continue to Bless You As You Bring Blessing to the Community
Linda C. Mayo "President of Gilmore Homes"
"Billie Holiday Celebration"
4-10-2015

Zahrah

May God continue to Richly Bless You!!!!!!
Kathy M-R & Family
4/10/15

Rose Sanders Ellis
[illegible]

May God Continue to Bless all of your Endeavors
Continue to Be a Blessing in the Community
D Bradley

Good Eating
R+G Bond
4/11/2015

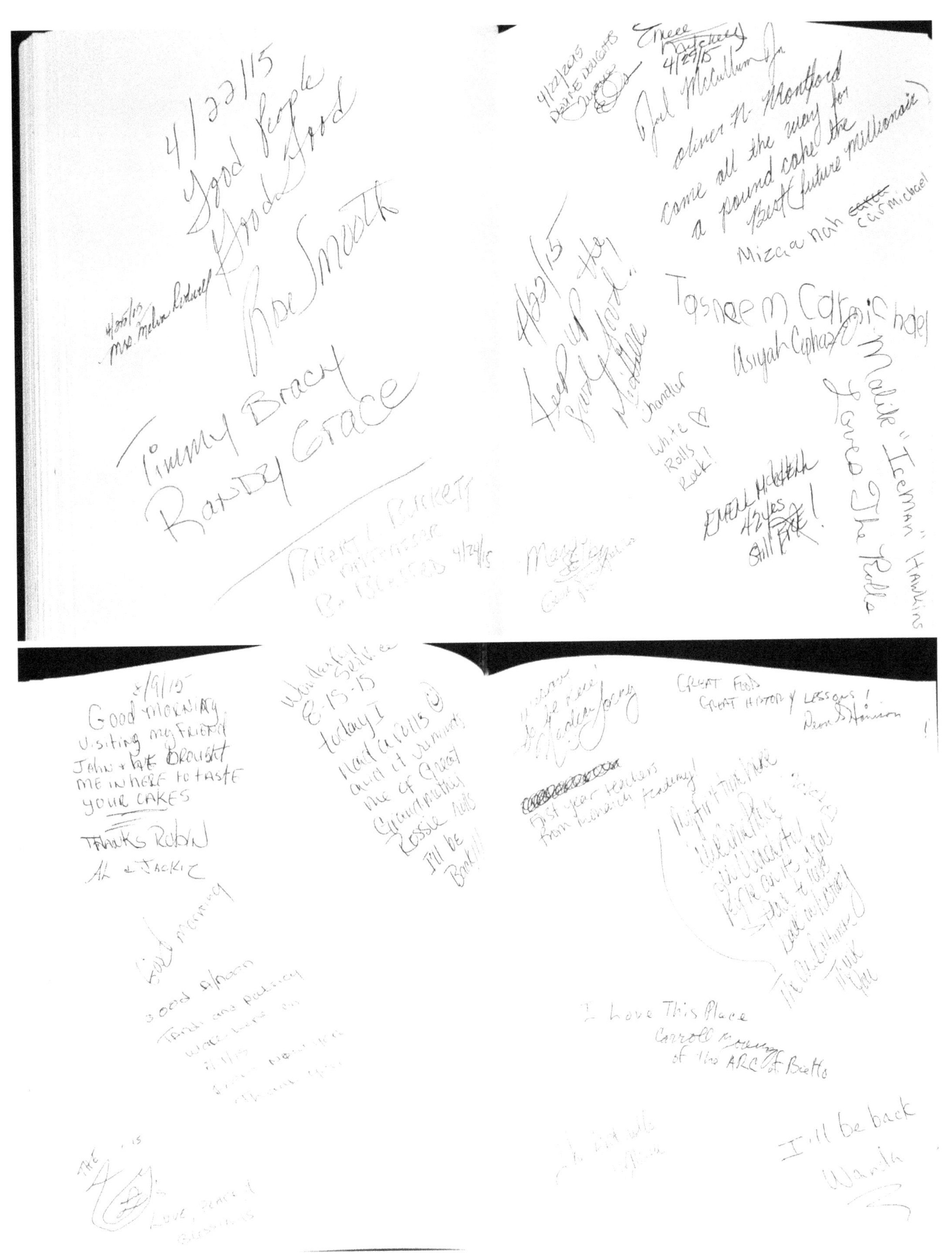
4/22/15
Good People
Good Food
Timmy Brach
Randy Grace
Oliver N. Montford
come all the way for
a pound cake the
Best future millionaire
Asiyah Cephas
Malik "Iceman" Hawkins
White Rolls Rock!
Good Morning
Visiting my Friend
John + Pat Brought
me in here to taste
your cakes
Thanks Robin
Al & Jackie
Great Food
Great History Lessons!
First year teachers
from Monarch Academy
I Love This Place
I'll be back

8-16-15
always a Pleasure
to be here and see good
People and good food.
Jeannie Williams.
Birthday girl next wed

8-16-15 Sunday God Bless
Veray good Place
Bakery goods are Melting in your
Mouth - Keep up good things for all
thank you.
Mrs Mable J Wright

Wonderful
Robin Moore
smile

8/21/15
First Time
very interested
8-22-15
Paul Nixon-Bey
God Bless!
DJ 8/21/15
Oneeda
#ALL Lives Matter
08/29/15
ALWAYS FAMILY,
THANKS FOR YOUR
FAITHFULNESS!
THE TUBMANS
8/23/15
GOD Bless!
Forever-n-Always
his children
B.H.
Pastor Samuel
Rev Brandy
God Bless
My First time
Here N I
Enjoy the sweet potatoe
God Bless
Ave. Bakery

Awesome Place
The Jones

Thank God
for this Bakery.
A Wonderful
What a wonderful
blessing to our neighbor-
hood community. God
bless!!
A.J. Shelton
8-30-15

Keeping it Sweet!
8/30/17
Ben Hall

Awesome
Baked treats 8/30/15
T Maddox
Nothing but
love. From my
Sister & me!
Vinita & George
8-30-2015 (20th Street)

Awesome Place
of Business
Emily Williams

9-Sep-15
Wow! Just to think,
I travel to other cities
to see important historical
sites and this is my FIRST
visit to this bakery and
I'm 61 years old:
A.L. Carter
(The irony of it ALL!)
And I live 5 minutes
away!

Celeste James
Was here
& Enjoyed
the decadence!
9/3/15

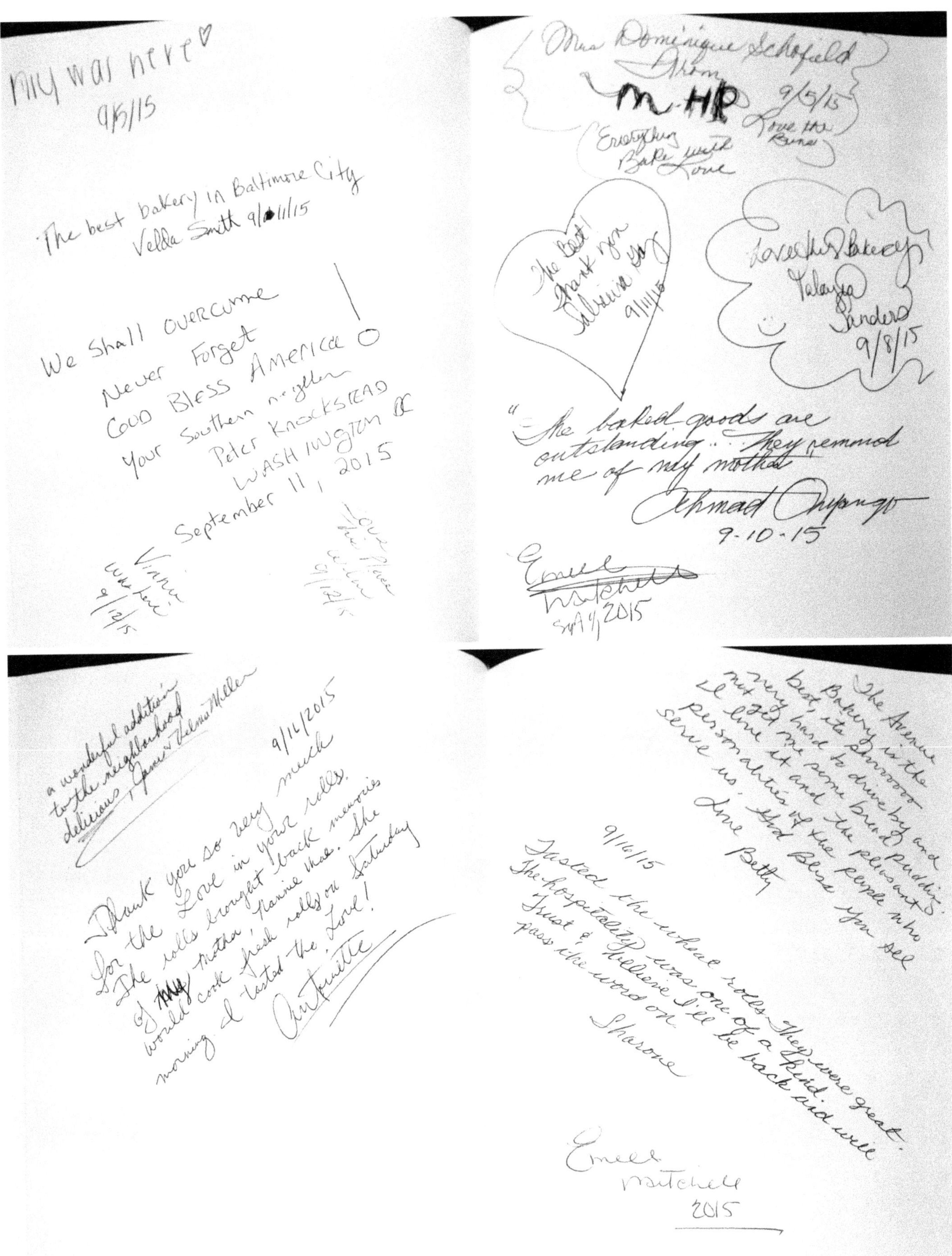

was here♡
9/5/15

The best bakery in Baltimore City
Velda Smith 9/11/15

We Shall Overcome
Never Forget
God Bless America
Your Southern neighbor
Peter Knockstead
Washington DC
September 11, 2015

Mrs Dominique Schofield
9/5/15
Love the Buns

Everything Bake with Love

The best! Thank you
Sabrina
9/11/15

Love this Bakery
Talayja Sanders
9/8/15

"The baked goods are outstanding... They remind me of my mother"
Ahmad
9-10-15

Emell Mitchell
Sept 9, 2015

a wonderful addition to the neighborhood delicious, Miller

9/16/2015
Thank you so very much for the Love in your rolls. The rolls brought back memories of my mother, Nannie Mae. She would cook fresh rolls on Saturday morning. I tasted the Love!
Antoinette

The Avenue Bakery is the best, its sooooo very hard to drive by and not get me some bread pudding. I love it and the pleasant personalities of the people who serve us. God Bless you
Love Betty

9/16/15
Tasted the whole rolls. They were great. The hospitality was one of a kind. Trust & believe I'll be back and will pass the word on.
Sharone

Emell Mitchell
2015

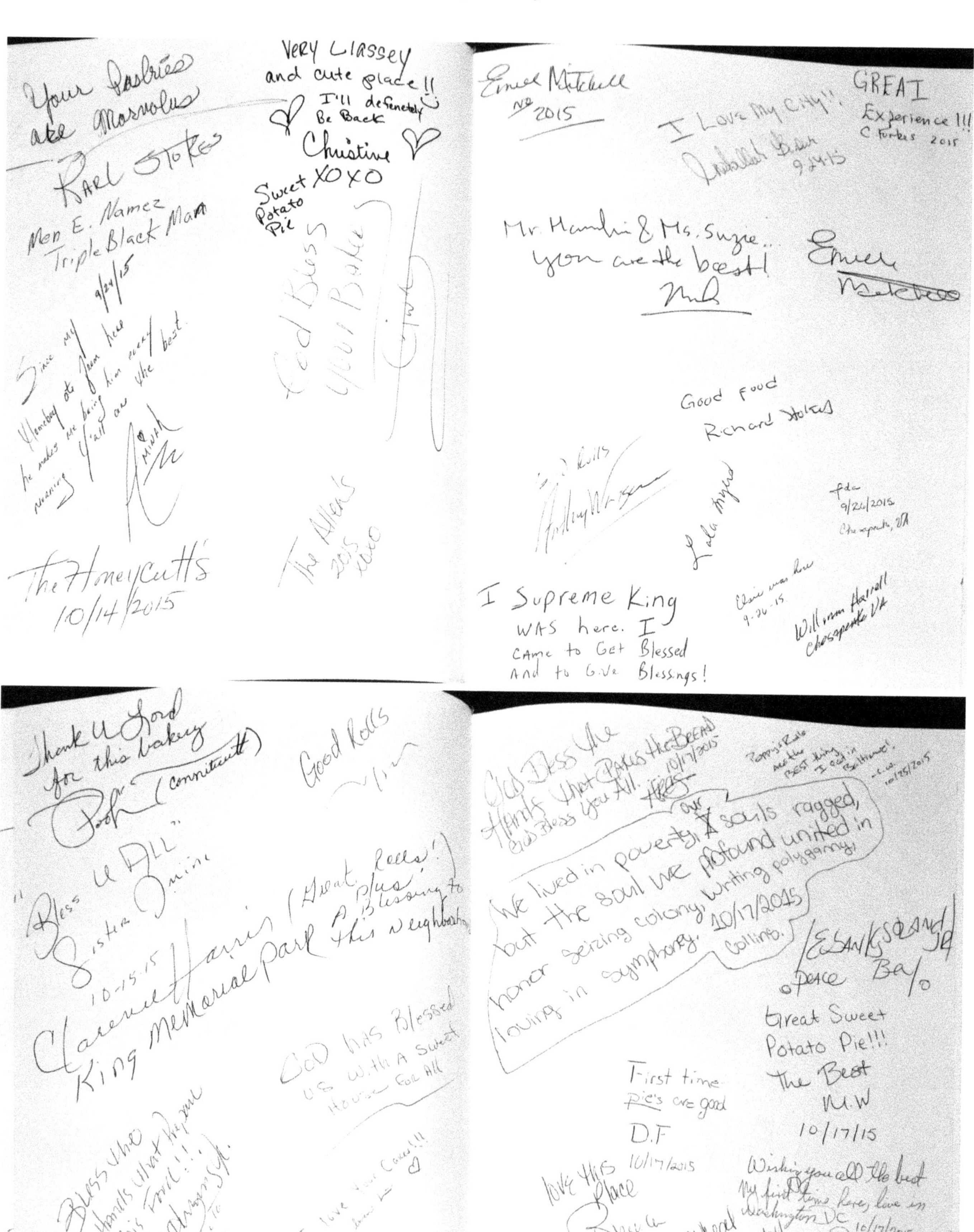

Your pastries are marvelous
Very classy and cute place!! I'll defenetly be back
Christine
Sweet Potato Pie XOXO
Karl Stokes
Men E. Namez
Triple Black Man
9/24/15
God Bless your Bakery
The Honeycutt's
10/14/2015
The Allen's 2015
GREAT Experience!!!
C Forbes 2015
I Love my City!!
9-24-15
Mr. Hamlin & Ms. Suzie... you are the best!
Good food
Richard Stokes
9/24/2015
I Supreme King WAS here. I CAme to Get Blessed And to Give Blessings!
Thank U Lord for this bakery
Good Rolls
"Bless U ALL"
Sister
10-15-15
King Memorial park
God has Blessed us with a Sweet House for All
I love your Cakes!!!
God Bless the Hands that Bakes the Bread
God Bless You All.
10/17/2015
We lived in poverty, our souls ragged, but the soul we profound united in honor seizing colony, writing polygamy, loving in symphony.
10/17/2015
Collins.
Great Sweet Potato Pie!!! The Best
M.W
10/17/15
First time pie's are good
D.F
love this Place
10/17/2015
Wishing you all the best
Washington DC
10/17/2015

11/12/15
Poppy Rolls
were excellent

Potatoe
Pig
Apple
Fort Laud., Fl. 33311

Tayia S. Walker
11/19/15 I love
this place!
Baked goods, wonderful
information about our
wonderful people!

SLICK-Q
WAS HERE

Smells LIKE
DAY in HERE
11-6-15
I pray that the LORD GOD
will continue to BLESS
your Bussiness

SHEKE
Nice Cinnamon
Rolls
FRIENDLY Ladys

Smells so good,
Tastes so good,
God Bless the
Bakers!

HAPPY
BIRTHDAY!
MARTIN
HINKSON
(15)

I love the
white Rolls

Kia

Tyler

Thank you
smells great

Kent
S

KILAM

Carolyn
Stat

open
some
time

Baltimore Afro-American
Our Freedom Now
Fords DISCRIMINATES AGAINST AMERICAN CITIZENS
Welcome TO GWYNN OAK
EQUAL TAXATION
EQUAL EDUCATIONAL OPPORTUNITIES?
The Baltimore Post
MOB HANGS, BURNS NEGRO
Man's Toes Cut off by Mob at Salisbury
WE SHA
OVERCOM

THE SPHINX CLUB
Baltimore Afro-American
VOICES SHOUT OUT
Freedom
DISCRIMINATES AGAINST AMERICAN CITIZENS
Welcome TO GWYNN OAK
EQUAL TAXATION
WHY NOT EQUAL EDUCATIONAL OPPORTUNITIES?
The Baltimore Post
MOB HANGS, BURNS NEGRO
Man's Toes Cut off by Mob at Salisbury

THE AVENUE BAKERY'S

LOGBOOK #4
(2015-2018)

Welcom To
"The Avenue Bakery"
Home of Poppoy's Rolls

Please share your thoughts!

KEEP BAKEING what YOU'RE
BAKEING baby GOOD and SWEET

EDDIE

Dec. 22, 2015
Merry Christmas & Happy New Year.
Your the BEST BAKERY For the Holidays.
GOD BLEST!!
Wardell & Sharon
Barksdale!!

12/23/2015
Merry Christmas!
Donna & Wayne Randolph

[illegible] All at Avenue Bakery!
[illegible] the blessings!!!
[illegible]

I love coming here, because you don't get to
see a part of history. Something they don't teach
in school today. #BlackHistory #WeComeFromKings+Queens
Love And Peace To Everyone Ms. Taylor

Thanks so much for the work preserving the
neighborhood. Dr Debora Johnson-Ross
Bridge Ed [illegible]

Ben Dorsey 3601 Ednor Rd Balto MD 21218

Derrick Moore – "Support black business"
#Black excellence -one love
#Peace and Prosperity

Trishawna Wallace
#love our History

Veronica Jones
#Love #Live #Laugh

Love your
melanin
skin – Denzel
Hall

I love coming here because, it
feels like home –
Al-Karim

May 5th 2018
I stopped by the Bakery for the first time today the lady who waited on me was delightful & pleasant I be coming back again and I know I will enjoy all the "goodies" I brought today
Brittany ♡

May 5th
Awesome Bakery
Fresh Rolls Pound Cake
& the Pleasant Service
Was Great!!!
Xnielle

Keep Doing what you do Best Always
My Family Bakery

I have been trying to get here for a year. Very Excited
Dawnita

I been driving pass here several times saying to myself I'm gonna stop pass one day. So today was my day, and it was a pleasure. Great Service. I'm a big supporter of Black own businesses, we need more of them and help each other to succeed greatness.
Keep Going
Keep Striving
Tawanda
t.harvey101@gmail.com

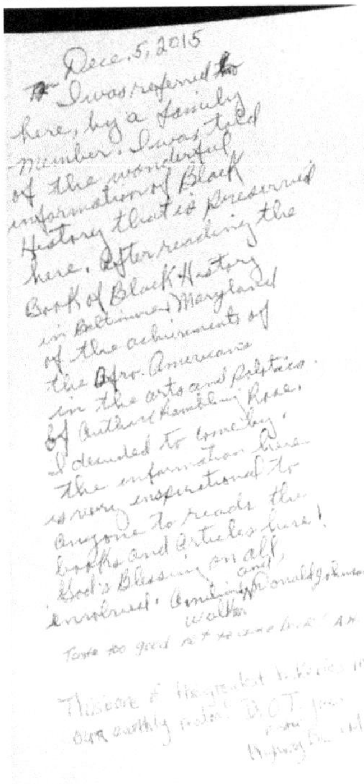

Dec. 5, 2015
I was referred here, by a family member. I was told of the wonderful information of Black History that is preserved here. After reading the Book of Black History in Baltimore, Maryland of the achievements of the Afro-Americans in the arts and politics of Author Hamlin Rose, I decided to come by. The information here is very inspirational to anyone to reads the books and articles here! God's Blessing on all involved. Amina Donald Johnson and Walter

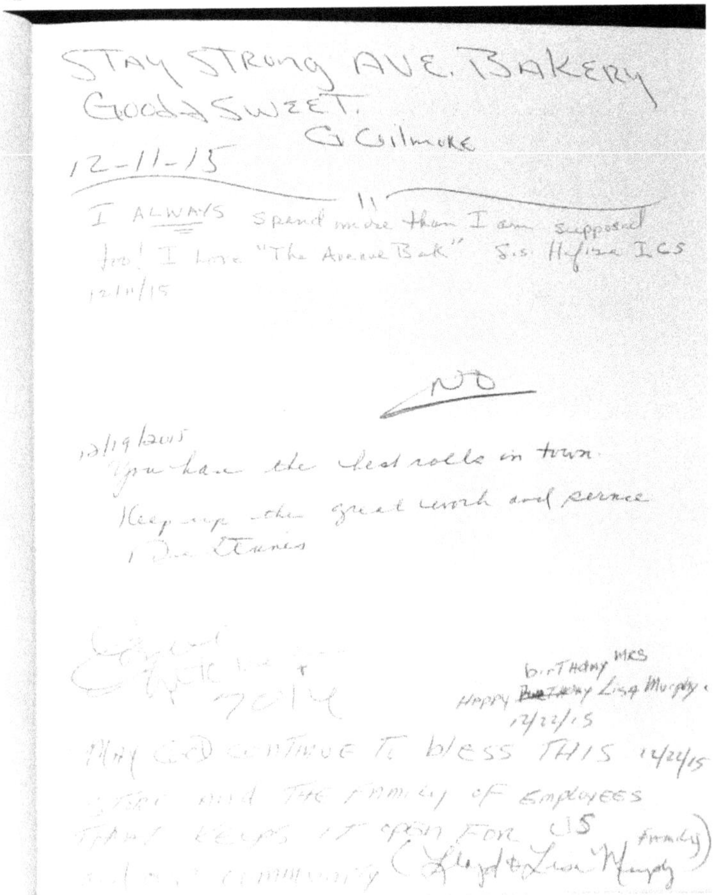

STAY STRONG AVE. BAKERY
Good & SWEET.
G Gilmore
12-11-15

I ALWAYS spend more than I am supposed too! I Love "The Avenue Bak" S.S. Hafiza ICS
12/11/15

ND

12/19/2015
You have the best rolls in town.
Keep up the great work and service
Dee Evans

Happy Birthday Mrs Lisa Murphy.
12/22/15

May GOD continue to bless this 12/24/15 ... and the family of employees that keeps it open for us ... community (Lloyd & Lisa Murphy family)

God Bless
Nice Spot
May God
Bless Yall
May God continue to bless you in this work
January 22 2016 we are here getting Ready for Snow with Sweet Homemade Treats from Eastside
Tastes So Good!!
2-3-16
1st Time @ The Bakery Gonna try the sweet potato pie Hope its Good!!!
Roslyn
P.S. To be Continued......
Thank you
Happy, Blessed and Prosperous 2016
I'm important
Best Wishes Always
Taylor
I Love
Buns Delicious
Feb 1 2016
May Allah Direct You'll in Great Ways
Great Desserts
Roland Park Middle School
2/11/16
Thanks!
Peace & Blessings
Trey
More Than just A Bakery
History
Food is Great Too!!!
Marcus
2-5-16
First time here going try the Sweet potato pie
Feb 5 2016
Great Food
Feb 6. 2016
Good Minister
William
Feb. 5. 2016

James H Fuller
04-13-15
Feb 12th
Sweet potatoe pies
so yummy!
#1 "The best bakery"
Leroy
Feb 11, 2016
Look at Chapter 2 Judges Verse 3
God blesses whom he Choses and Curse's whom he pleases But he Chose this dwelling to bless—
prophtess Charmaine 2010
2-13-16
Black History Month
2016
Thank you for keeping the legacy.
2/13/16
Love the Ladies @ Penn Ave Bakery! Thank you for the smiles + fabulous treats!
Feb 11
Stay Black In Mind + Soul
My Bros. + Sisters
Bro. O.
Best wishes to A Fantastic bakery
Fantastic Bakery
The Best Smoothies In the World!!
Sweet po
Love The History
Thanks
Good Baked Goodies always
Brown Power
The Rolls taste like I died and went to heaven
Ummm! 1st experience 2/17/16 will def be returning
check out our FB page
www.facebook.com/groups/
support black business
#blackbusinessmatters
So Special!
20 Feb 2016

Black is Beautiful
I support Black Businesses
Power to the People!
peach cake is marvelous!
Best rolls in B-more!
Shaw

Baltimore Youth Organizing Project
Approves of this business!
#Keep up the Good work 2/20/16

2/20/16
All the way from North Carolina we were truly blessed during this visit. We will be Back
The Reid's.

THANKING YOU
MR Gordon

Vietnam Veterans Approve
Mark Griffin 2/20/2016

These rolls are full of love just like the people who make them ☺

This wont Be Our LAST Time Here
Keep up the good Work
Odell Grant Jr and Family

Thanks for a job well done 2/27/16

Autumn Hughes was here

I'm from the youth organizing project

My First Time Here and I Love It
#Black owned businesses rock
Akia Jones

Olivia Williams
♡ @ 1st Sight

God bless you real good!
B.A. Dugger

Johnny Shaw
Victorine Q Adams Community GARDEN

Butter Pound CAKE
YUMMY YUMMY GOOD TO MY TUMMY
GOD BLESSINGS
BEVERLY

THANK YOU!

Thank you
your Cakes are The Bomb.

Thank you ☺ Ralph King

DJ TRAY

"Simply The Best"

VERY good
KEEP UP the good work

3/5/16
Life, Health and Strength!
V. Hazel Hopewell

Dinner rolls are awesome! You can taste them too!

03-11-2016 ☺

CONGRATS ON FIVE YEARS IN BUSINESS

Kia & Marci Myers

This place is rich history

Love yall

Love The History

It brings the Love Back!!!

Keep on moving

Alright you all

Karen ♡

Love yall

XOX

Gwen

Love yall

4Eyes!!!

MTA

THANKS

Love your Bread???

3/26/16

West Baltimore, comes back home!

S. Williams

S. Harlan

And you know this!

DR Z

The Best Baltimore has to offer

Eri English

Burke 06-05-16
&
Deondra

BRO
1514 N. Mount St

Good Luck
Love This Bakery
Larry Hall

Keep up The Good
work you are Doing
R. Cox

Don't go
out of Business
Love you
2016

your muffins
are awesome
thanks. Brianne
Peyton R. Gaines

The peach
bread pudding
is to die for. I
enjoy my Sunday
drive to Pennsylvania
Avenue

Kendy

5-18-16
We haven't
stop coming
since 5-4-16
We just love
the pie and
the coffee
kitchen
&
Passion

5-4-16
We love your
sweet potato
pie
kitchen & Passion

5-11-16
We came
back for that
good ole
coffee
and
sweet potato
pie
kitchen & Passion

Wonderful

This is great
Thanks

Dottie Conaway

Latasha Bowman

Heard wonderful
things about u
Came to see
myself
Cookie

Russell

Kelly
&
Tasha

Free WOP
I love you!!!

Thomas
Lovelist

Love this
Place!!! - Jasmine
4/29/16

Russell

I love this
bakery!!!
Walker

Puggy

Raisin Donuts Da BomB !!!

Donald Ed

Thanks for the invite, James!

5/7/16

very nice!

LA 4 Life

Rickey D. 125

Service with a SMiLe

Thanks for sharing your story! -Lee

Taste Band

Smickey

Please Stay Pleasant
& Beautifully Black!
We Need more like you ♡

He Shall
Shine upon
You and your Business
shall grow = make sure to
tithe your 10% unto the Lord
Be Blessed
IN All you Do

My First Time,
Delicious!!!

L.A. Coffey

Keyshawney
Martin

My
First
Time

Thanks for a
Great location in
our community. This is my
first visit & not my last!
Nicki Cheeks
The Green Group Baltimore

I ride from Towson
Maryland to support
the Greatest Bakery ever!!
Keep up and Thank you
for servicing the community

came from ATL, GA for your
great Bakery.

Best place
to stop in
town!
Sam Little

my first time
A Great Place
2016

The Best
Better than
ALL
the Rest
Ness

To Our Best
Friends!
God Bless!
and Continued Blessing
Jane & Pop

Ain't muffin
but a thang!

How Delicious!!
Great food & Customer
Service
from DC

I heard about you
all the way in Harlem!
Congrats on 5 years!
Cheers to 5 more and 50 more!
Peace & ♡ K.T.

Every time I come in
there is always something
delicious waiting for me to
try. Keep up the excellent
Baking.
What A Blessing to the
Community. Delores Bradley

GOOD GOOD
Arlene Green

Greetings from Genevieve & Carole Wilson! We plan to purchase 150 books!

Thanks for your hospitality! Bill & Paula Bolton Hill

Kelly Crudup East Baltimore "2016"

Willie Davis Waxhaw, NC

Janie M. Reddick Charlotte NC

Carrie Barnes Charlotte, NC

Rev George Erwin Charlotte NC

Delores Easter Charlotte N.C.

B. Adams, Char. NC

Christine Erwin Charlotte NC

Betty McLeod Charlotte, NC

Rosa Erwin Charlotte NC

Betty Stewart Charlotte, N.C.

8/26/16 Charlotte NC !! Thanks for the Tour and much success in the future re-establishing the area

Pearl was Here Thx Good Service

May The Lord Continue to provide you with a blessed increase year to year Howard Dansplatt 8-27-16

This is Great!! Saundra Jackson Aug 2016 Charlotte, NC

Keep up the Good Work on our History Thanks

Cassandra Hunter

Richard Elder

God is good

Hey Jim!

Veronica

Dana Martin 330 Roland Ave Balto. MD

Arielle & Carde & Naima Was Here 12:48PM 8/31/16 and again on 9-2-16 @ 12:40am

08/31/16 Linda Weaver Edmondson High '68

BALTIMORE BLUESMAN – QUINTON RANDALL 26 years old

(Free)

Antonia Perdu the Poet

Rena Stewart Johnson was here

Glenn Payne 9/13/16 Nothing But Love

Allison Robicelli ALLISON@ROBICELLIS.com

Kysha Shaw Kyshashaw44@gmail.com Wed Sept. 7th 2016 @ 11:40am

Linda Stewart, Balto, MD lmstewart42@gmail.c

(Ellwood's Mother) Rhonda DiLane Balto. MD 21217 Rlane7@jhmi.edu rhondalane21@gmail.com Saturday September 10, 2016 12:28pm.

Greetings from Cleveland, OHIO St Mt Carmel Church Group Tour 9/2016

Sean Berry-Bey Seanmonet.bb@gmail.com Sun. 9/11/16

Congrats on 5 yrs GOD Bless your Family And your business, You are truly a blessing to the Community of Baltimore, [illegible] 9/11/16

Congrads 5yrs and counting
Otashika Albrecht

Amazing! Rochelle Kane 9/15/16
Wonderful Glorian Fields-Short 9/15/16

Will be Back
Loved it

Colleen Montgomery
+ Mike

To God give the Glory 9/18/16
Stay Blessed Carol Burrell

Thanks
100 Black Men of Maryland, Inc

Rebuilding The Royal
One Brick at a Time
Mykel Hunter 9/16
Radio Mike Mobin

Matt

Make more Buns

Thank you Matt

9/24/2016
Good Morning
Jackson

Need to come back!!
Chris

RICHARD GIBSON
"OK"

Enjoyed myself
purchasing my
sweets today
9/23/16
Sharie May
&
Matt

2016
MY FIRST TIME
HERE, AND WHAT A
GREAT PLACE!
ERNEST YATES

Tommy Woodard
Bass man 2016
God Bless

Keep Achieving!
Barry

God Bless this Bakery
Rolls taste just like Grandmothers

Always good to see good people
10-29-16 Peter Conway

Deacon! Lucas Please send me
some picture of Birthday cake to my
EMAIL ADDRESS: ROBERTDLUCAS0181@
gmail.com

Reach for the joy
that rises with every morning Sun! B.H.

Ocean and the TV of
history is enduring
Dr. G

11-23-2016
Happy Thanksgiving
we Love your Rolls and
other Baked Goods

Donna Anderson
+ Robin Parker

Rosetta
My Love 12/1/14

Mom
23/16

A Very Special
Place
I'm happy
Mother

Dr. Ken
GOD ALWAYS BLESSES
— DENNIS D. HARRIS
Dr. Greg
Battle

THANK YOU
FOR PRESERVING

May you Continue to
prosper & be blessed
A great place.

Peace & blessings
Linda Weaver
Edmondson
Class of '68

Train Up a Child—When They're Young

It's always been my belief that to make a difference in a young person's life, one needs to start early, well before they hit high school. Sometimes well-meaning organizations get involved with high schools, trying to capture young folks to join their companies. Such is actually a disservice to companies and students. We should be concentrating on middle schoolers because that's when kids make the decision to drop out of school. After that, all they're really doing is waiting until they turn sixteen, so they can drop out legally. We must ignite these young minds as early as possible to make a difference in their lives.

On my mission, full-time a UPS as the new District Community Relations Manager, I joined the Junior Achievement of Central Maryland's board of directors and convinced UPS to spend $4,000 for two years to implement a Junior Achievement program called The Economics of Staying in School (TESS). It was the beginning of me working with school principals and various company department heads to create Job Shadowing and other learning/networking opportunities for youth.

I met Maggie Masters, who was involved with Teach for America. Maggie was also one of the proofreaders for my memoir *A Baltimore Story on a Roll: A Baker's Recipe to Revitalize Historic Pennsylvania Avenue* (2020). Part of my mission was to connect our youth/schools with the history and legacy of the community in which they lived and operated. Maggie was busy convincing Teach for America that to spur empathy and effective teaching, it needed to acquaint new teachers/educators with the lives and neighborhoods of the students they are teaching. For Maggie and me, our merge was made in heaven. I quickly availed the resources of UPS, and later when The Bakery came into existence, I availed

its spaces and resources to Job Shadowing, and I instituted my own classes to teach students about my business, baking, math skills and commerce.

Colin Powell's initiative called *America's Promise* crafted the Job Shadowing Program. At that time, I was a board member of the Maryland Mentoring Partnership, which was instrumental in implementing Colin Powell's initiative. As a result, I was able to convince my UPS partners to host students from schools within our district, which included Maryland, West Virginia, and Delaware, to allow students to shadow our managers and supervisors in various departments. Because of my relationship with Booker T., I was also able to get other businesses with which I had relationships to climb aboard. As I was setting this up, I was able to get UPS to pay for the transportation of these student field trips. All the participating businesses provided lunch for the students.

Mrs. Brenda Hamlin and former Ravens Safety Ed Reed

The next connection to cross my desk was with The Ravens. Mel, my district manager called me in his office again. "There is a football player by the name of James Trapp [at that time, of the Oakland Raiders]. He had partnered with UPS in California. They were running the program out there. [Upon a trade] The Baltimore Ravens signed him up as a safety."

The Ravens program, partnered with UPS, was titled *LORDS*, which stood for *Leadership, Order, Respect, Discipline and Success*. I introduced Trapp to Booker T. and to the then principal, Ruth Bukatman, with whom I had been working. The way it went was that each homeroom class had a football grid. The students earned points or gained yards based on attendance, behavior, and classwork.

Hall of Football Famer, Ravens Safety Ed Reed taking in the sweets, delighting customers

And the class that had the most yards got to go to a Sunday home football game. UPS paid for T-shirts and all the tasty fixin's of a tailgate party, prepared right there in the stadium's parking lot with a UPS truck positioned as a supply-hub and backdrop. Soon James Trapp was traded to the Jacksonville Jaguars, and the game ball was handed off to the Ravens' Safety Ed Reed. Reed, who had a Football Hall of Fame induction in his future, already had been active, encouraging youth. When UPS made the decision to move on to a different project, my nonprofit, The Royal Theater and Community Heritage Corporation (TRTCHC), picked up the ball. And, to this day, TRTCHC and the Ed Reed Foundation continue our partnership and program at the Booker T. Washington Arts Academy (its new name). A part of this partnership includes our tailgate parties at The Ravens football games and Ed's sports activity days held for the students on the Booker T. campus.

Press coverage at The Avenue Bakery

Keep on Keeping on

11-16-16 Stopping By to get some yummy sweets!!

Thank you for being here Rocky

A quietly strong ... and a winning ... quality

American place w/ great smells :) yum. Liz

Good Luck &

God Bless You

Come here all the time from over East

Carl, Stuart, Frances, Eleanor & William
The Hodgins Family
Visited on 25 Sept 2016
This store is a local extension of the newly opened National Museum of African American History and Culture

Blessed and Highly Favored!!
Honored to be in the Presence of Baltimore Greatness - Taking Back all to Detroit!!
Regina Ann Campbell :) 09/26/16

... Coppin State University

Awesome place, Thanks for hosting us! Aaron Goodman - Detroit, MI

Good to see sustainable black businesses

The Avenue Bakery is evidence that a business enterprise can thrive in our community. The investigation ... the history of the African American ... All the Best, Joseph Haskins, The Harbor Bank

Everything at the Avenue Bakery is Awesome!!! T. Maddox

Seph-Lova
- 2016 -
- Humanitarian Music -

Paul "Doc" Coleman
Penn Bakery is excellent
Oct 5, 2016

Christian X King
- Worth the trip
393 NE Kettle St Oak Harbor WA 98277

First Time in the Bakery
Love you all & God Bless You
... James G. Young Balto. Md. 10/7/16

Jerry & Ann
4-Ever
Angela & Angela
10/7/16
Love This Place
The strawberry danish is (Bomb)
The white breads are delicious! 10/9/16
Thank you for your continued love of us and support. I'm so grateful to see Black business in the City I can see myself here.
Danielle 6/22/17
Good Sweets!
God Bless!
A Great Baltimore Resource!
Delicious!
All the best -
Congrats 5 yrs n Countings
Good Luck
There's no one else like ya!

2016
10-15
God Bless you
Mary Bailey

04/02/17

10/27/2016
WITH LOVE
FROM SWEDEN

2016
10-16
I AM BACK!!!
GREG.G.

MARVIN

2016
My frist time
Will Be Back
Kitty

Hello! 10/27/2016
I walked in
Glad to see Blacks in business
I truly ask My God
bless your Establishment
& you All with
Good health
Prosperity
Patricia

Tommy Woodard
Bass man 2016
God Bless

Keep Achieving!
Barry

11/13/16
God Bless this Bakery
Rolls taste just like
Grandmother

Always good to see good people
10-29-16 Peter Conway

Deacon: Lucas Please Birthday cake send me
some Picture of cake to my
EMAIL ADDRESS: ROBERTDLUCAS0101@gmail.com

Reach for the joy
that rises with every morning Sun! B.H.

So clean and the TV of
history is Exciting
D.G.

Thanks for being here Rolls & all just Great like Grandma. Love Kotee

I came for the history, & came many more times for the [illegible]

12-4-16 Wish we had discovered you sooner. [illegible]

Thank you for being here, representing the cause and presence of Africoid people. This who we are. This what we're about. May the Creator bless this establishment and all like it.
Bro. N. Chambers-EL, the Moor
Dec 10, 2016

Such a beautiful Place
Deborah Lloyd

Renard Moore Hardware Plus

I AM BACK AGAIN SHOGUN'S
GREG. GILMORE
DEC 10-2016

Peace Much Growth Queen Shelnith

Thank You for Be here Dawn

This place takes me back to the good old days when life was simple.
I appreciate the memories that you represent.
Keep up the good work.
Sheik R. Wimberly-El, DM

Bro. Marrow-El, D.M.
Lost is good, better to be found in the Heart of Allah at anytime... Rest and awaken!
Peace Peace!
Salamisha my Brother

12/4/16 Love them everything they make

Love this place

Timothy Johnson

U guys keep up the good work May GOD Bless U All
Earlene Cooper
B'klyn N.Y.

Happy Holidays to [illegible] Inc. I Don't [illegible]
[illegible] wish everyone [illegible]

I will be arriving the age of 46 on Dec. 23. All I ask for is peace and to be with my grandkids, Kapria, Ravelly and Baby Day

12/22/16
Holiday Blessings To All Supporters/Friends of the Avenue Bakery. May the New Year bring You Joy, Good Health, Prosperity and New Friendships.
Blessings Always,
Vocalist/Poet
Thomas Carter

This bakery is the Best

12/30/2016
May God continue to bless lovely ligia. Keep doing good
Love Always
Pearl 1st time shopper

Saturday Sept. 2, 2017
Been trying to catch the place open + I Made It!!
JH

always comes here to get my Raisin buns love this Places and The Peoples who works here Pat Giles
9-7-17

12/30/2016
Thank you for a wonderful experience
– Adreanna Fleet
God Bless!

Happy Valentine's Day!
to
the wonderful folks
at
The Avenue Bakery
from ALL who
Love you
Great that we have
you "right here" in
Baltimore

12/30/16
Thank you for the great rolls!!
– [illegible]
1st time shopper

12/30/16
Pastor Lewis
God bless!

Thank you Vivian + Doc from Annapolis MD - Enjoy the bakery good. Keep up the excellent work.

Great rolls and service!! Lawrence 2-9-17

Well worth everytime I stop.. The best thing That happend on the P-Ave

Mary Trueheart 1st Visit 2/11/17

I LOVE IT HERE! The food is AWESOME

JQ

Heritage, History, Hunger All here 4 u 2 Enjoy. Keep up good spirit! R Burns 6/26/17

James 8

Phillip Hamilton "17"

I love the Bakery Best 2017 The Best

Congradulations

Congratulations!

Keep Up the good work

This Place
Has shown Love &
Great place to the
community. May God
Bless & Grow This
Establishment and
May People come here
for peace & increase.

This Place is Fantastic!
C'est Fantastique!
¡Es lo Fantastico!
Das ist Sehr Gut!
Len Williams
A Benjamin
Friday 9/1/17
• [illegible]
• [illegible]
• [illegible]
• [illegible]

9/1/17 - Heart's Palace ... Detroit!

9/9/17
It been a Pleasure to have eaten at this black owned & operated establishment. Love

We need this place! These treats are awesome
I love it here
Toyia @ JCPenney's @ Eastpoint

My husband & I love this place. It has the best sweet potato pies. They melt in your mouth.
Awesome Place
The Wilsons

Thank You for Having a Great Team and Business!
Pleasant events with A Teaching Class!

Tracy Mck & Marcellus Sin.
Towson, MD

My Mom made me come in today while we were out from PA.
Nathan Jefferson
Gwendolyn Richardson

Love the Acorn Berry
Love the Smoothie
Keisha Davis

Fmoig @ K4mcrOn (zero)

Thank You From The Mitchell-Hargrove Family

Amy Terrell
You have Good service May GOD Bless.

I told you I was coming back when I had some money because everything is delicious and everything [illegible] sample them

10. Avenue Bakery
Heavenly Churning 8 of you guys
Enjoy every Bite of your ...

10. Ave Bakery
(Now) Known
As the "A"!
Black
W.L.C.
all ways
Gold St.

To
The Avenue
Bakery Owners
& Staff...

Wednesday
February 22, 2017

I am very impressed with this facility. It is, by far, the best enterprise that I have ever seen! It is clean, orderly and professional. Without tasting anything, I know that it is all good. Thank you for your efforts, workmanship, hospitality and most of all for the presentation of our history and culture! God bless you! Dr. William A. Benjamin, International Business Consultant
(Former Talk Show Producer & Host of Profiles on Africa - WEAA Radio)

2-24-17
Very clean, quite impressed, my first time but I will visit again. Emily ...

I Love The Rolls and The history
Duani Dorsey age 10 2-25-2017

Jim,
Keep the vision going.
It's going to happen.
Bill

Veronica Broadnax
So excited to have a Black owned business in the neighborhood. And such a professional atmosphere.

Simmons & Day Softball Team
Baltimore, MD

Thanks for the tour really enjoy it

Authenticity, Creativity, Wholesome, Delicious, and made with that Black Love. Best Place In Town

You Just can't eat one

Very Mild, tasting

I LOVE this BAKERY
MARTIN H.

great time
Kenneth

You are terrific! The avenue lives.
Larry Jackson

Love it here
Dorbie

First time here and I will be back

First time Here
the Harrell Family
3/5/17

Great Service, Great Bakery
D. Sh[illegible]
3/[illegible]/17

I Love coconut cake

We love this Bakery Thank You All

We love the Ave Bakery The Davis Family

Santos Lekgatoane
From South Africa
I am Zulu/Sotho

Saturday, March 11, 2017
10:40 a.m.

Hey Santos Dumalong! This is William Benjamin
My first Radio Guest on Apartheid in South Africa
WEAA Profiles on Africa
1985-2000 15 years
Check me out at
www.[illegible].com

Mr. & Mrs. Joseph & Thelma Samuels 1st timers

Thanks for your Service

This Place takes me back to the 60's when we had bakeries on every corner it seems like! Signed
"Customer for Life"
Denny & Duane Harris

Bonjour...
The Avenue Bakery in French...
La Boulangerie de L'Avenue
Dr. William A. Benjamin
Samedi le 18 mars 2018
Saturday March 18, 2018

May God Bless Hill's of Catonsville
Greetings from Atlanta by way of B'more
Stay Blessed - James Stewart EWING

Brother Hamlin,
Great Job! You've made us proud. Keep up the good work!
God Bless
LeRoy Young

3/25/17

Um! Um! GOOD East Baltimore
March 26 2017

I from Phila MAY
Love this place

"KEEP ON KEEPING ON"
Rock

God Bless

3/25 First time here, but definitely not the last. Fully supportive and proud of the movement.
Annapolis, Md

Love the food
MARTIN H. "2017"

dmoneyz sweets was here Ful of Fire

Here for cake!

Love Helma & Joe Great Bakery

SWEET POTATOE PIE'S ARE GREAT!!!

Great and rich history moment!!!
Love this Bakery
BASIR Nice
Former Marrah Broom Dance Student
Di Martin - FL Granddaughter
Alexis Snell and Nathan Jefferson
I Love this bakery
1st time here but will be back (Queen Anne County Kent Island)
3/25/17
My First time in this Amazing Bakery
Black owned & Black Love + 2017
Brian
Me and My stomach are loving these treats
I Love this good Food
Aiyunna

Taking delicious rolls to The
"Great City of Pittsburgh"

Donnell Jones from
Park Height

Rosie X Lola
from A providence Adult Day
We love your bakery!!

Margie Firedevereaux
Soooooo... Happy to find A Real
Bakery again — Love it — will
tell others + be BACK many, many,
more times God Bless

Crown 300 Franklin St
Baltimore Maryland 21229
410 566 4827

Jessica Novak - Delicious
artexchangegroup@gmail.com + Thank you!

Peaches + Winky Camphor Well worth the
3308 Laurie Rd. 21244 trip.

A'Ameen I. Ahbdallah Quaiuzzii
Peace and Blessing to all of Allahs
Instruments and Helpers
Only Allah has the power to
Give and Take for his use
May all praise and glory
be to howAAh

Thank The Lord for your success.

Oasis on Penn Ave
Thank you for your hospitality
Visit Baltimore

Mr. & Mrs. Martin
On the Avenue 4/22/17
Thanks for your warm
hospitality.
Best friendliest
Bakery in
Baltimore

Thank you for [illegible]

Refreshing!! the coffee, the [illegible] ... and the hospitality

I love this bakery
especially since it is
in the community

Best Wishes
This is my childhood neighborhood!!

Elaine Simon President
Combsbern Council
443-869-1835

le 28 avril 2015

Michael G. Middleton Sr.
Thanks for your Help + hospitality for Cheryl

Mari

You guys are the BEST! Customer service is unlike most nowadays. Thank you for caring on our legacy and keeping history of our people ALIVE! Love you!

This is my first time coming here but definitely won't be my last, # supportblackbusiness
Ms. Toy

BIG DADDY !!
Hope y'all last forever

I love the [illegible] for the [illegible] keep the good work up [illegible] [illegible]

On this day of 4/28/17
I love the Bread pudding
Best in the world
Yours truly
M. Whitted

Love the wonderful warm loving experience. Jean!!

Jean - keep the faith! and your vision.
Bill Henrick

THE ONE & ONLY
THE AVENUE
MR Ben

Charles Weaver
4/5/17
The Best Table of All

My first time here. Love the warm feeling given!
Donna Waters

Veronica Love

PEACE & BLESSINGS
PW
2017

You are the best
Luv Y'all

Great experience for first time visitor! Brad & Monique Bradley
From Hollywood Florida will be referring our friends & family
God Bless You!

I [illegible] was here [illegible]

DOC Annapolis MD

ViVian McCown

Being from D.C. in the 60's I can appreciate what little I remember of the Ave., back in the day. Thanx for the memories
G. Darby

Williamsburg Brooklyn NYC

B-more

Sylvia Morgan 6/17

PARRIS GARDNER
FROM NORTHEASTERN SPRING
GREAT EXPERIENCE!!

Mrs. Alfreda Brown Matthews
Upl. MD.

God Bless wall
Larry Newton from King of Deliverance Holiness Church
1200 N. Fulton Ave
Bishop John Jones

The Avenue Bakery
Home of Poppay's Rolls
2229

6/19/17 Your food is awesome ☺ Renia

I love The Avenue Bakery
Hafiya ICS!

6/7/17 marjuanah R. martin i love this place
marjuanah ICS

6/7/17 Thank you so much for having us in to hear and learn from you! – Simon

6/7/17 So excited to try your treats!
– Celine

6/7/17 We skipped a lot of plans to come here, and it's well worth it

6/7/17 Thank you so much for your hospitality, knowledge, and tasty baked goods! We so appreciate you staying open late for us and sharing history with us. We will be back soon!
Simon, Maggie, Abby, Esther & ...

6/7 I'm hungry for sweets! Bush... Ruskell

6/7 Thank you for your sweets will be back soon – ...

6-10-2017 My first visit, I'm so excited! Debra ...

6-10-2017 My girlfriend told me about your bakery! Just happened to be in the area. Yummy!!! Debora Brockington
Baltimore, Md.

06-10-17 Enjoyed the sample and the hospitality
Neal Brockington

6-11-2017 I came back! The best cake I've ever eaten! She must use a special kind of flour + sugar. Too Good...
Debra G.

Keep on Keeping on!!
Rocky

6-16-17 my 1st visited didn't know it was here – I'll be back ... Elvie

6/16/17 I Just Love This Bakery J. Watkins

6-17-2017 The food and service are GREAT!!!
Michael Robinson : Cleveland, Ohio

Doc Vivian
Annapolis md

Glenn Cooper
6/20/2017
East Baltimore

Vivian J. Storey
11 Slade Ave #516
Pikesville, MD 21208

6/22/17
The Best Bakery in town
u know how I know once u come back for more of anything u know that its good

Bassir the Baker
I love everything about this Bakery

Congratulations!
Art chit chat & chew

Great Sweet Potato Pies
Carolyn

Robert Thompson
Dallas Texas

Congrats on bringing the past forward. We love what you've done with the place!
George & Stephanie Brooke
We will return

the food's great!
Heaven
6 30 17

Love your baked goods
... Pete ...

Thanks for the history lesson!
George - Houston, TX

What an inspiring & educational experience to become acquainted with the history of Penn Ave. Thank you, Jim, for executing and for remaining faithful to your vision. You can be nothing but successful!
Melody Martin San Francisco July 1, 2017

Always ♡ a visit to the Avenue Bakery
Great Partners, Delicious Coffee
and Wonderful People
Stephanie Delgado

ED HYMAN
JUST CAME FROM ST. Louis MO

Amazing! Thank you for feeding us and teaching us some of the history of West Baltimore
Sincerely,
Sophia Rosenfeld
(Urban Teachers)

Hardware Plus

Harriton Gobeh
Born Liberia
Raised New Jersey
Ooh-roh

Dina
Bernard
Carolina

Thank you ♡

Kofi Kulu - The Alameda
Peace + Many Blessing

Nina the Original Party Girl
Baltimore's Exclusive
Celebration Technician!
May God continue to bless
this wonderful black
owned business!

A#

Good to be back in B-more on the Ave.
Little Rock, Arkansas

Mrs. Bella Johnson 6/8/17
Such a Wonderful mission
& place
May God continue to bless your service
to the community & the world!

A wonderful food experience that I would do again!
Edmond T. Yates
7-11-17

7/1/17

God's blessing And Favor in your life.
Diane Wattley

God Bless This Place With Your Grace
Love RaRa

God Bless sending many blessing
Matt Dylan Carr

May the Lord bless your business and it exceed your expectations. May He meet every need, and answer every prayer. In Jesus Name.
Laker - Dallas, TX
7.27.17

God is Good all the time.
Nettie D Crocker

Be Blessed
Dawson

Have Heavenly Cleaning Svc, LLC
Has checked in again
we so love you guys

Mercredi le 19, juillet 2017
Wednesday, July 19, 2017
French - Bonjour
Spanish - ¡Hola!
German - Guten Tag
Pennsylvania Avenue Bakery
Thank you for the history!
Best Wishes!
Merci Pour L'histoire
Meilleur Voeux
Dr. William A. Benjamin
Profiles in Africa WEAA
1985-2000 88.9 FM
Morgan State University

H. R. Mack
Sandtown legend

Jaranne Medlock, North Carolina

Shaquanna Dotson
R Dotson
3128 Piedmont Ave
Baltimore MD 21216
Rodney Dotson
Shaquanna Dotson

Thank You! Came All the Way from Arizona Just to Have Homemade Goods!
God is Good!
Regina
7/23/2017

Thank you 07/30/2017
Word of mouth brought wonderful service & bakery items
Kept me
Marian Gayle

8/3/17
I love you guys

Angine #52
Bmores Fire finest!

I'm ever greatful for your detication, and your comitement to make your brand the in the most & east product that being giving your love to the community is and has been the responsibilty of restoring that which was slowly slowly loosing your help in restoring makes all the difference.
Sincerely
Kip Hall

LOVE
- Sterling, 10
Bermuda

Great Place We needed this
Cassie Hemming

Good Luck
We need a
Place like this
Jerri Bright
My Neighborhood

Thank you
God's Bless you
for all you do
T. Green 8/20/17

So glad to be here. I brought my 88 yr. old mother today. She loved the Courtyards. AND the wheat Rolls ☺ oh yea
Thanks for being so kind.
Alexis Morton

Pleased to see us
Prosper Staff
Much Success

The Best!
Khari Hayes
Silver Spring, Maryland

Beautiful Place
First Time here
Me & My Brother
Charles + Gerry
8/20/17

Been a long time coming
thanks

Tashaun & Octavia
1st time here 8/4/17

1st TIME
LIL Thomas

"Nice"
C. Stanley WAS HERE
STAN THE MAN
MERVO 1980

Baltimore born & raised but living in Portland, OR. Everytime I come home, I come here. Love the food, the atmosphere, the history.
Thank you
Patricia W.

Thanks
For Great Desserts
Peace Y. Muhammad
8-24-17

Thank you for a wonderful experience and the pastries are very good
8-27-17

Thank you for providing a space for us to remember our heritage (who we are and where we can go to achieve greatness.
Rhonda Elsey

Shelley Franklin
1207 James St 21223
Baltimore Maryland 410 493....
Everything taste Great
I will be back soon everyone one greeting us were pleasant and kind
I will be back and I'll bring some people with me. "2017"

★ This will be a face you'll see quite often ☺ ★
Cynthia Franklin

Thank you for helping us to remember how wonderful we are!
President Emeritus, Payne Theological Seminary
Aug 25, 2017

The 'pound cake' are heavy with Love!
I cannot wait to buy 5 more
8/25/2017

The Bakery is an amazing place ...
It is truly an honor to have been able to visit the bakery and purchase some of the fantastic rolls and cobbler.
Many thanks to ...

It's a blessing to be served by folks who really care about our community & provide such great tasting sweets.
8/25/17
Hilda Harrison

Thank you for all your sweet treats and your commitment to excellence!
The Talleys

9/6/17

May Allah Guide and Bless this Bakery, the owners, Employees and their Families, This Community and Keep the unity amongst us all. Ameen

Tonya Brown

May Jehovah continue to Bless you All.

Much love to the poppay Rolls

It's my Lucky Day

Rolls are ♡

Luv Chase

9-9-17

9/9/2017

I Really Enjoyed the history And Jazz show I haven't been here in a while but I sure will come back!!!

Thanks for the memories

"Ms Regina Burlatt" Robert Burlatt sister

P.S. Yours food is delicious

Sat 9-9-17 6:30pm

Hi, I'm Alma Burkett from 518 N Pine St We live over 56 yrs Debra, Jeanna Lee Burke Home for every Thank You

Sang at The Bakery With Aaron Rhimes 9-9-17 DC Beautiful Spirit Mr Hamlin one of a kind

Good Morning Family. It is a pleasure to come to such a wonderful establishment. It was just like grandma house. Heavenly Bless

9/21/2017 Very nice Bakery people & Great Biscuits. Angela

9-16-17 Good bakery goods Continue to keep it going. Peace & Blessings Rochelle Las Vegas NV Boulevard Baltimore

9/21/17 Loved, Loved, Loved This Joint. Blessings towards your success. Virginia Ruffin L.A. CA 9-10-16

May God Bless the Bakery & all its Staff

GREG HILL ALWAYS KEEP LOOKING UP ↑

Glad to See You Keeping The History Alive.

Thank you David Johnson

9-16-17 Food looks delicious, can't wait to try it! From Washington DC The Hales

Praise God for this Business and may it be prosperous in the future. Rev Wayne Green

A Baltimore Uprise is what we need set the captives free. May God Bless you, and every one who enters your establishment. Marcus Hall

Bishop Simmiel Williams
One of the greatest bakeries
I've ever been to.

Alma Hicks from California. Glad to be here. Black business is special —

Hello, Barbara Gibson. Glad to visit your Bakery.

AMA BADU - LA, CA. ☺

Rosalie Jones was here and from Los Angeles CA
enjoy so much thank you

Ostree J. Griggs was here 9/2017
from Compton Cal

Much success [illegible]
many blessings [illegible]

GREG GILMORE, 9-16-17
GREAT PEOPLE
GREAT BAKERY

9-17-2017

Best Sweet Potato Pie
Pebbles 9-20-17

9-21-17
God Bless

Good to Come to a Very nice Place. 1st Time Charlotte

The Best

9-20-2017

9/21/2017
Rosie was here from LA Great success to y'all ☺

Lamechia + Melvin Scott
Compton CA
9/21/17

Jean McDaniel Boatright
Compton Calif VIA Watts where the old South Line / Sadie V. Thompson H.S.

Jennie Buchanan — Los Angeles CA — 9/21/17
[illegible] — Los Angeles CA — 9/21/17
Alma Malone — Long Beach CA — 9/21/17
Mary Shipp — Los Angeles CA — 9/21/17
Donna Daley — Hawthorne CA 90250 — 9-21-17

Enjoyed looking at the beautiful art. E. Potter L.A.

Kenny & Co
9-22-2017

Waldo Davis
9-22-17

Delicious & inspiring!
Georgia [illegible]
9/28/2017

Janet Butler
MOM MOM'S HOUSE
May GOD Bless your Business
9/30/2017

[illegible]
Your Generous Donation

A treat 4 Body & Mind Truely a sweet blessing 4 me
Thank you.
andre

Clayton [illegible]
Baltimore/NYC
Thanks!
9/29/17

Mizaarah Makini
LOVES Thank you

Proud to support an establishment that heralds our history
Dr. Worley
Church of Christ

B-more

Thank you so much for your hospitality and the cakes. Tanya Ke 9/28/17

Dr. Greg says it's the Best spot in town — 7/2017

Thank you for being
an amazing asset to our community!
The tour was awesome!
Rams • Parrots
Rod.

10-6-2017
Love What ya doing
Photography for the Arts
and other things that Matter

Bc-More's
Best
Ave Bakery

Butch & Sons
Shoe Shine

Love · Peace
+ Blessings

Peace & Blessings!
The Best Ever!
Love the Summer
Jazz

Beat The Streets MD

thank
you for
making this
Bakery

T@BY:D Love you

Just Stopped Ray
in the neighborhood!
Best Bakery in the State.
Great Job James!
Del. ~~Kent~~ Hyper

Great Bread,
Cunbre

It's Really Good!!
KL

10/21/17

Linda Weaver

Dawn Neal Montgomery County
love the sweet potato pie

Good Morning 10/25/17
:)
My Favorite
Baked Goods!!
Thanks Avenue Bakery
For Loving the people
May Allah Bless You and Your Family
©Tanya Brown
"2017"

First Time here
& I must try Somthing
and I hope it's good!!

EVERYthing was
Great Ronald Byrd
God Bless this STORE :)

Been coming here for a while
now and I absolutely
love it. The service, the
atmosphere and the quality
of the products is second
to none!
Love you guys
Ray tup!

10/28/17
First Time.
Loved It!
Marsha, Tony & Tyler

FIRST
TIME HERE!
MTA Mobility
Woman
BLACK Woman
PROUD!
Ms. Suzie is AMAZING
a wonderful inspiration
to me as a
BLACK
WOMAN!

11/1/2017 12:00
Finally Made it here
Lovely Ladie's + Baked Goods
Carlos & Theresa Moulden

11/2/17
You Guys Are the
best. God Bless you
Charles

Liam Davis
Council President Young's Office
11/9/2017

One 'L' Michele
2017

Baked Goods R The Best
From Senator [illegible]

Love Them Raisin Bun's

Love the Rolls
xoxo
Monica

First time here Nov 9, 2017
Heard desserts are great. [illegible] mine now.
Bridget

[illegible] you have seen the mother of [illegible] thousand things. [illegible]

[illegible] Veteran Employee

Love this Place!!
[illegible]

I love the yeast Rolls and the sticky Bunns
Love this Place
Stacy [illegible]

2017
Rena Sweeting
[illegible]

Fabulous history and rolls!
A great Baltimore treat
[illegible]

God Bless you, forever and ever
The Davis's

Love This Place
Much Blessings!
Pam

Love Y'all
Russell

[illegible]
Nov. 16, 2017

The Avenue Bakery is Everything!!
I'm so Glad I found your bakery
Um Um Um... Um... Um... Um...
EXCELLENT!!!
LHM (Lord Have Mercy!!!
Good Food
Thank-you
Avenue Bakery is Awesome!!
A GREAT EXPERIENCE
RJ
Hardware Plus.
Love this place!!
Dudley

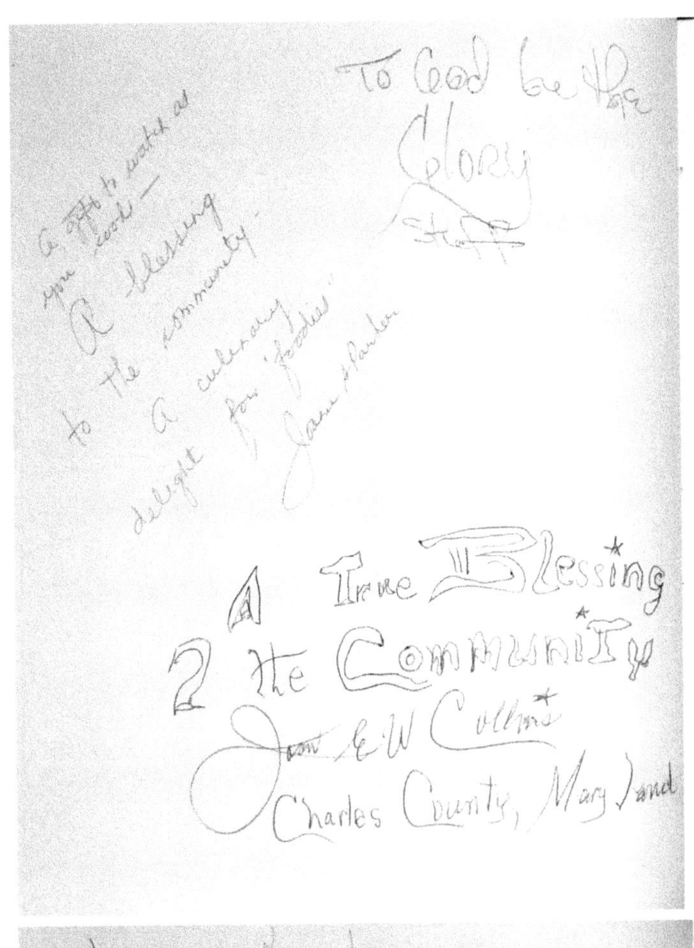

Bonjour et Siyabonga!
de La Part de
Dr. William A. Benjamin
le 22 Novembre 2017

Prince Miles
nephew of Douglas Miles
Bishop

Very Good Place Green
See you soon
11-2017

Don't ever leave the neighborhood
we need you
George Spencer

11/28/17
Continue to support Black Businesses!

11-29-2017
May God Bless

So happy for this bakery in our neighborhood. God Bless you Dec 2017

Keep on doing Baking Thanks

This is a remarkable place we need 100 more just like this

Great Black Owned Establishment with delish baked good

Great food Great people Johnny

(Heads)

Great black owned store with great friendly employees and staff

Talia Whitehurst I love this black owend store. 12/17/2017

Happy Holidays, To a wonderful group of people and a delicious baking. It's a blessing to have you in the community. Much love ♡ Betty

Continued Blessings

Happy + Merry Christmas Blessed Person to a Blessed Establishment May God Continue!! Karen Y. Jones

HAPPY HOLIDAY GREAT JOB Roddell

happy holidays Big Quan

"Happy Holidays" God Bless you all and I'am thankfull Mr. William H Miles Nephew of Bishop Douglas Miles I Love you all

Happy Holidays Merry Christmas Happy Kwanzaa Keep up the GREAT job!!

High School Sweethearts Soaking up The Avenue and Beyond

It's something to behold when I think about how years of my life's observations went into my revised vision to prove that commerce could thrive on The Avenue and that the community would eat it up—and support it. It was second nature for me to incorporate all I had learned while working at UPS. I knew that valuing customers would be key. As a young student in junior high school, one of my teachers, Mrs. Hardy, caused me to love history. I once harbored a dream to become a history teacher. I knew that honoring the legacy and history of the Pennsylvania Avenue Corridor, its activists, legacy, and surrounding communities—West Baltimore as a whole—would become a part of my new vision. And that thought did not only belong to me.

My wife, Brenda, and I have known one another since we were young. In West Baltimore's Booker T. Washington Junior High School (now known as Middle School), shared Mrs. Hardy's history class. "It was during the one year I went to public school," Brenda joked.

My wife had been educated in Catholic Schools, but we both grew up in the same neighborhood and we both grew an appreciation for history in Mrs. Hardy's classroom. While I eventually honed a career at UPS, learning all about business, customer service, and community outreach, Brenda had a career as a librarian, honing the exact same skills. Ironically, she retired from the Carroll County Public Library (after sixteen years) in April of 2011. The Avenue Bakery came into being on August 15 that same year.

James & Brenda Hamlin Wedding Day

James and Brenda Hamlin in their Sweetheart days

James Hamlin's High School Days

About Brenda's love, devotion, and acquired expertise, baked into years of elbow grease that she has put into the business, by my side, she said, "We're family. We believe in supporting each other." She conceded that while building a bakery "really wasn't my thing; no matter what *I've* always wanted to do, he [James] has always been there for me. So, I tried to put whatever knowledge or skill I had together to make things possible for him."

One might say that it's the sugar that puts the longevity in our marriage.

Brenda's years at the library, catering to all types of people, put her in sync with working in a depressed area. People from all types of backgrounds and social and economic challenges walk through the doors of The Avenue Bakery. "And you have to learn how to treat people, no matter what, with dignity," Brenda commented.

Displaying excellence to the community has been our goal, we work hard to demonstrate the difference between a hustle and a business—doing things in decency and order. Often, out-of-town visitors will come in and assume that we're only the face of this operation, that there is someone else—outside of our community—running the show. We quickly set them straight. Then delight them with a Poppay's Roll sample. Thus far, it has ensured repeat customers. Visitors return, bringing family members and friends—especially during holidays and family gatherings. And when the daily grind churns uphill, I sneak a peek in our legacy logbook to read the comments left behind. They always fuel me for another day.

Another early memory gained in my youth that went into my vision to build a bakery came from patronizing a local restaurant called Haussner's that stood in East Baltimore's Highlandtown. As young adults, Brenda and I respectfully enjoyed the landmark eatery that previously didn't serve African Americans—its food, its atmosphere, and its décor. Nearly every wall was covered with eye-gripping portraits and scenes that conveyed stories of the German proprietors' old country, a husband-and-wife team—their history. Their art collection was not only expansive and expensive, but it was also legendary and rivaled area art galleries. My young mind, for years, also took note of its cleanliness. I mean it was simply absent of dust. And its claim to fame was its strawberry pie. Haussner's was in business from 1926 to 1999.

In October of 2016, *The Baltimore Sun* reached out to me to engage in a special celebration of landmark eateries, no longer in existence. Its request of me was to recreate Haussner's strawberry pie. I was happy and honored to do it.

The *Sun's* reporter, Sarah Meehan, wrote this:

> Avenue Bakery owner James Hamlin didn't change much about the strawberry pie from Haussner's when he was re-creating it. But he did double the amount of pastry cream in the filling and substitute cream cheese for decorative whipped cream.
>
> He remembers the Highlandtown landmark as a restaurant to bring out-of-town guests, and a place with a menu so vast that customers could dine there for an entire year and never have the same food twice. He also fondly recalls the dessert case, where items like the strawberry pie could be found.
>
> I am a dessert person," he said, "so I walk in the door, and they have this showcase ... it's like, 'Let me in the case!'"

It also mentioned how *"The building was recently demolished to make way for apartments."*

Roll Prep Hamlin

Strawberry Pie, Haussner's

Ingredients

- Cooked Pie Shell
- Strawberry Glaze
- Strawberries
- Pastry Cream
    - 1 cup of Milk (scald)
    - 3 Egg Yolks
    - ¼ Cup and 2 Tablespoons of Sugar
    - ¼ Cup all Purpose Flour
    - 1 ½ Teaspoons of Vanilla
    - 1 ½ Tablespoon of butter (softened)

Instructions

Set aside scald milk and softened butter. In a bowl whisk together the egg yolk and sugar until it's light in color and very thick, then beat in the flour. Pour in the warm milk into the egg mixture and blend well. Pour mixture into a saucepan and cook stirring with a whisk over low heat until it comes to a boil. Get the lumps out but make sure it doesn't stick to the pan. Remove from the heat add vanilla extract and butter. Cover with wax or (parchment paper) so it doesn't form a skin. Allow to cool.

Spread the pastry cream in the bottom of the baked pie shell. Pour in ½ pint of strawberries, cover with glaze, add more strawberries and cover with glaze. Decorate with almonds and whipped cream and cream cheese.

Today, when customers walk into The Avenue Bakery, they will experience the influences of history and Haussner's in place. Visual art abounds, the history being highlighted is of the African American culture, achievements, activism, and entertainment renaissance. Because the goal is *to feed your face and your mind* in a clean environment that smells heavenly.

All my observations that life has afforded me are seasoned with my individualized concepts, such as The Bakery's inviting display case in the lobby and its specially designed work area to let customers see the magic being baked. There are no workers taking customers' money and disappearing behind closed doors to fetch confections.

This leads me to another one of my life observations. This one came to me as a young family man and became destined to seep into my decades-later plans for The Bakery.

When my son, James (affectionately nicknamed Hammy), and daughter, Lin, were young, my wife, Brenda, and I loved to spend family time enjoying The Inner Harbor. This was back in the eighties and nineties, when The Baltimore Inner Harbor, which would soon be dubbed Harborplace, was in its heyday. We often visited a fudge shop, located in the food pavilion, called, The Fudgery.

A *Baltimore Sun* reporter, Catherine Rentz, covered its closing in 2018. Here's an excerpt of her story:

> The Fudgery, the singing fudge shop that opened in 1985 in Harborplace and helped launch the careers of Baltimore R&B bands, will ring its bell one last time at the close of business Sunday. Current and former Fudgery employees will join in a few final songs in observance of its last day of operations.
>
> "This is a very sad day, but it is also a celebration" said Reggie Linnette, a general manager with The Fudgery. Linnette managed the store during some of the Dru Hill days in the mid-1990s, when then-Baltimore City Community College Prep classmates Mark "Sisqo" Andrews, James "Woody" Green, Tamir "Nokio" Ruffin and Larry "Jazz" Anthony worked summer jobs at The Fudgery.
>
> "They would draw huge crowds," Linnette said, "Probably 50 or 70 people would huddle around the railing." The quartet practiced their R&B tunes together while serving candy. They developed an audience, competed in local talent shows and later became known as Dru Hill, after the Druid Hill Park neighborhood.
>
> "We'd do these little Fudgery songs and had these little skits we'd do while making fudge for the audience," Nokio told USA Today in 1998 after they became known as one of the hottest R&B male bands.

Singing Icon Patti LaBelle and James Hamlin share a moment backstage

Visiting The Fudgery, you could buy fresh fudge and other chocolate goodies, and, yes, you could see the young Black guys and gals (often teens), working hard, slicing the fudge and whatnot, preparing the store's wares of goodness. The workers were also charismatic. I observed them efficiently serving and interacting with their customers, having fun—laughing and singing their rehearsed tunes—while they managed it all. It was a favorite spot for my children.

That image of customers being able to see, right there in the kitchen, things happening, we adopted that concept, the open-kitchen atmosphere, from what I had observed years prior. When I thought about the design of The Bakery, The Fudgery, stowed in my bank of wonderful memories and life experiences, sprung to mind. It's just another example of how the past experiences you've had in your life can culminate to create something productive and beautiful in your future.

We've also been known to hand out a hot, buttery-roll sample, placed on wax paper, to inquisitive passersby. That idea, we gleaned from restauranteurs in the mall or in Baltimore's famed Lexington Market, handing out tasty samples among the crowd. It's the best form of culinary advertisement.

Our customers can come into the lobby or stand outside and look into the big windows. They can see us preparing our baked goods. They can see our rolls coming out of the oven. They can see rolls being buttered and buns being iced. Customers will not stand at a front counter, watching employees disappear behind swinging closed doors to prepare their baked goods out of sight. At The Avenue Bakery, everyone can see where the magic, the hard work, and the love happen.

A Press Interview of many

The Press takes notice

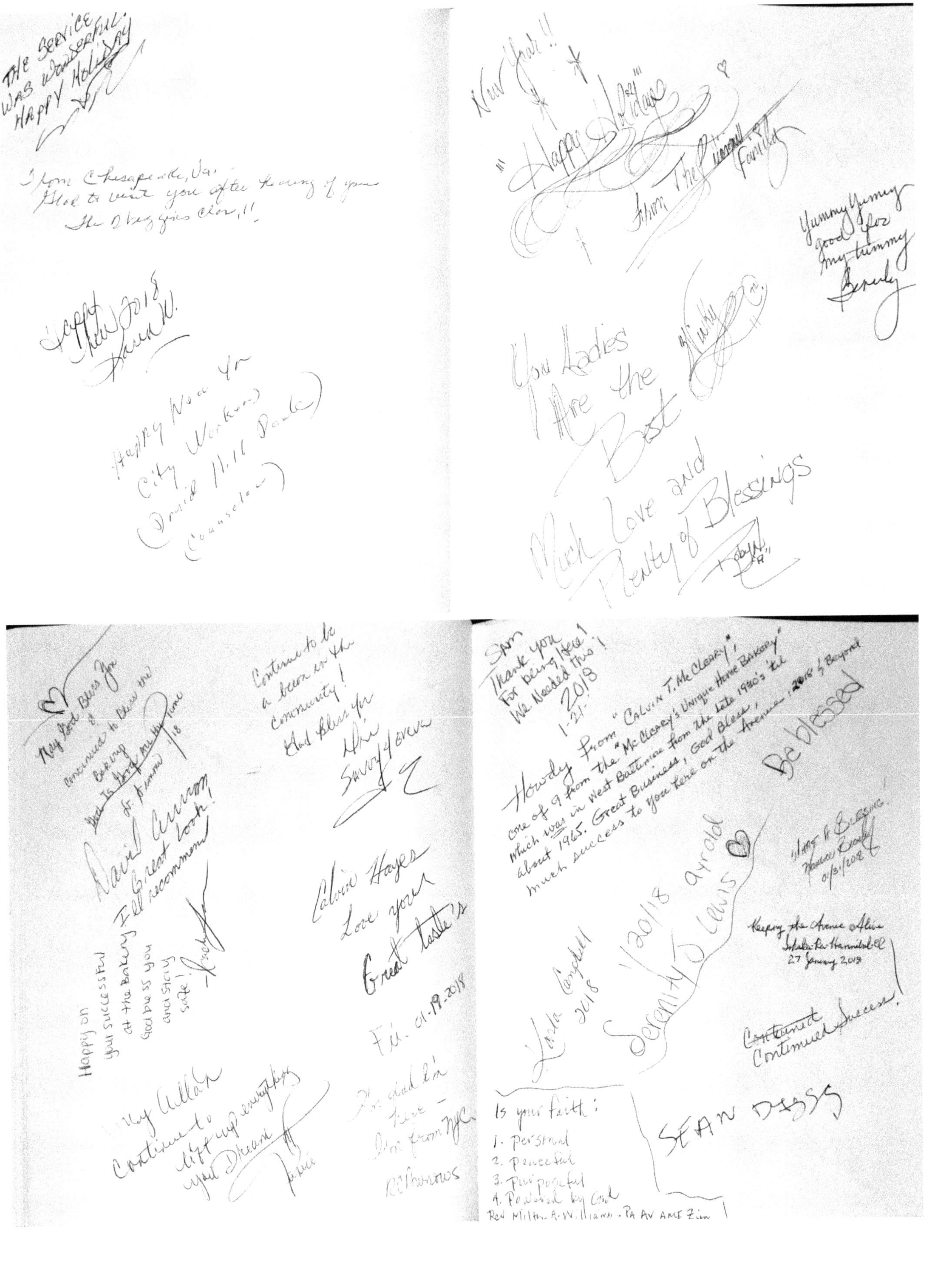

THE SERVICE WAS WONDERFUL!
HAPPY HOLIDAY

I'm from Chesapeake, Va.
Glad to visit you after hearing of you
The Diggs girls Chor,!!

Happy New 2018
Karen W.

Happy New Yr
City Workers
(David Hill Park)
(Counselor)

May God Bless You & continue to bless the Bakery

David
Great look!
I'll recommend!

Happy on your successful at the Bakery
God bless you and stay safe!

Continue to be a beacon in the community!
God bless you

Savoy forever

Calvin Hayes
Love your Great taste's

Fri. 01-19-2018

Continue to lift up everything your Dream

I'm glad I'm here -
from NYC

Sam
Thank you
For being Here!
We Needed This!
2018
1-21-

Howdy From "CALVIN T. McCLEARY"!
One of 9 from the "McCleary's Unique Home Bakery"
which was in West Baltimore from the late 1930's 'til
about 1965. Great Business, God Bless,
much success to you here on the Avenue, 2018 & Beyond

Be blessed

Many Blessings
01/31/2018

Serenity Lewis 1/2018 9yr old

Karla Campbell 2018

Keeping the Avenue Alive
27 January 2018

Continued Success!

Is your faith:
1. Personal
2. Peaceful
3. Purposeful
4. Powered by God
Rev Milton A. Williams - PA AV AME Zion

SEAN DIGGS

Norma Jean Fortune
God Bless!!!
YUM
YUM
We love this
PLACE
2018
Jackie
Fullbright
was here
from Detroit Mi
2-1-18!
Good Luck
God Bless
Rita Cooper
2/3/18
Love
from
Sean
Yum Yum!
Lassiter
2/8/18
Today is a good day
today is my birthday
with my mother
2/8/18
Today is a good
day. The devil thought
he had me, But God!!!
P.S. Thank you for this
delicious bread pudding
Leonard Coples
Wonderful place, Good atmosphere
Thanks
2-10-18
Good Luck
Linwood Clopton
2-10-18
Good Morning Neighbors,
from your neighbors
ON Calhoun ST. - Accross
from historic Frederick
Douglass High School,
it sure smells Good
in here.
God Bless
YOU ALL
S. Cromwell
&
Family

2.10.18
GOOD PIES
Apple Dumpling Gang
Lenny, Rob, William
Billy, Curtis

Best Wishes
+ Blessings
Duncan
Donut's
Crew

2/16/18
It is recorded in the book of Psalms 78: "That the generation to come, we see the change in our world because we no longer understand generational responsibility. May we remember this truth for the generations to come

2.15.18
This is a very good bakery.. & it's African American Entrepreneurship
Great Pastries & Bread & Smoothies
Tammy Weeden
The Ragin Family

Self Actualization
Self Esteem
Safety
physiological
Part I.
Thank you Lord I made it
2/18/18
J. Mooney

Jarm Rue love
Brother Lydell Craig
I love That sweet potato PIE
William H. Haskett
Union Baptist Head Start

Jocelyn Baker
Thank You Jesus for such an Awesome Business. May God continue to shower Blessings Upon you your Family & Business in Jesus Name
J. Baker

2/25/2018
"Remember Our Chains"
sermon by Pastor Williams
Pa Av AME Zion Church

"KEEP KEEPING ON"
Rock

Rev. Dr. Andre Humphrey
Trauma Response Team

THE Best EVERY

Blueberry Muffins are the Bomb!

Tonya Riggins
Shawn Blackwell
03 Mar 2018

3/08/18
What A Treat to visit here.
Frances M. Gill

3/9/18
The Answer Has Come!
Receive, Receive, Receive!

Always A Pleasure
Edmondson Class of '68
Linda Means

3-4-2018
My Grandad
Brought me hear
And everytime I come
I buy a little something
extra just in memory of
him. I appreciate the
memories everytime.

Love EVERYTHING
Lemon Pound Cake The
best !!! Kim Peace

Marion & Jane 3.10.18
were here
and glad about
it, too!

Todays is my
First Time in here
But I can tell you that
It with out a doubt won't
Be my last time!!! I Love this
Shop!!!! 3/10/18 - Redd's

Love the chocolate
cake!!

First Time
The Smell Got
me. Love fresh
pastries
Rosalind Miles
3/15/18

Thank you for existing!
Love, Shadae' 8

"Deserts are delicious"
Shay

WOW!
My first time here and
I am extremely impressed
especially with the visual display
of history (Profound) I will be back.
- The rolls mmmgood!
Evangelist M. Johnson

Zion Sweetwine 3-18-18

Renee Sweetwine was here on this glorious afternoon
3.24 pm 3.18.18

Such an awesome place. Learn history while
enjoying great food. Thank you for giving back
to the community 3-18-18 [illegible]

You have the Best cakes/just like mom's
T. Wms
3/23/18
9:10AM

History, History, our History
This is more than a bakery
it's a history lesson of our
past pointing us to a bright
future. Love this bakery
& I will definitely be back!
Rhonda Hunter
3/23/18

3/23/2018
Iesa Tahqwa Ahmad Ibn Adama
[illegible]

AGAIN THANK-YOU ROSETTA NEWTON

Thanks for the wonderful service!
Clinton W. Hanley

Once again thanks for giving your good
service Monday

Thanks for the delicious baked
goods, we are obsessed with the rolls!!
Love from Brooklyn, NYC! :)
Cris + Coco

Best Bakery in Baltimore!
—R. Johnson Jr.

"KEEP ON KEEPING ON"
Rocky

I just come here to smell the food! No, the
bake goods are on fleek!! Best Bakery
in Maryland - Keep up the Good Job!
Rhonda :)

KEEP ON KEEPING ON!
Rocky

Thanks for good custumer serves!

– "Jomeca & Chinab Kitchen & Catering" April 2018
Pound Cake & a Song

Thank You ALL
3 Level Cake
Arlene Green

The Best
IN
Baltimore City

Albert
Sweetwood
Family From West
To East
Baltimore 4/21/18

Love You

I Love your
rolls Thanks for History Lesson

Enjoyed the tour and the folks!
Amirah

Love your pies
BB

Your rice Pudding is so good

I Love Baltimore
its great
its Fantastic
R Chamberlain
2018

19 April 2018

First time here. Looks full of good and full of history 4/20/18

Historical Greatness displayed!!

Awesome place!

Great Place,
Friendly, Courteous
employees
Wonderful baked
goods!
Blessings to you
and your business
4/22/18
Bernice Blake

Walter Hiss-Abbotston

Like Pennsylvania Avenue
So much History – We need
to bring back our History!
(So many memories)
Christian

Brought back so
many memories

Best Wishes!
Monty & Steve Howard

Thank God
For the Sand Town
Coming back
Again

We Appreciate the Love, that you put into your Bakeing Keep up the good Work

Andre T. Marshall

Cheers from K.C. City Keep up the good work!

The Rolls are Fabulous

Valerie Cousen

I Love your Rolls

Mr. Hugh Carry

I love everything about this Black Owned & Operated Business. My favorite is the sweet potatoe pie, cakes, pound cake, rolls well everything :). Keep up the great work.

Dee 2018

Thought that you had closed down

Glad you had NOT. Stay Open

Love this Place - The 4/2018

Our 1st Time Visiting, CAN'T WAIT TO TRY OUR BAKED GOODS. GREAT HISTORY - KEEP UP THE GOOD WORK

This place is truly amazing! Everything is simply Awesome!! Kim '18

2018 ©

The Poppoys Rolls are the best Item Here

Jon

of Southtown back in the Day Everything Awesome!! 2018

THE AVENUE BAKERY'S

LOGBOOK #5
(2018-2020)

Welcome To
The Avenue Bakery
Home of PoPPay's Rolls

Share your
Thoughts

Good Time To Be here
1951

what a wonderful bakery & landmark!
– Alicia 6/6/18

The family here is amazing. Love and generous is an under statement.
6/2/18
visit from NC

Great history!
– 6/6/2018

wonderful stories & amazing town
Bentley, 6/6/18

delicious rolls!
– Mara 6/6/18

Coffee + shot Espresso
Boom!

Thank you all for the amazing pastries + sharing this amazing history with our students!
– ABBI 6/6/18

Coffee + shot expresso The Best pick me up in the universe
2080

A true Blessing
on Sunday after
Church I try to make
it every week Rasin
buns and Bread pudding

Hey♡
I'm back again♡
I love this bakery♡
Please keep on doing what you do♡
Keep our culture alive with the
positive flow that is always here
Thank you,
Leyia @ JCPenney's salon
of Eastpoint Mall

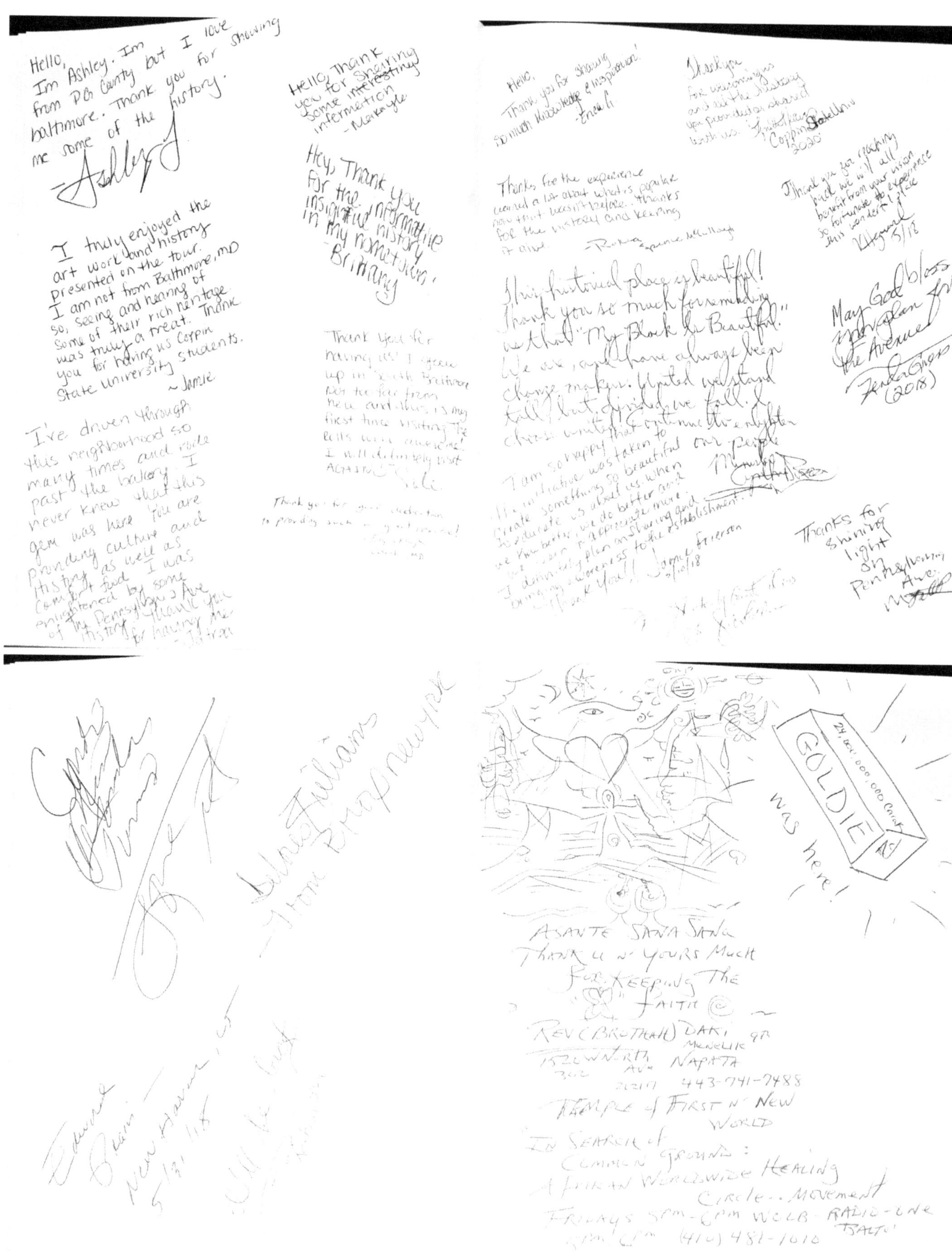

Hello, I'm Ashley. I'm from PG County but I love Baltimore. Thank you for showing me some of the history. -Ashley

Hello, Thank you for Sharing some interesting information -Mckayle

Hey, Thank you for the informative insightful history in my hometown. -Brittany

I truly enjoyed the art work and history presented on the tour. I am not from Baltimore, MD so, seeing and hearing of some of their rich heritage was truly a treat. Thank you for having us Coppin State University students. ~Jamie

I've driven through this neighborhood so many times and rode past the bakery. I never knew that this gem was here. You are providing culture and history as well as comfort food. I was enlightened by some of the Pennsylvania Ave history. Thank you for having me.

Thank you for having us! I grew up in South Baltimore not too far from here and this is my first time visiting. I will definitely visit AGAIN!

Hello, Thank you for showing so much knowledge & inspiration! -Erica G.

Thank you for welcoming us and all the history you provided and shared with us. Coppin State Univ 2020

Thanks for the experience learned a lot about what is popular now that wasn't before. Thanks for the history and keeping it alive.

Thank you for reaching back we will all benefit from your vision so fortunate to experience this wonderful place 5/18

This historical place is beautiful! Thank you so much for reminding us that "My Black Is Beautiful." We are, and have always been change makers. United we stand tall, but divided we fall.

I am so happy that I was taken to this initiative. It was something so beautiful. I definitely plan on sharing and bringing awareness to the establishment. Thank You!! Jamie Frierson 5/10/18

May God bless your plan for the Avenue (2018)

Thanks for shining light on Pennsylvania Ave.

from Brooklyn New York

New Haven CT 5/31/18

GOLDIE was here!

ASANTE SANA SANA
Thank U N' YOURS Much
For Keeping The Faith
REV (BROTHER) DAKI MENELIK
443-741-7488
TEMPLE of FIRST N' NEW WORLD
In Search of Common Ground:
African Worldwide Healing Circle... Movement
Fridays 5PM-6PM WOLB RADIO-ONE BALTO
(410) 481-1010

Carlton Eley
6-1-18

Keep the vision
keep the faith. Your
work to preserve the
legacy of activism and
achievement in West Baltimore
is important and needed
Daniel J. Gilmore
6-1-18

Love all your treats

6-2-18
May Allah keep
My blessings upon
Establishment.
Muhammad

What a blessing to see our black businesses
May God continue to be with you
6-2-18

6/2/2018
It was such a Pleasure
to Visit this "SPOT" of Maryland's
Greatest Personalities!

Good Folks
Good Food
What more do you
need? I Love this
Place!

The Hardy Webb Family was here
Sarah
Thelma
Janice
Jemma
Jamir
2018
GOD BLESS THIS PLACE!

Thank you for displaying
our rich heritage!
Plus, delicious desserts ☺
Peace + Blessings
Charles + Christopher

11/3/18 C. Hudson
It's good to be back
KTHEPLUMBER
Ramona
Love The Apple Pies
Nov. 3, 2018
Happy Birthday
Collin Scott
Ashley Owens
Best Wishes!
Wishing you joy and prosperity.
Hoping you will recover soon.
May God continue to bless this bakery for many years to come and let this place be a blessing to all of B'more.
Scott Family
East B'more
2018

God Bless This Place in our nice city
at Matchup's
People of
Goodmorning Peace and Blessings
Blessings & Thank you
visting from Georgia
I will Be Telling Everyone to Visit!
Thank You For such a wonderful Experience
The Davis Family
Good Cake all day!
Happy Holiday
Love You Ladies
I'm so in Love with this Bakery
Thank you for Bringing Back the Memories
Love Ya
Sharon
Leslie St.
First time Customer everybody!!
Support The Ave Bakery
1st Time at this Bakery
God Bless
USCG / DHS
United States Coast Guard
Dept of Homeland Security

Mural by Cisco Davis in The Avenue Bakery Courtyard

Enjoying Jazz in the Courtyard

Insa & Lorenz
from Germany
... guests from Bruce have been here.
Great Place

Thanks
You Good
Cake
Love
Always!

Thanks for
Serving our
Black Community.
I really like the
idea of supporting
your business

We've been coming here for many years and thank you for serving the community so well.

-John + Rita Crooms
7/15/18

NY
It's so good to have People
Rember our Heriget LOVE YOU
Michelle Davis From
SANDTOWN
WINDCHESTER.
7/15/18

This is A blessing a Bakery In the heart of Baltimore City the food is Great !.

Let us eat cake :)

"What a wonderful" Blessing to have come to West Baltimore The Baked Goods are Awesome!!!

Thank you Lord for Breath and Live And Laugh Life.

The Bagel is outstanding

Great Food All The Time Can Never go wrong Thank you

The Bakery This has Become A very special place For me to come Bless God you Christine 2018

Thank you Food Very Very Very Good Good Price Ttine here ever Very Good

Thank You God for Today We wake up and see the light

Thank you for the delicious Fells Cakes Blessings Always!

Very Happy to support your business

Love Rhonda

Happy to be here at Hamlin Bakery

Makayla Scott

The St. Louis "Mo." Posse!

Raymond Sulé Murphy

Raymond Murphy

Suraiyya Cazembe

Taj Cazembe (I'll apply for job when I move up here!)

Kim Murphy

Family of Groome Givens

God Bless & Protect!

Support BLACK BUSINESS

Anthony Amos Jr

God Bless

THIS PLACE IS THE BEST THING THAT HAPPEN TO PENN AVE

HARVEY

COFFEE + SHOT OF EXPRESSO THAT WE LIKE

© 2018

Peace + ABUNDANT BLESSINGS! XOXO Khadijah Paul

Anita Moore McQueen

Bro Robert "Keke" McQueen

Baby Sarah

First time coming here & love your bakery 2018

8-18 Esther Living God

8/2/18 Hum Hum Good.

The best Bakery in Town!!

Love this spot

8/3/18

Makayla

Schmuz

Thank GOD for great bread pudding and a great life! HyonLife TM

God Bless You!

!! KEEP ON KEEPING ON!!

Rocky

Brownes Cute Pie

Thank You Every Day for my life with my family

The best Muffin!

Keep on Keeping on

Shanks

Pickett 8-4-18

Peyton

Great Pies! Ant. 8-26-18

I Love the Atmosphere!!

It was wonderful watching you prepare our breakfast. Thank you. (Micca's mom)

Jonelle 2018

Peace + Blessings to everyone! Love,

The First time was Heaven. Now me & my family are lifetime customers! "Minister E"

Calvin Harris New Tomorrow

Big DADDY Spencer

Thanks and Bless

Kim (Shorty)

Thanks everyone

I checked It Out Janette

IT WAS SO GOOD TOO COME DOWN HERE AGAIN Love Elaine

Thanks with Love

My First time here 8/12/18

I Love it here one of the best places in Baltimore City! Rasheeda

Im here for my birthday 08/11/18

Wonderful Job Keep Up The Good Work

Everything is wonderful Thank you for opening Here

Kanard Early

My first time here 8/12/18

3-18 - 8/23/18 MY FIRST time was bliss. Second time is heaven

GOOD LEMON CAKE
Spoon
Came by many years ago. Enjoyed your rolls. Reminded me of my mom's. Glad you are still here and that I was able to come by again.
LOVE APPLE PASTRIES
David J.
Love Sweet Potato Pie
Love this place!
THANK YOU for all you're doing to make this community sing again! Love this place, love these rolls, love Pennsylvania Avenue!
♡ - Kate
delicious + Peace
Good Good
Peace + Blessings
Delish!
1- Merci Beaucoup French
2- Danke Schon German
3- Gracias Spanish
4- Mamnoon Farsi
6 - Siyabonga Zulu
Thanks for being very gracious to me + my Guy. I couldn't wait to come in here.
Lemon + Butter pound cake
09/05/18
Amazing Baked goods and service
Thank You!!
We are from Trinidad & Tobago
Anthony
Wow!! Love The food Service + Coffee.
9/8/2018
THE ENGLISH FAMILY GR
Tarsha and Daryl was 9/12/18
KEEP ON KEEPING ON
Destiny and Wanda was here ♡
What a blessing to see!!
Eleanor Walker - New york city
It is a Pleasure Here!
Historical 2018

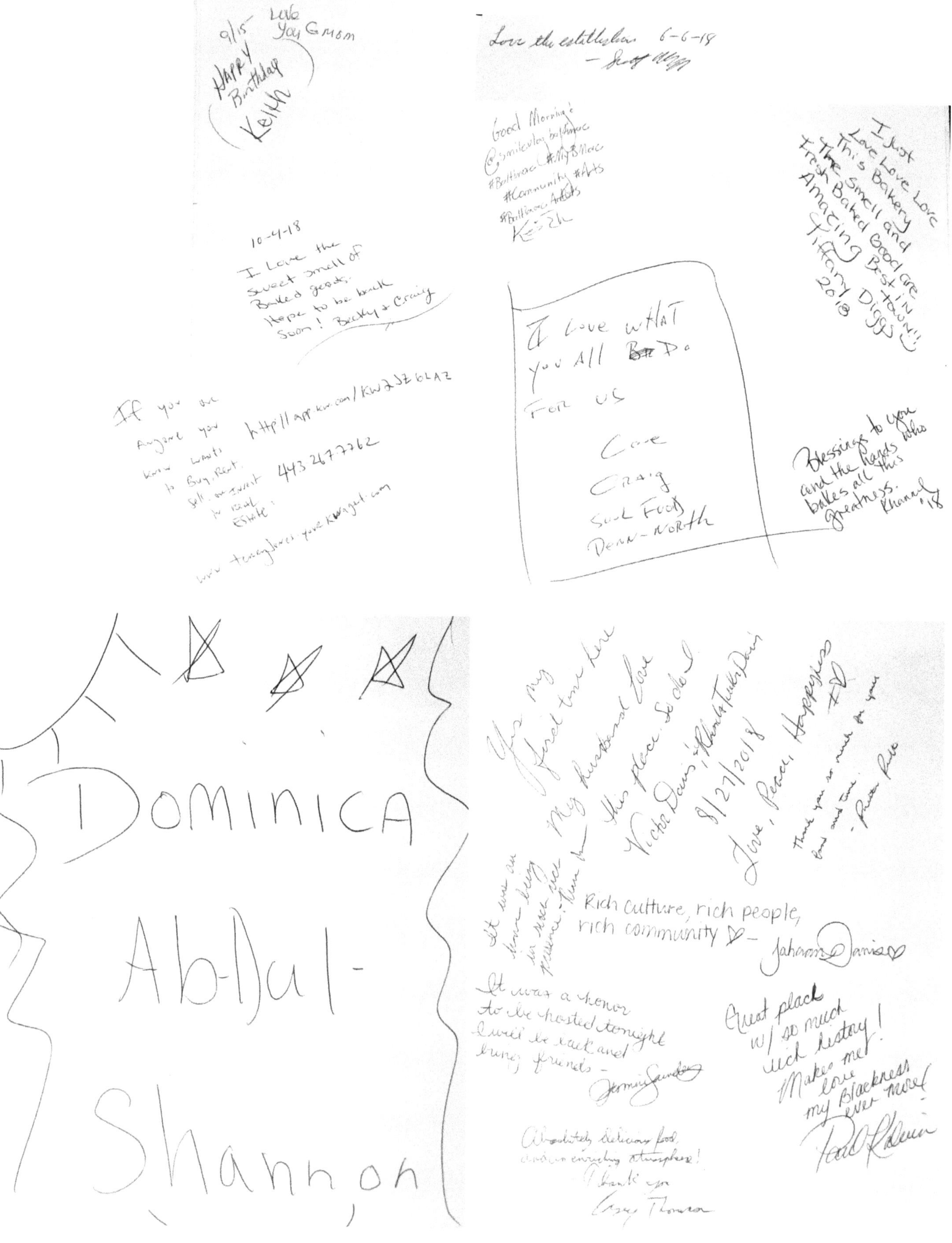
9/15 Love You Gmom
Happy Birthday Keith
Love the establishment 6-6-18
Good Morning!
#Community #Arts
Keith
I just Love Love Love This Bakery The Smell and fresh Baked Good are Amazing Best in town!! Tiffany Diggs 2018
10-4-18
I Love the sweet smell of Baked goods. Hope to be back Soon! Becky & Craig
I Love what you All Do For us
Love
Craig
Soul Food
Penn-North
If you are Anyone you know Wants to Buy, Rent, Sell, or Invest In Real Estate:
443 267 7262
Blessings to you and the hands who bakes all this greatness. Khanna '18
Dominica Ab-Dul-Shannon
Yes my first time here
My husband love this place. So do I
8/27/2018
Love, Peace, Happiness
Rich culture, rich people, rich community
It was a honor to be hosted tonight
Great place w/ so much rich history! Makes me love my Blackness even more!
Absolutely delicious food and an enriching atmosphere! Thank you

We came all the way from East Baltimore. Cake is delicious. 1st time.

The People's attitude in this Bakery is very awesome. Their hospitality is very decent. ☺ 2018

Good Service Love it

Very Good Service Great Bakery Oct 2018

Smells so Good

Your Grandson came for a surprise visit!! I love you!

Clinton, Mark Good Place

Glad I stopped. Elymore @ DC!

My mom sends me in here... Love, Love the cresants 11/1/2018

Kathie Bermuda

Marva Robaina nice visit from Bermuda.

Bermuda Nice!!

Great Place First Visit Won't be my Last!!

10/20/18 1st time here and the cinnamon buns was everything. Lil Sammy & Wife

We came all the way

Mike B-more my first visit and won't be my last I finally made it Here!!

11/1/2018 We Bless your Business and the prosperity you represent in the Community. Joyce & All Wings chase

Donnell Moani

JUNE

Best Bakery Ever Oct. 2018 Fan Loyal Customer

God's Peace be with you always John & Peta Cusse

10-31-18 Wonderful Bakery

Dominica

"BTaste AND SEE" Rachel C. Evans

Thank you for making my holiday complete. 1st time here... hope not the last #RICHRee

B+B Barbara Evans

Thank you for being my Ministry Spot - Ernest M. Rand... Nov 10, 2018

1st time customers Russell, Babe "2018"

NOV 17. Happy Birthday MARTIN H.

Arlene Sterling is my mother she looks like me but life made her hide who She is a lovely mix lady from west baltimore

God 1st Kids after that

power in they name God is Great!

1st Time Vistor Excellent Service the staff is fantastic

Dominica loves all women and kids!

Deacon Sherman

Thank u 4 the History Lessons I'm From NYC! I learned About Baltimore! F. Bookman

Thank you guys for doing what you do Taylor B

One Large Coffee & a tater Muffin (Riding)

A rose bud in a concrete jungle; I like coming here. - Arthur S. Sands - Mizoram.

The Best in B. More Rolls Buns etc.

Amazing to see how far history has come & We still are striving to be one in Love!!! Malcom

I TRY Not do tell "GOD" How Big my problem is I tell my problem How Big GOD is. Dec 12/1/2018

Fred D. Elliott Cobbler

"Book" Reconnecting by "Me" Coming "Create" God Bless You! Love You! Thanks for ...

Eden A.

my 1st time here 11-30-18 and returned 12-1-18 the pies, rolls are soooo good!! - The Overtons

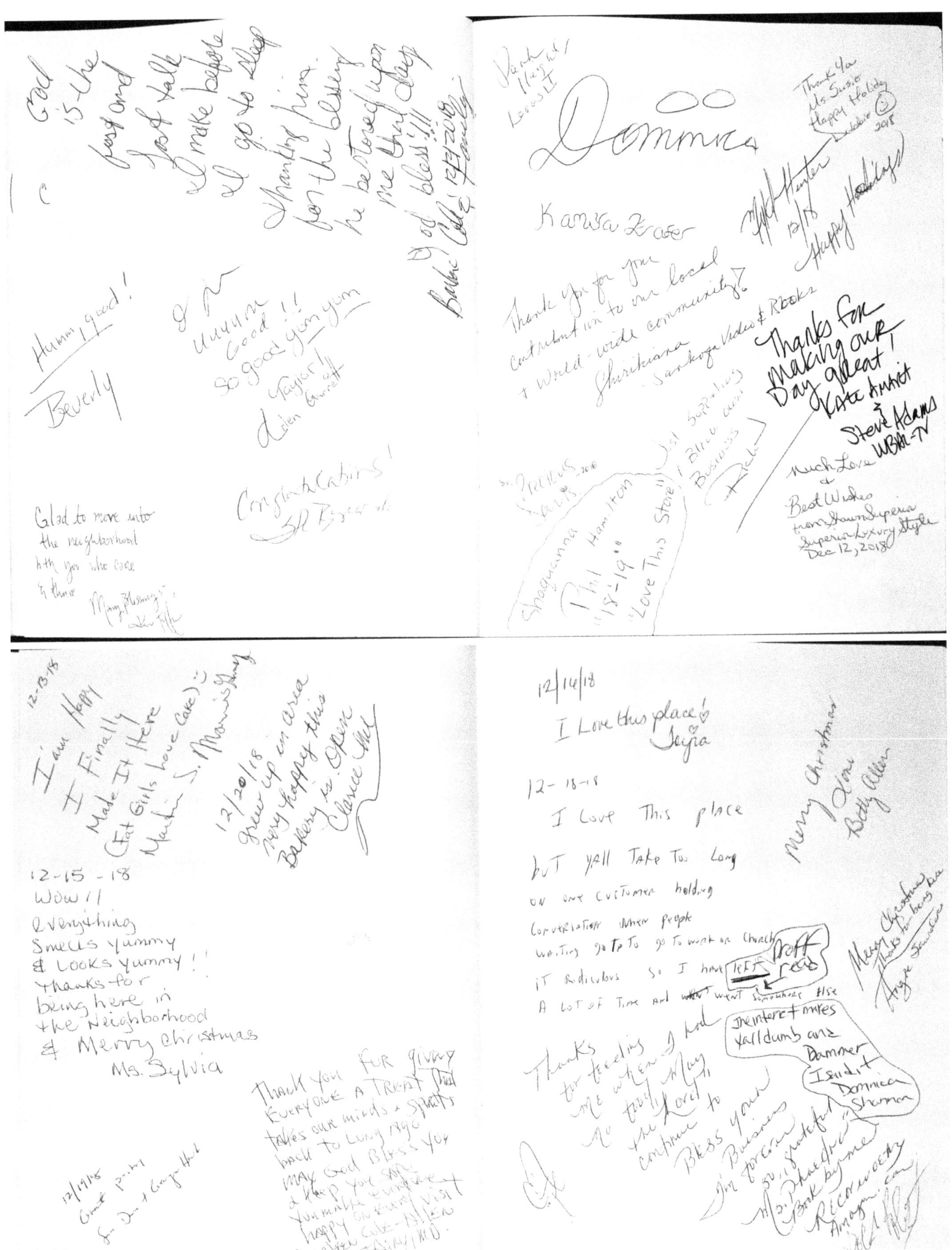
God is the first and last talk I make before I go to sleep
Thanking him for the blessing he bestowed upon me this day
God bless!!! 12/17/2018
Humm good!
Beverly
Uuuum Good!! so good yum yum
Congratulations!
Glad to move into the neighborhood with you who care & thanks
Many Blessings
Thank You Ms Susie Happy Holiday 2018
Thank you for your contribution to our local + world-wide community!
Happy Holidays
Thanks for making our Day great!
Kate Amato & Steve Adams WBAL-TV
Much Love & Best Wishes
Superior Luxury Style
Dec 12, 2018
Love This Store!!
12-13-18
I am Happy I Finally Made It Here
(Fat Girls love cake!)
12/20/18
grew up in area very happy this Bakery is Open
12-15-18
Wow!! everything smells yummy & looks yummy!! thanks for being here in the Neighborhood & Merry Christmas
Ms. Sylvia
Thank you for giving everyone a treat that takes our minds & spirits back to long ago
May God Bless You & keep you safe
12/14/18
I Love this place!
Merry Christmas
Love Betty Allen
12-18-18
I Love This place but y'all Take Too Long on one customer holding conversation when people waiting got to go to work or church
it ridiculous so I have a lot of time and went somewhere else
Thanks for feeding me when I had no food. May the Lord continue to Bless your Business
Merry Christmas

3/14/2019

MOVA

men of valuable action

MBFC

founder Antoine Bonnett

This is such a Good thing your doing here, so much History, I Love it.

Rosevelt Boone

wendell Holmes

you are the best out of all the rest JazzyBlue

Dan Vincent
Kenya Vincent
Summer Vincent
Michael Kyo Vincent

We love y'all thanx

Learnin To LIVE Again L2LA.org
Non profit

Thanks so much — Larry

God frist!

Dominica Shannon

Hola

Gods Only

Hi

Sem orson!

Im 32 now

1st

Thank You!

my Kids

Dymonnae

Kamiya

Tiyonna

Mother

are my heart

Ms Abdul-M

Dominica Shannon

was here again!

I ♡ z the'l caks and Pies.

love always

Dominica Shannon Abdul

fondly Chaplain Linda

The Very best of Baltimore! Thanks for the memories and delicious Treats!!

friends of the Toms family Phillis Williams Ida Mae Williams we love and miss you dearly

yum

Lil Rick B.K.A Cookie Man
"All bake goods R-Good"
ALWAYS STAY TRUE 2-4
Never-Rest proclaim the best ever 2-76 Finest

So Awesome. Jason

Raynard Parr

Love it!! 1.19.19

Karen 1/19/19

Cynthia 1/19/19

Chrissy Love #Secondvisit Dec 29th, 2018
Apple muffin & Strawberry Mango Smoothie

Tony #Firstvisit Dec 29, 18 Very kind people

Counselor from (Park Heights)

MARTIN HINKSON 2019 January 16 MON

AKA Chopper Long Time Coming

I came Today Ricky Barnes

I came today me and my BaBy! to get a buscity
Thomas Kelly

COME All THE Time Best BAKERY on THE EAST COAST! Riddell 1-20-19

Ralph Simpson 1/20/19
Newark, Delaware & Foster City, CA

Bread Puddin' like my momma's :) Sm

Mayzella Corley 1/20/2019
Raised on 1300 Brunt St Baltimore the Royal. God Bless left in 1973.
When they tore it down

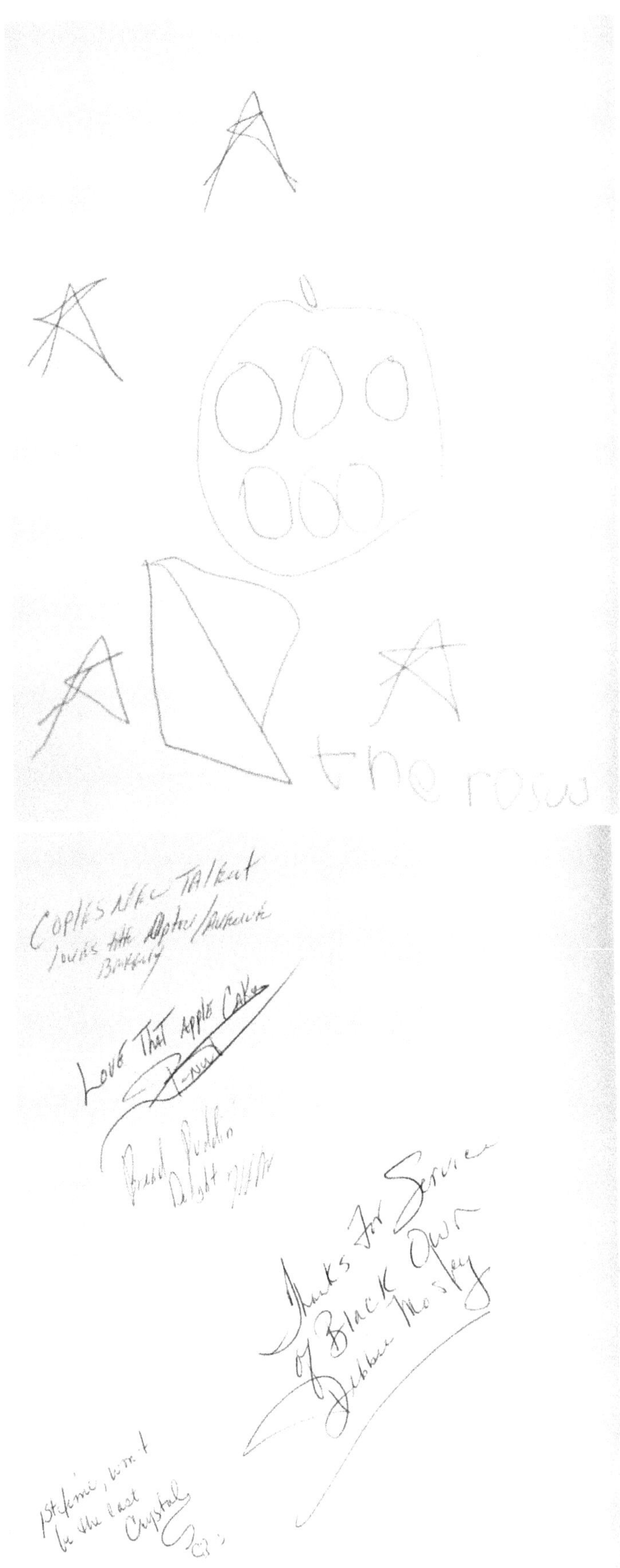

M2M
Faces Going Places
8-29-2019

Debra
Howell

Great Place
I Love U All

Love Your Pies

Love everything
Ebony cool!

Cheese Cake
+
Bread Pudding
Awsome. Kenny
&
Karen

1-26-19

I walk in and the place was so clean. I was very please to see that may you continue to always have success

Mamie Pearce

"Here Again, Love This Bakery"

Bernard Lea

Here for the second time, enjoyed everything

B Jones

2/1/2019

Came to visit a week ago and back today! I'm SOLD! So proud of my ancestors and the owners, may GOD continue to bless you!

I LOVE AFRICAN AMERICANS! (all of them)

Damara

I just can't stay away

D.O.T. Jones

Food for The Soul!

T. Tilayo

410-926-7812

D Barrett

may God Bless you

Black & White Lives Matter

Rickey Barnes Was here 2-3-19

Allaah Akbar!

God Bless You

Bishop Kenny Tol

MWC

2005-2019

Paula McDowell was here

Bedazzled Treats & Catering came to Visit

White Rolls/Wheat Rolls, and Apple Cake, Oh My!

Believe it or not, in 2005, a year after I purchased the Old Baker's Hardware, while I was envisioning administrative offices, a community master plan indicated that the residents desired a bakery. And while Poppay's Rolls were a hit in the community, my mother's sweet potato pies came to mind. Although Mattie Virginia Waymon, my mom, had passed away in 1999, I knew that she would have declared, "You can't have a bakery without sweet potato pies!" Ironically, while she was alive, I could never mimic her tasty recipe. But finally, in The Bakery, I mastered my own technique for an original sweet potato pie recipe. My customers had declared that whenever I opened our doors, sweet potato pies were a must.

As I think about The Bakery and the journey to today, many things come to mind. Yes, I have been baking my rolls for years, but I only baked white rolls. However, now I bake wheat as well. The beginning of the wheat roll came about because of a question by Baltimore's former Mayor, Sheila Dixon when she visited us. One thing about her is that she is very health conscious, and she has a regular exercise regimen. As I remember it, on her visit, she got a taste of our rolls and loved them. Her question to me was, "Do you make these in wheat?" Thanks to her, we offer them in wheat and white.

A Press interview

Recently, the former Baltimore City mayor, Ms. Dixon, did some reflecting of her own that made me smile with gratefulness. She shared, "I watched you leave UPS, which is where I met you, to take on this dream of opening a bakery—because of your passion to please others through baking and showing black people that they could accomplish success and create a business that would have a tremendous impact on the community!"

As we began developing our menu, one of our customers, Rene' Wartman, worked for the Baltimore Police Department. On her visit, she mentioned that one of her aunts, who used to make a fantastic coconut cake, had a recipe that she was willing to share. Although we didn't end up using her aunt's recipe, we have to have coconut cake for our customers.

We have had thousands of visitors over the years from all over the country and beyond. Another visitor who comes to mind who impressed me was Dr. Keiffer Mitchell of the political family by that name. I believe it was a few years before he passed when in one of our Legacy Logbooks, Dr. Mitchell sat in our lobby and completed an entire page reflecting on his family and his experience in The Bakery.

Some years ago, one of our customers asked me, "Do you bake Jewish Apple Cake?"

To which I replied, "no." However, that same year, Brenda and I took a weekend vacation to Philadelphia. She wanted to visit the Liberty Bell and other historical Philly sites. We visited the Reading Terminal Market downtown. We encountered a bakery booth and happened to see apple cake, and we bought a couple of pieces. We did not taste them until after dinner that night in our hotel room. It was fantastic. When we got back home, I looked up a recipe online and tweaked it. Soon after, apple cake became a huge hit with our customers.

When we celebrated our tenth anniversary, I reflected on so many people who helped make our business what it had become.

Nostalgic Look at the bakery

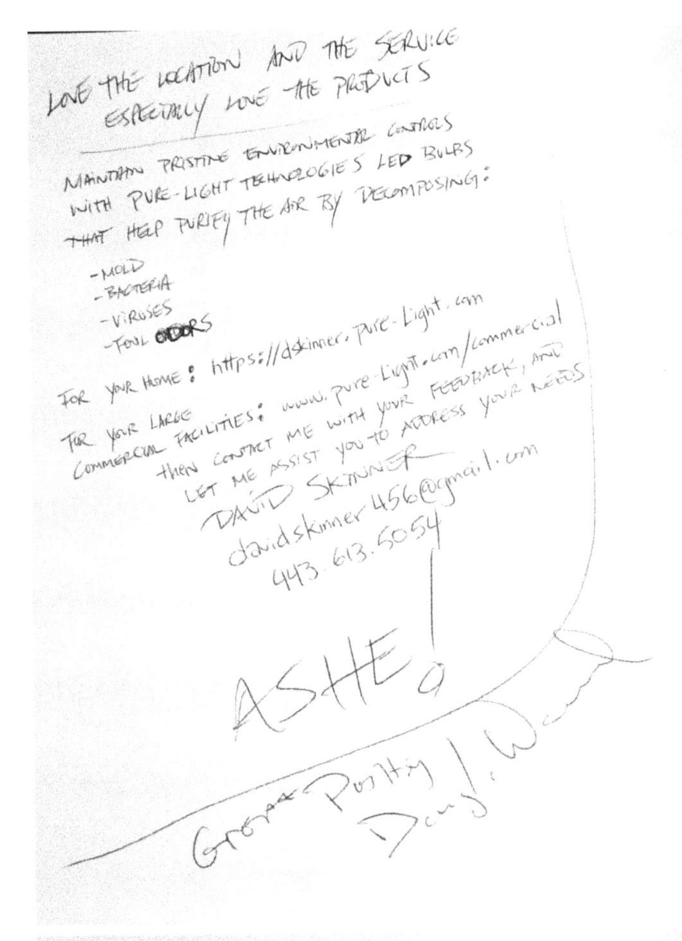

This is by far is a place of nothing but → Love!!

2/9/19

This was a wonderful place to come too!

the coffee is great!!

Some body Help me !!!!

2-9-19

Bro Louis
2-9-19

all the way from California! -Zuniga family
Great Service - Love this place
Wish you the best!
Jesus Love!!
Good Luck for the future
BHM 2019
Peace be unto you
Back Again Yusuf Rushdan
Abdus Salaam Jersey City
Deborah Kinsey 2019
Born + Raised Baltimore Bred First Time @ this monumental Bakery. Too Black + Too Strong. Thank you for continuing Black Excellence.
J.N.
Exploring Baltimore
Thanks for the great smells
Best Cobbler in B-more City
I love this place! Open a tour of the neighborhood please!
It's good to be Home At The Ave.
Good Luck
Great Job.
EVERYTHING LOOKS AND SMELLS DELICIOUS
"Love your Baked Goods" "Gained Weight But So Worth It!!"
this place is Heaven sent
God Bless
From the Members of Nickel Dime "Engine 52" All love here and Taste 7 heaven.
God bless you All. I will always support your Business
PEACE-N-BLESSING ALVIN THOMAS JR.
This is A good Place to get coffie
Kia Black
From S.C.I.T. We love u keep it com

Hey! Here again love this Spot's Sweet Delicious Yam-Yum Darlene

Love your Pound Cakes
Ms. Nita

O.M. -the- (Counselor)

I have to Say Thank You!!!

Ms Taylor Thank you

IN 32 years today is my first Day here!!, and Im addicted already Great Service Smelling Real Good in here!!

We Want Rolls and we want it now!!

"WE LOVE whats going on. Peace, love and GOD." (The Christopher Family) Eugene Jeanine, Najee

Surprisingly, I haven't been here in yrs now that I'm back I've gained 10 lbs eating these rolls
xoxoxo :)

Thank You God Bless for the things you have done to the Ave. The Hall Family

MY NAME IS GARY I BEEN IN THIS AREA 69 YEARS THANK YOU

3-9-19
Coming in today for Something "Yummy"
Sylvia - Calhoun ST.

LARRY M. LYNCH, SR
JASON BROOKS

Thanks so much! Debra Joseph

so wonderful! Vanessa Harris

3-14-19
I Love to support our Black Owned Business's
The baked goods taste amazing!
Terri Mac

Paulette Medley (Everything is wonderful)!!!

Jasmine "Mchp" 3 Meek "Supporting Black Owned Business"
510-486-1680 "Meek"
667-216-7050 "Jas"

Brooke

Bria, Green Family with Love

Patti Pasture's Florist
(443)850-2763

3/20/19

Everything is sooo, Good. God Bless this Bakery.

Neece

(MAR. 21, 2019)

Young Sir Nathan, were granted his 1st opportunity here within this historical bakery treated to a beutifull slice of the tridiltional (cheese cake) greatly appreciated thank you all to all my bros & sisters friends of the bakery Penn. Ave.

Yes yes y'all!

I just want to say thank for your service and commitment to our culture and community

Monica Cooper

Always good to come back here Pat Cake and I Thank U never leave us

3-23-19

God is able to do far above and exceedingly more than we can think or do! Keep doing it. Great Job!!!!...

Heads

Dru. Heights

Great job

Good Food !!

[illegible]

LOVE COMING HERE!!

1 Coffee

1 Riding Muffin

D. Suite

wonderful everything you doing!

Rebecca Miller

Akron OH

GlAD I CAME

Kim

LOVE THE Food

3-28-2019

Don't close Please

We Need You

Love Love Everything

Terrie T 2019

Nice 2019

Love Twin

"4 over" Singletary

3400 KENYON AV

Balto md 21213

This is a coffee is really good here Wolf

Coffee Good

Penny was here #Detroit 5/2/19

Avenue HAPPY

2019

Steven Motich – Akron, Ohio – 4-6-2019

May God Keep Blessing This Bakery!! Shirley Craig 4/6/2019

Peace + Blessings Stephanie 4/6/19

The Best cookies

Peach cobbler 4/7/19 is The BEST!

~@Prettygirll Cori

Keep in going

Follow me Slime!

This my first time here and im loving the peach cobbler!! – Skipsnay 4/7/19

Fritz G JNG property solution Best in town

dinner rolls are bomb!! – bmore_los Follow me on ig.

"Bread Pudding IN TOWN HANDS DOWN"

Thank you for providing fine treats and history. God Bless Shaunt. 4/7/19

May Allah always Bless you

"Thumbs up on the cookies". Ethan Richmond

Every thing in this store to eat is very Good!! I have a couple of favorits bread Puding and the pound Cake is awsom!!!... May GOD continue to bless the hands that cook's and the wonderful women that work and serve us!!

R. R.

May God Blessed This Store, And The People who Work's Here, For I Fell well come here Thank's

All is in order! My love is Good! Thank you!

Brother [illegible]

I love you! uh Wonderful Bakery from Peanut Butter & Jelly

Thanks

Will enjoy your goods

[illegible]

4/09/19

It a lovely place

Thank you

Rosemary & Theresa

2019

Florida

Monica

Florida

2019

T-Bone

Love from Jeri & Steph!

Jow — Kept Baking its good

4-27-19 Smith

4-27-19

Thanks for Coming to this Communite!! Love your Baked Goods!! Wish you Continued Success!!

4-27-19

Loved the Vibe & the genuineness

Love left

Much Continued Success

Black Businesses Rock

Ofegini Shabazz

Aminyah WAS here!

Amazing Bakery

Best Peach Cobbler EVER!!

We read about this bakery in the Book
"111 must see places in Baltimore"
We were Blessed enough to meet the
owner 'James' and got a tour & learned
about the History of Pennsylvania Ave.
Thank You! [illegible] Indianapolis Indiana

Visiting this Wonderful Bakery [illegible]

Love my [illegible] City of Baltimore
Mrs. [illegible]
4-2-2019

I love this Bakery

This is the Best BAKery in town!!!

Black Owned!

Best Bakery "N" Maryland,... Cynthia & Kenny 2019.

Love Our Bakery Harvey D. Burrell 5/1/19

1st time I will be back 5/1/2019 Turner

Yummy! Yes... Indeed. Very Tasty! J Hawkins! 2019

rode 3.5 miles for the smiles a happy stomach

I Enjoy Supporting This Bakery. May Allah Grant This Place much success. Tanya

The Love of My Life 05-03-2019

God is Good! Mr. E. G. Hopkins

I love your Bakery! Every time I ride by & catch you open I stop. Keep up the good work

CIC

(DJ)
Paul Knight
Best Buns N Town

May God Continue to Bless You and Your Business

Kevin D. Brown
(Dalto)

Riding Muffins are here!!!
DSJ

If I'm free, its because I'm always running.

Jimi Hendrix

The "Shermans"
First time here
Love it!
James and Michelle Sherman
2019

This Bakery is lovely and Song Stafford Lorraine had the pleasure of 4/4/19 entertaining there

Best Bakery in Baltimore
5.10.19

Love you! [illegible]

The IDea is to write it so that the People hear it and it slides through the Brain and gose Straight to the heart

Change is Not an option It's a must. Bit good OR Bad that is the Choice you have to Be Good or Bad But you must Chose

Love Yall

A wonderful bakery, a wonderful project. Godspeed!

Jane Cochman + Bill Found
Toronto, Canada

how good !!!! (Great party!)

5-11-2019
Jennifer Renee Markey
This Are My first time here.
[illegible] strong

I love Black History month the other week I went to a musem about black History I wish travon martil was my big bro or even Emitt till and I wish my grandma was Harret tubman

Black History

Wonderful Place!!! Best Wishes!!! PEACE 5/11/2019 Jim Jones HARLEM N.Y.

The Allen's Love This Place 5/11/19 Not my First time

WONDERFUL!!!

Today, my sweet tooth, I can't explain, other than I had a sweet tooth, I experienced NOT 1 But 2 slices of Carrot cake. To sum it up: Scrumptious!! 5/11/2019

Visiting the city for the first time and fell in love with the soul food and all the baked goods 5/5/2019

Love You Guys 5/16/2019

My favorite spot when I have a sweet tooth Avenue Bakery never fails!! I Love your Sweet potato pie 5/16/19

Now we Know! 5/18/19

I Love the rolls!

Best Place EVER!!!!

I Love You Your Cake!!!

My Nose, say yes they will smell good.

It Smells delicious in here. Smells like 10 Birthdays!!!

IN 1972 PROF TWILEY BARKER OF UNIV OF ILLINOIS AT CHICAGO INTRODUCED THE CLASS ON CONSTITUTIONAL LAW TO THURGOOD MARSHALL & "THE LAW & SOCIAL CHANGE." THANK YOU JUDGE (RET) MICHAEL & GRETCHEN BRANDT, PEORIA ILLINOIS

Eric C Hamlin 5/25/2019

Jermaine Jackson

I Love This house

Mrs Couplin Nothing But Love Keep Up The Good WORK

MR. TRAVIS D Robinson "2019"

Mr. Steven C.

Charles

Quentin Mays "2019" "The World Is Yours"

Eric C Hamlin

Love was Here w/ ORIAH & ... 5/25/2019

thank you for serving the community!! LEE HARRIS 05/25/2019

Christa Carter - 5/25/2019

Stacey Curtis 5/25/2019

... Love ...

I Love all of the Desserts Made here Thank the lord we have you all 05 19

Happy Birthday NICA Baby

Dominic to me

Shannon

[illegible]

NICA DA Gemini ...

Paulette + Ceelia Was here on 6/1/2019 God Bless

Keep Hope Alive
For (God) Allah is He love Jazzy Blue

Have a Blessed Day

All I'm writing is just
What I feel That's All
I just keep its almost
Naked And Probably
The words are so bland
Jimi Hendrix

Fatima Kamara 6/5/19
Turquoise 6/5/19
Angela Zhu

Don't Look Down on anyone, Unless you are picking them up.

Devin Lucas 6/7/19 - Atlanta GA
+ Family 2019 Durham, NC
Bull City
Ricardo Andrews Ricardothe_bakersman IG 2019

Karina M.
Love your Sweet Potato Pies

I like chicken !! & Fortnite & GTA !! & For last the peach smoothie!!

Dillon
Bobby Back
Paul Jr
2019

I love This Bakery, It's VERY, VERY INFORMATIVE! 6.8.19

I'Am so glad that we have our Barkey Back ANS god bless your Keep it going don't let It go.
Love Michelle Davis
900 W Lexington

Love Supporting Local Black Businesses!

The book of 111 Places you have to go in Baltimore bring us here, and it really worth the try love it, will come here again for sure!
Clera 6/19

I Love this Baker it has the Best Choclate Cake every. Thank yall for being here in the Neborger Hood
Tina

WesT DUGG

God Bless this Store In this Hood

THE #1 BAKERY
My 1st time
Specialty Cakes is Awesome & the BEST!!

Power to the People. Stink
Fan of Huey P. Newton
Reverend AL Sharptun
Reverend DR. Martin Luther King
Non-Violent Protest don't work
I will have my SAY
I will get on my soap
box and speak
Record MESSAGE
Send to all TV, Radio
News centers - all states of
the union on tape
MESSAGE is As follows:
To the Nation - United
States of America
still RACIST against
Woman of Color

Happy Saturday

Good Eating!

I LOVE COMING Back TO
MY OLD Neighborhood AND
supporting This store!

Another Great Black OWNEd Business
Peace and Blessings - The Bransons 7-5-19

"IT'S THE BEST THERE IS"

follow me through the hate, follow me
through the lies ~ Barry Sherrell

London and Drew and Mmaa and
Aunt [illegible]
Happy Fourth of July

The People who is crazy enough
to think they can change the
world are the ones who do!

GOD Bless

Its Always good
to go!!!

First Time Here!!
and I'M SO Amazed
don't know what to Look
at the writings on the wall
or the deserts
KIMIA ☺

David J
Best Cakes
~
Bread
Ever!!

YESSS
the Best
Bread pudding

James Hamlin, Jr., James Hamlin, Brenda Hamlin, Belinda Hamlin and her son, Brandon Sorrell

Once upon a time on The Avenue...
ROYAL
ALWAYS
A
GOOD SHOW
ON A ROLL
A Baker's Recipe to Revitalize
Baltimore's Historic Pennsylvania Ave.
James Hamlin

THANK God for another Day Head in his world! Love U. Jesus, Always Summer Time! 6-7/12/19

Thanks + Congrads again Jim, Teraye UPS

Amyah was here!

Thank you for your service and smiles :) -Morris family

You bring life

Ange was here

Clayton G. (AKA) clay

@Pr3tty.mya —

God Bless you for this vision to maintain our heritage & Rev. Katrina Futrell Blessings :)

123

Thank you for a great welcome & fantastic treats Fondiswa Dlodlo Khondine Dlodlo & Kweku ... South Africa

Dwight III

Barren Cunningham

Dennis Jackson

Iyanna Ruffin

Azzurena

"96" (Bruce Lee)

Tatyana was here

youtube @ xoxory — Ryan here foreva

fm ~ @Pr3tty.mya —

4.28.19

Wow! The biscuits were so Good. Malkia

Jake & Carolyn Eldridge Baltimore MD 21210

wonderful Rolls Pecan Pies / Bean Pies

God bless this business, Wonderful place Roz Harris 10-14-2019

Rev Artis 1428 Linwood May Blessing Be upon U all +

Blessings & Thank you for Staying in West Baltimore!!! The Shivers Family 2019 + Peace

I ♡ city life.

Thank you! Live Baltimore

Black Arts + Entertainment District
Congrats Penn Ave deserves our best efforts to honor its legacy and the work done by our ancestors.
7/22/19

Best of Luck!
"Buddy" Hughes
Arch Social Club Inc.

Thanks 4 all the things
you'll put up with for us/me
and I will not stop until it's
better for all us

Qreem Marris
King Edin SIRRAH

Alan Berthy
love this place
Best cookies
Ever!

I Love This Place

Best Pound Cake ever

Love is always here

To James & team, keep up the great work, in the bakery & beyond. You're an inspiration. Byron
Ottawa, Canada

Such a wonderful experience at this lovely bakery
God Bless You
The Shields family

Shrella Baden Lee & Marc Lee will be looking forward to attend the Jazz Series

Hi I love the people and cakes

Love it!

Sweet Cookie

I'm so grateful to have a African American Bakery in the neighborhood
May God continue to Bless your Business

"RECOVEROETS BOOK"
Support my Book "Recoveroetz" Amazon, Kindle, coming soon to you!
"CRACK" my True Story, State of Addiction

So bad I came when the baker is on vacation!!!
But it smells Good!!

Mad I needed a strawberry shortcake today
8/8/19

My fat friend is eating cake early in the morning!

Thank you! So Much for Exsiting! This Place is a Breathe of Fresh Air! Peace & Love Kimi

Thank You!! Nothing Like Black History of Our Own Town! This place contains so much knowledge! Ariel

This is my 1st Visit and I'm tickle to life... Continue the OUTSTANDING work in the community

Friday, August 9, 2019

This Bakery is The Best Pleased to Have you in our Neighbor Hood. your Pastry are the Best Mrs Marion Ringgold 8-9-2019

Those rolls won't make it far out of the door with me. — Chris Grant 8/14/19 — Daniel Palmer

The best anchor institution ever! We all need baked goods. [illegible] 8/14/19

Love your baked Goods! They are the best ever! Aasha 8/9/19

Thank you Avenue Bakery! Kali-Ahset 8/14/19

Best ever Kamar 8/9/19

Awesome Bakery Ed + Pat 8/14/19

Thank you. J. [illegible] 8/14/19

I'd rather be messed up and messed in the hands of the Potter, than to be simply be messed up
Elder Christal Harris
Penn Ave. AME Zion Church
8/11/2019

May Jehovah Bless the poppay Rolls
— Janae!
8-10-19

May God Bless your Business 100x over
8/11/2019

Tasty rolls & fascinating history
Thank You!
Frances

Y'all Guys Are Great!
Be Back
8-18-19

This is the best! Lisa from Pittsburgh

Joseph Sullivan is back buying buns and cakes (They are the best)

Very Good 8/15/19
Service
Pastries off the hook
5 stars

8/17/19
Still going Strong all the best!

Education is power!
Keep up the great work!

God Bless! Our History
I'm excited to be Here
S. McLeod
8/11/19

"Great Job You Guys keep up the Good Work"
8/15/2019

5 stars
Vottah
8/14/19

@maddisonmariecosmetics
Lip glosses 15 year old CEO

Great customer service
Camille Winston

OMG Good ASS Biscuits!!
8/16/19
Will be back to get More!!

God Bless You.

Elaine Clark
8/17/2019

Keep up the great work!
— Washington DC

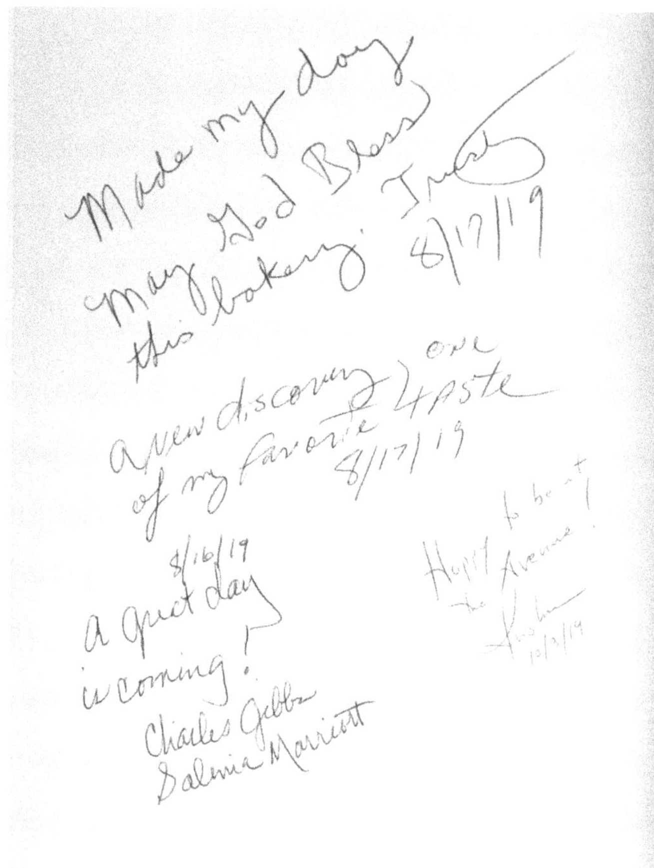
Made my day
May God Bless this bakery! 8/17/19
A quiet day is coming!

Made my day
Tracy Sibbs
Love Y'all
Sweet Potato Pie
Continued great success!
Kurt Schmoke
Mayor, 1987–1999
I'm the sugar without the Pie (Sweet Ms. Toni)
8/23/2019
Thank you for sharing the history of Sandtown and Pennsylvania Ave with us
– Shanee' Sibblies
Realtor w Exit Flagship

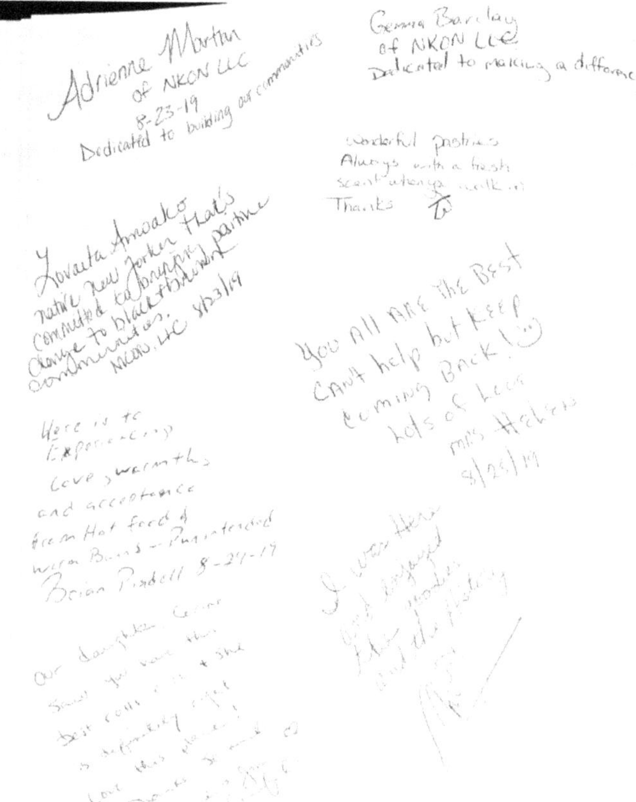
Adrienne Martin
of NKON LLC
8-23-19
Dedicated to building our communities
Gemma Barclay
of NKON LLC
Dedicated to making a difference!
You all are the Best
Can't help but keep coming Back!

Thank you for all you have done for this community
May GOD continue to Bless The Avenue Bakery 8/26/19
Thank you for your great service
Love this Place!

This place smells sooooo AMAZING. Very nostalgic :) -Kelly Palmer

9/8/19

Been a while but decided to stop today. Love what they do and the baking is delicious

Donna Burston

9/07/2019

STOP BY TO BUY ME SOME CAKE + PIE for Lunch + dinner, and Brown in Serve Rolls! God BLESS in House All the Time MR. D. G. Hopkins

BLESS This House All Way's MR Hopkins

9-12-19

Here's to beautiful celebrations of LIVING history!
- Julia Robinson (new to Baltimore from Ohio)

Thank You!
87 KC Chiefs

Love you!
20 HOF 19 9/13/19

9.13.19
We love The Avenue Bakery and The Hamlins! :)
Robert & Luanne Medley & Grandson Zach & Zavy

Best flow in Baltimore

Much Love! - Desoto Texas
RoParrish :)
NBATV | NBA on TNT
NFL Network

Thanks a lot
9-13-19

Thank you
Welcome thanks for all the blessings
D. Bydume 2019

Hello and Thank You!
I had such a wonderful time with the ladies!!
I am from New York and I will be Back!!

Thank you. We love your cake. Brandy Davis

Best Goodies in town!
BigD163

Safe streets
Sandtown

Stop shooting start living yeah!

Pastor Boyd Whipple
the Historic Mount Hebron Baptist Church
Baltimore, MD

Medina Tyson
from ATL →
Best Rolls in the
Country!

09/14/2019 3pm

Ms. Brenda,
Would you
be so kind to share
how the top of lemon &
pound cake is so—
well it has a different consistency
on top. Can you tell me how
you do it please?
I'm just kidding! Ha! Ha! Ha!
Ha! I'm kidding. Happy cooking
A baker never reveals her
secrets. Hope you got a little laugh
from this. Just being silly that's all...
nothing more, nothing less. :)
+ Shannon * Shannon
& Only Shannon :)

Safe streets
Sandtown
MB :)
Street living I did

1 Best
Sweets In Baltimore
the old Avenue
Favorites
Just like I was
a kid
Q Brown

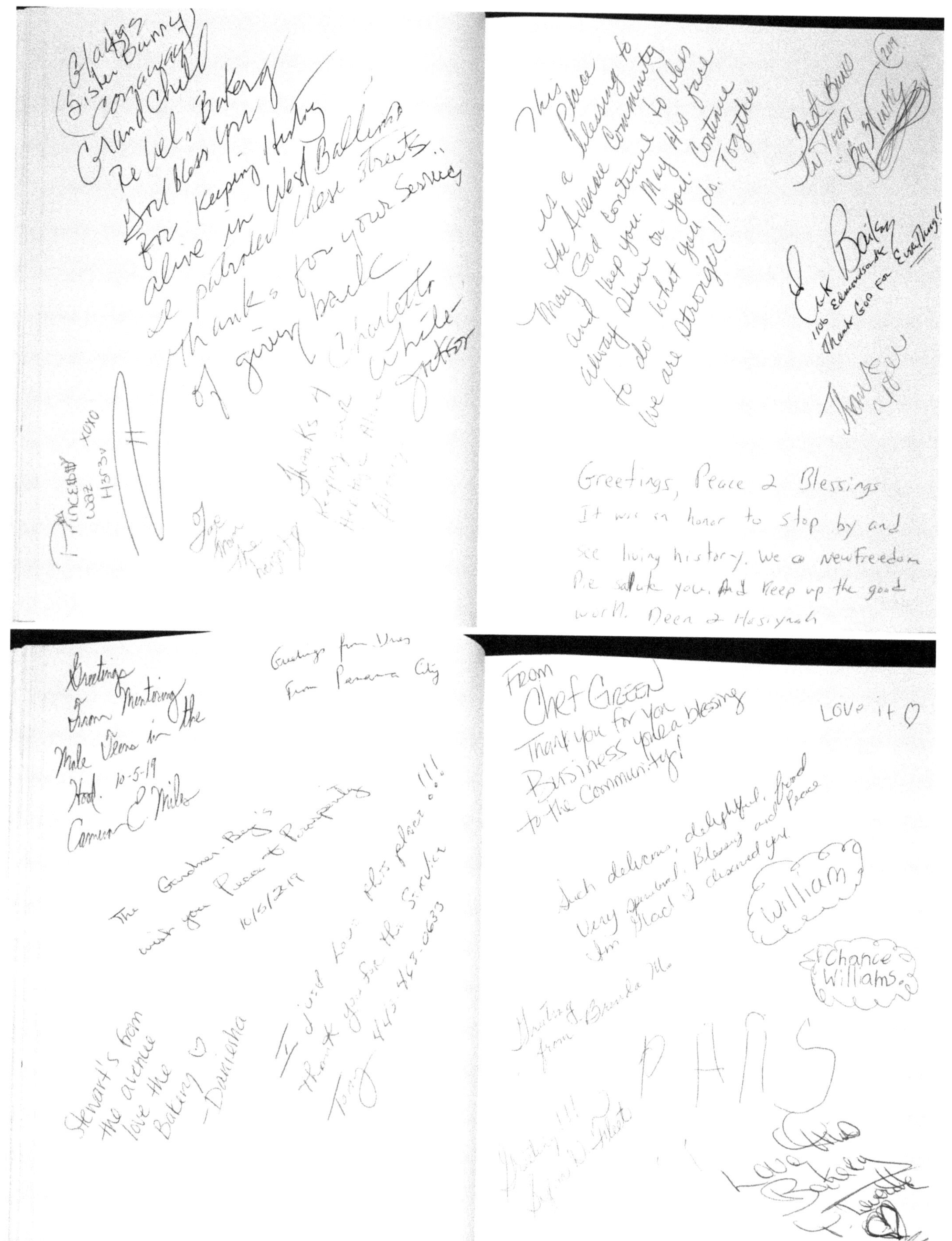
Grand Child
God Bless you for Keeping History alive in West Baltimore
Thanks for your Service
of giving back
Charlotte White-Jackson
Princess XOXO
This Place is a blessing to the Avenue Community. May God continue to bless and keep you. May His face always shine on you. Continue to do what you do. Together we are stronger!!
Eric Bailey
Thank God For Everything!!
Greetings, Peace & Blessings
It was an honor to stop by and see living history. We @ NewFreedom Pie salute you. And keep up the good work. Deen & Hasiynah
Greetings from Mentoring Male Teens in the Hood. 10-5-19
From Panama City
The Goodman-Bey's wish you Peace & Prosperity
I just love this place!!!
Thank you for the Service
Stewart's from the avenue love the Bakery ♡
From Chef Green
Thank you for your Business you're a blessing to the Community!
LOVE it ♡
Such delicious, delightful food
William
Chance Williams.
Love the Bakery

LOVE
This PLACE
BAby AL

This place smells INCREDIBLE!
Thank you! PS> Thanks for the
♡ [illegible] history

Hold it down for
Upton 100

I. Simba Upton
Resident
PCV Ecuador
17-19

This place is Awsome
Upton Resident Nancy

Love

100

Ericka W.

I come here Love
The coffee and The
vibes

(Counselor
is
Here)

[illegible] Jr & Family
Thanks for being Open!
KaKa Pgh 412

I enjoy every opportunity to stop here
and have coffee and a pastry, and I bring new
customers at every opportunity
R Goodwin
rontgd@aol.com

Proud members of Engine Company 52
Keep pushing '2019

Happily supporting this historic establishment

Keep Pushing a change is gonna come

Loved it here
Tevens
10-18-19

rich history, incredible bakery
-Nidia (Puerto Rico)

Crystal Williams
Stay up homie
Keep that backbone in your afro!

Wonderful place.
Keep on keepin' on.
-Laura P.

Beautiful place! Thank you for the history & experience!
Magnus & Madison Jones

What a stunning history & inspirational effort to revitalize!
– Tausha

Thank you for sharing the history
-Anah

Amazing history

Be back soon ♥
Dean O'Neill

Craig
5 years old
10-18-19

WAS Friday
57.
2019

Love the Ave

Andrews Washing Repair
1615 Pennsylvania ave

Mary Foreman
AKA Miss Mary the Frozen Cup Lady
504 Gold st,
1008 N Arlington

Charles Foreman
Moving & Hauling
504 Gold st

My Book
"Latisha Thompson"
AKA Family
"LADYBUG"
Just Lov the Avenue
3505 Erdman Avenue
Baltimore MD 21213
(Anita)
557 Presstmanstreet
Baltimore MD 21217
"Informations"
Peace And Blessings!!!

Wonderful to be here
Edna Mack

Everyone at No Boundaries Coalition says Hello!

Black Box Radio
BlackBoxRadio.com

Thomas G Savage, SR
"Thomas the Great"
11-1-2019

Woods John
Park heights (15)
Best in town
Michael
Love ya LOL

Dr. Jawad Abdullah

Ms. Lady
LOVE EVERYthing
they make its wonderful

Kassidy
Khloe

D.J. Was here!!
Nov. 3, 2019
God Bless
Put God first in all you say & Do!!

Ms Booker

Love them Rolls

Hello There

Cake

Pizza

Busneiss

Have fun

Pennsylvania for life
Tyrone Tisdale
Thank you

TAVON

J Jones

Get it

Douglas

LOVE

Yes Indeed!

Earl -N- Tasha

Niyah B1

HOME SWEET HOME AVE BAKERY

Good

Im back fave spot!!!

Coffie

Love

Love

Love

Best at what they do

Lots of Love XOXOXO

God is Good!!!

"Charlie" (Lots of Love)

Thank you for playing an important role in the (our) community! Coppin Students K. Carter

Concerts, Visual Artworks, Legacy Lessons, and Community Concerns

I had been involved with mentoring and bringing enhanced programs to Booker T. Washington Middle School since 1996. The Bakery gave me more opportunities to engage the students outside of the school walls. We were also able to add other schools as well as elementary, high school, and college students throughout the Upton, Sandtown, and Druid Heights communities.

The Royal Theater & Community Heritage Corporation
Presents

The Courtyard Summer Music Series

A Taste of Contemporary @ The Avenue Bakery

Singer/Songwriter/ John Milton Wesley returns to Pennsylvania Avenue on August 17, 2013 for the first time since he completed his latest work in print, **"The Pennsylvania Avenue Heritage Trail Tour Guide Booklet and Map."** Wesley , a graduate of Tugaloo College **is known as a "soulful" performer who is as much fun to watch, as he is to experience vocally.** The gifted musician and songwriter **once performed with Duke Ellington and** his **orchestra at Carnegie Hall on April 4, 1968 at the age of 20.**

Also Returning "The Firm" serving up the Brass!

Saturday, August 17, 2013, 4 p.m. – 8 p.m.

2229 Pennsylvania Ave, Baltimore, MD 21217

FREE! ALL SUMMER LONG, featuring performances by Baltimore's most consummate musicians and performers

Light fare and drink
Available for purchase throughout the afternoon.

DONATIONS WILL BE ACCEPTED TO HELP REBUILD THE ROYAL THEATRE "*One Brick @ A Time!*"

www.Royaltchc.com   www.TheAvenueBakery.com

We held baking and business classes at The Bakery, and we donated and mentored children in need. In collaboration with The Royal Theater & Community Heritage Corporation (TRTCHC) we set about the task of educating our community on the history and legacy of historic West Baltimore. As a result, The Bakery has been designated a mini-museum, showcasing the heyday of our ancestral past and African American legacy builders from all walks of life—political/civil rights, cultural, and in entertainment of the 1930s, '40s, '50s, and '60s.

Back in 2011, Kathleen Sherrell, our architect, Brenda, and I—we all got to work creating The Avenue Bakery. I've never claimed to be a visual artist, but I came up with a preliminary rough draft drawing and handed it off to Kathleen. She got me.

We dedicated our courtyard to The Royal Theater & Community Heritage Corporation (TRTCHC), a nonprofit

MEDIA ALERT

Friday April 10, 2015
1:00P.M. – 2:00PM

Unveiling of a One Of A Kind Photomontage

"Billie Holiday A Life In Music"

100 Year Celebration of Her Life Work

THE AVENUE BAKERY
2229 Pennsylvania Avenue, Baltimore, Maryland
Sponsored By The Royal Theater & Community Heritage Corporation

MEDIA RELEASE

Poppay's Rolls 200,000 and Counting

You're Invite

The 5th Year Anniversary Celebration of The Avenue Bakery On Historic Pennsylvania Avenue
Saturday, August 13, 2016/4:00p.m.

MEDIA RELEASE

476,446 Poppay's Rolls and Counting

You're Invited
The 10th Year Anniversary Celebration of The Avenue Bakery
On
Historic Pennsylvania Avenue

Saturday, August 14, 2021 At 4:00p.m.

Courtyard Concert Series Fun at The Avenue Bakery

we formed in 2005 to rebuild the Royal and revitalize historic Pennsylvania Avenue. The very first piece of artwork that we unveiled was that of The Royal Theater, which was crafted by artist Cisco Davis. Every year since, we have unveiled a piece of artwork or photomontage that depicts the history and legacy of the community, The Bakery, and offers the neighborhood visual encouragement with history lessons to boot. One of the most impressive pieces is the 18'X28' foot Civil Rights photomontage adjacent to our parking lot. When I purchased the property in 2004, there was a liquor sign on that wall that I vowed to remove. Over the years, we have folks like historian and graphic artist Stuart Hudgins, artist Peggy Seeney, author and columnist Rosa Pryor, and photographer and author Amy Davis contribute to our exhibits.

In an attempt to give folks a snippet of the atmosphere on The Avenue during the '30s, '40s, '50s, and early '60s, we allowed TRTCHC to host summer concerts in the courtyard. They were dedicated to an era gone by. The Bakery has become the site for community meetings and an official tourist designation for Baltimore City. It attracts visitors from around the world.

Baltimore's tourism industry ranks third in our city, boasting 10 million dollars annually. Many of our visitors and local customers alike make it their business to sign our welcoming Legacy Logbook, standing post in The Bakery's front lobby. Outside of The Bakery, that menacing telephone-booth-thing, once representing when ne'er-do-wells perpetrated illegal commerce, became a thing of the past. Having it removed was one of my first business to-dos.

Our continued goal is to build a theater, replacing the unjustly demolished Royal Theater, in which top entertainers can clamor to entertain and audiences can flock to see. In 2019, we had proof that the dream could become a tangible reality. When we began The TRTCHC Concert Series, held in The Bakery Courtyard, we had never imagined how its popularity could grow so quickly. During the early days of the concert series, our area bands played pro bono because they knew what we were trying to accomplish—a safe and entertaining outlet for our community. These days, we pay the musicians and vocalists who appear, and though we may not be able to pay them a lot, according to the world of entertainment, we are overrun with requests to perform. We receive phone calls, musicians leave their business cards with us, and we receive emails from all the rich talent in Baltimore and beyond who want to perform in our concert series. And it's a blessing. By that same token, our audiences steadily grow as well.

One of the reasons why entertainers say that they want to play here is—location. It's *Pennsylvania Avenue*. Musicians are well aware of the history and legacy of The Avenue. Musicians love the atmosphere we've created in the courtyard, made complete by attractive greenery and murals that honor historic African American icons whose stories have been colorfully etched into the 21st Century. And then there's the clientele. Consistently, a diverse crowd (young and old) shows up for our concerts. We have White. We have Black. We have various ethnic groups—sipping, eating, clapping, and jumping up to dance when the live music overtakes them. Then we have the back-in-the-day crowd, returning each summer because of the nostalgia factor. They come to honor what once was and to show their support for what could be—if we keep at it.

The Royal Theatre Community Heritage Corporation
Courtyard Jazz Benefit Series
Proudly presents

A September Taste of Jazz
Featuring
"The Firm"

Light fare and desserts
by The Avenue Bakery
to benefit Baltimore City Youth Programs

Sunday, September 16, 2012
4:00p.m. - 8:00p.m.
(Rain date: Sunday, September 23, 2012)

in
The Hamlin Family
Courtyard Garden
2229 Pennsylvania Avenue
Baltimore, Maryland 21217

****

Contributions of $35 or more
are requested, most appreciated and tax deductible!

2012 Jazz Announcement, Concert Series

You are truly anointed! These rolls and baked goods are heaven sent. Michelle & Eugene Braxton

*Tastes like the rolls mama & grandma used to make!

a change is coming

Regie K Hunter
Sweat N Go
"Thank You"

Thanks for the great breakfast!! Pat & Richard

Brooke Thank you for the tour!!

Thanks for everything ♡

11/17/19

Bryanna Valentine
Thank you from Coppin

Thank you for every seed sown into the community
Noelle
Coppin State

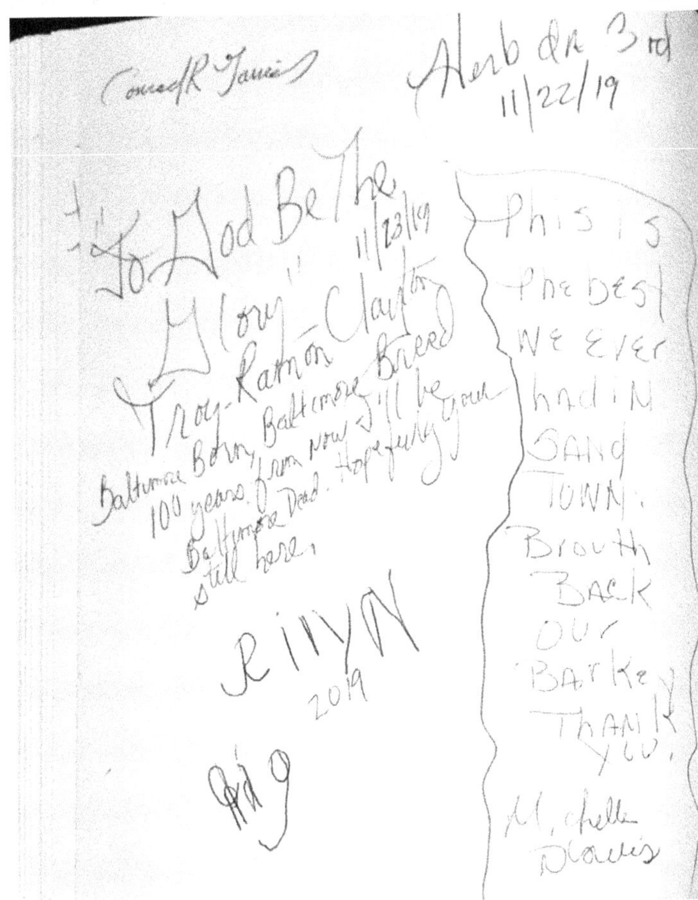

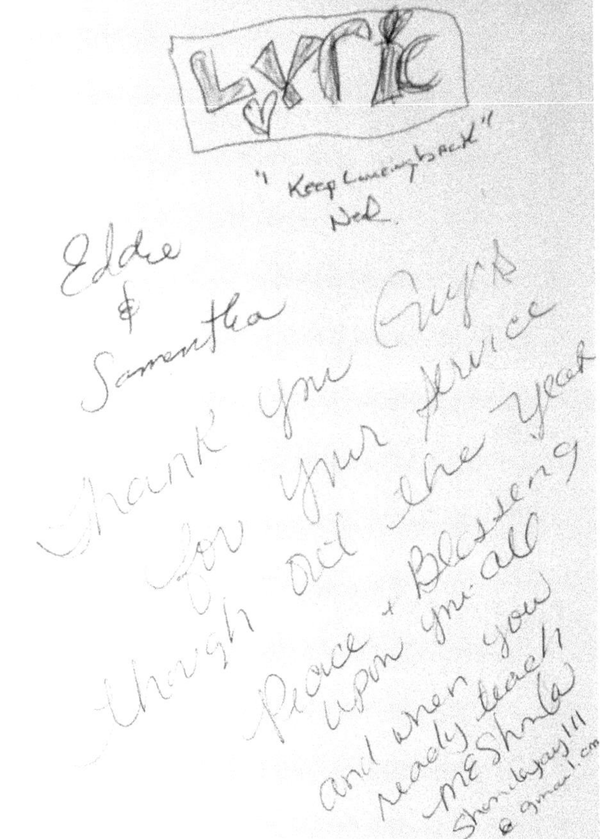

Happy Thanksgiving Voices of the People 2019 The Best Food!

Happy Thanksgiving
Abu the Flutemaker

Have a Great Thanksgiving
M. E. [illegible]

Happy Thanksgiving. The Avenue Baker is something I am thankful for - God Bless you all
[illegible]

Rochelle A. Arrington
Thanks So Much!

Thank You for your steadfast and unwavering business [illegible]

Delicious! [illegible] 12/5/19

[illegible]

646 373-1064
Saratoga Spring, N.Y Apt 811
12866

May the Holiday Season and the New Year be filled with an abundance of Blessings and Prosperity.
— Craig 2019

[illegible]

Love God!

Don Back Again

Thank

We're here exploring Baltimore!! [illegible] 12-13

First Time But Not the Last Time Happy Holidays Russell D. (NY)

Andrew's Washing Machine Repair

I took an apple cake & 3 Potato pies to [illegible] from Alabama for Thanksgiving and they were a big hit. Everyone wants more
[illegible] 12/13/2019

Seasons Greetings

Love, Love, Love everything here!
Marilyn & Greg

Blessings & much love
Wilhelmina

Blessings to All
Kitty

Greatest Pecan Pie ever. Cheapest prices all around
12/18/19

12/18/19
Shogun's
Love This Place
Greg Gilmore

12/18/2019 Bless
May The Lord ^ You All.
Amen. Madonna + Al Jones

12/19/19- My first time here! Big Mu Gotti!

12/19/19 I'm Always At
Home Here & Nothing But Love

12/19/19
Let Build on What We
Have Achived
Love
Steve

12/19/2019
Can't Wait til
the change come
to return the Avenue
to it High lights of a time
that Has passed
Revitalization
It will happen in the
next 5 years
J. Charles

12/21/19

Happy Holidays 2019

Debra HOWELL

12/21/19
Smells Very
Good heard so
know it tastes good!
Lovely I'll Be Back
Friday.

12/23/19
Amazing to see
my people and the opportunity
to this welcoming space
It also smells Amazing!!

12/23/19
Smells like
My Mother's Kitchen
I'm back because
these rolls taste
just like her rolls!
Thank you

12/22/19
My Dad worked at
Samsons Restaurant.
He baked rolls there, He taught me
how to Bake them. Everyone loved my rolls,
until I found this place two years ago.
I haven't baked a roll since then.
Samson's rolls were good, But
these Rolls are GOOOOD!!!
David Carpenter

Hardware Plus y'All We Love
Merry Christmas

Dan + Claudia Zanes — we're here from Brooklyn NY.....
Delicious!! Happy to be here eating!
XXXX

Wayne Morton 2019

Happy Holidays!
No Boundaries Coalition
12/29/19

"Happy Holiday's food is good customer"

Suggestion: Always _(Attention) to Detail is Key.
Customer Service
your taking to long to complete order's here:
We are waiting too long in the lines
please learn How to Move faster Thanks.
To a longtime Customer who would love to keep Coming Back

The wait time is over 5 minute for a cup of Coffee.

"Happy holidays"
Semaj
"Chid"
Great food

Customer Service Is Awesome!
Thanks For Coming!!

THE AVENUE BAKERY'S

LOGBOOK #6
(2020-2022)

Welcome To
The Avenue Bakery

We appreciate your support of our business and mission to revitalize Historic Pennsylvania Avenue. We want you to enjoy our products and the History of our community that we have here for your education.

Feel free to express or jot down your thought and experience here with us. We hope you also share it with family friends and neighbors.

Sincerely
Poppay
James Hamlin

Scott 1/16/20
Family
East Bmore

Welcome Back
Best in the west
Roots & Us

¡ WELCOME BACK,
AVENUE BAKERY!
GLAD TO START THE NEW YEAR WITH YOU.
– Max from Medfield

"Leon Johnson
I will be back!!"

Glad you're Here!
Linda M.
from Chicago
01-16-2020

Hello again!
James & Brenda
Love
Bernie & Barbara Holman
(your old friends)
1/16/20

Oh, my gosh!
What an honor to meet you, Mr. James.
This place is beautiful.
I will be back!
-Sa'Toya Truss
17JAN2020

Thank you for everything
Xudeo. This place, the history, the rolls! the person (Jim).
What a treasure!
Thank you again,
Sarah G
from Brooklyn
Will definitely come back!!
1/23/2020

We got our birthday treats!!
1/23/2020

First time - not the last!
Misic
1/19/20

We loved our visit!

The best place to celebrate a birthday! Thank you guys!
Ben

1/23/2020 Glad we took the opportunity to explore the goods!!

CAN'T WAIT TO TRY THE ROLLS! HEARD ABOUT THEM FOR YEARS!

Aye!! It's Yay Nae Follow me on all Socails Yay NAE

MLK

God is Real? Thats for sure!

Love U Father! Always!
Ion Hopkins
Keep Loving Him!!!

1st Time Here!!
The Johnson family
Love everything about yall family owned Bakery! Will Be Back often!!

1-31-2020
To: Jim & Family
Keep up The Good Work

THIS PLACE IS INCREDIBLE "AGAIN" "MEATWO ONE"

YOU GUYS ARE AWESOME
OFC. RAHEEM

Enjoy the muffins luv them to the moon and back

Moski 02/04/20

Muffins the Best!!

Tom Savage Thank You

Hasan Abdel-Adl Thank You

Kenard Moulden Thank You.

Thank you for your love for Avenue and your delicious food

Providence Baptist Church

Thanks for the great food
Keep up the good work

Keep up the good work!
Thanks for the pies!
Lori from San Francisco, CA
02/07/2020

Make the Avenue Great AGAIN!
02/07/2020

Thank you for shining your light!
2/8/2020

Destiny
Dezzi Dez
2020
Much Love
Peace

2/15/2020
Black History Month
Love Always
Major Sharon K. Evans

Dear Mr. James Hamlin & Family, Saturday Afternoon February 08, 2020
Be Blessed all the time... Congrats to you!
I simply love eating your Outstanding and delicious wheat rolls. Thank you so Much... with a gentle effect. Lots of Love,
Jeannette Edmonds (Member)
Christian Love Baptist Church
4198 Falls Rd
Pastor Reverend Dr. Wm C. Bailey

Finally I caught this Bakery open!
D.N.

2/18/2020

Kashina Was Here

Peace Blessings Love

MAKE EVERY DAY A MOMENT & DREAM TO CREATE

BY AREL BRADY

My Love is FREE

I like the Bakery

May

Love the Bakery,
thank you!
Dr. Morales

Jacquelin Hill
Love the Bakery
and all you do
for the community.
Thanks for caring!

Baltimore's
Best
Bakery!!!
Thanks for all you do
for the Avenue!
Anthony Wilson
(son of Bernice)
2/15/20
(Back home from NC)

A Glorious Day! Thanks for all you do for the Community —
The Reverend Sandye Wilson +
2/15/2020
Newly returned home after 50 yrs!

2/15/2020
This event was awesome, the History. People I will never forget

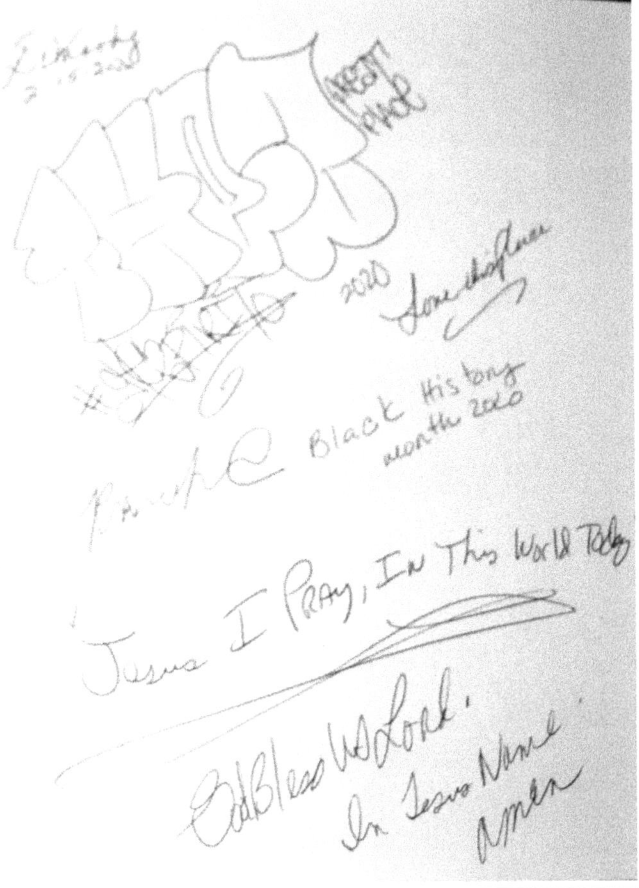

Nothing But LOVE Feb 21-2020

Genesis - 12:2
Randolph W
West Baltimore

A great Community Asset! Thank You for the Vision! Carolyn M. Mayor's Office 2/24/20

God's Blessings Always, Carolyn M. 2/26/2020

Thank you for all you do in the community. Much prosperity

2/26/20

3-7-20
Good Morning - Coming in for Something Yummy!! - Sylvia & Roger

Awesome visit the real community!

3/7/20

Best Bakery in Town - B-More
Bobby B-More
2020

Keep on

Ed Crosby
Lexington Terrace
VS. Navy Ret.
thank you for staying here
God Speed.
MR BONOS

yes ☺

First time here!

Love this Place

Mr & Mrs Corey Watters
Essex, MD
Keep on Keepin On!

2020
Thanks, God Bless

What A Wonderful Place and good Excellent Service
Delores Smith Catthee
-and-
Bishop Wm. E. Catthee
U.B.C.
1939 W. Baltimore
Baltimore MD.

Denise C.
My dad introduced our family to this awesome baking - I live miles away but don't mind driving here for delicious treats! excellent customer service
Keep up the great work!!!

J. GRAY
Filmmaker, Producer
moved to Baltimore in 1994 Excited to be working w/ Jim Fields on a project to bring more recognition to West Baltimore and The Royal Theater and Community Heritage Center
Mr. Charles —
GOD LOVE YOU

West Coast
Las Vegas
Steven Cobb

Excellent ♡ the Chocolate Cake
J.B.

Wonderful Bakery

Fantastic Display
Preserving Baltimore's History
Rev. Reba
and
Matthew

Great Place We Need more Black Business in our Hood.

Blown Away by the amount of information and history.
Thank you for preserving our story.

Blessed are my family. Love your cookies. Have a lovely weekend. Have a lovely week. they are the best makye you work day fun. wrote this with intelligents and love showntae Jeanette Brown family and friends Kids say thats write and thanks.

2/2/2020
the Millers Teenagers Was here at this great place I can remember as a little Kid How Beautiful life was we all served our own oh how I wish it gonna come to be as honorable as we use to be helping one another please lets NOT DIE this way ... C. Miller

10-01-2020
I Love Your Baked Goods... My Wife + I be Very disappointed When Ur Not Open. Thanks 4 being Here ☺ The Banks Family

I Came here on Sat. I came back today I love yall & everything is So good thank You
Louise Redd

I came because I LOVE BEING BLACK!
#ISUPPORTU ~Damaw (DOB)

Hello I actually travel from Towson area just for your baked goods. DELICIOUS

Alot of History, Black (Asiatics) Culture, Art, etc.
Troy X 2020

June Byron

I was told about yall
I love the homemade Rolls
And I will be back Louise Redd

First time here a friend shared Some of your Lemon pound cake
May Allah continue to Bless You
The Sike Mohammed family

First time here appreciate service love to support people of my color Business

Best Baked Goods in Baltimore City Oct 4, 2020

Mary and Charles Came Here two weeks in A Row So Delicious ~~so~~ We Are Hooked ♡
Baltimore Virginia 10-10-2020

Sandi Schutz - wow a hidden treasure - I'll be back!

My first time here. Heard So much about this great place
CSJ

I can not wait to try it. Never could catch you open. I am Here Yvelle

Best bun's in the world!!
A.N. T.M.

Every Time I Share ~~My~~ bake Goods from here I Share the Best of the Best
Shee

Taking in The Avenue Bakery's many history lessons

I support Black businesses as I should!
I love being black ~ Tamara
OOPS- A conflict Mgmt. firm helping our community with the OOPS of miscommunication!

I Enjoy coming here I Come a long way to get This
Frankie J. Lee

I really enjoy your bake goods mainly the homemade rolls the pound cake is really good I will be back St. Louise Kidd
Thank You

Staff Great! ♡ Ayanna

This is the Best Bakery I've every been too in my Life!!
My GOD BLESS AND KEEP US!!!
LOVE ALWAYS FAMILY
MRS C. BANKS
10-18-20

Congrats Joe x Kamala 2020 POTUS 11/7/2020

Jo Ann McNeill Scott Class of '68

Shari Parson-Bey was here NOV 7 2020

every step counts, every effort must be sincere

Oct 1 2020
Raquel Bailey
Love coming to this Bakery every Sunday afternoon with friends & Family
Beautiful staff!

Oct 30.
Hope y'all had a great Vacation
Miss y'all but hope y'all had a safe and good Vacation — LEE 2020

Remember coming to Pennsylvania Ave as a child ~ 1957. With my mother at the Charm Shop. Because of Apartheid in Baltimore, she would get dresses hand made. Could not shop downtown.
Phillip Bo[illegible]
10/30/2020

Thank you for your service! STAY Healthy! STAY SAFE! STAY Blessings

30 October 2020
I am always grateful for your model of a great family business, in a great facility, with a really great team – You and me are blessed – God stay with you – Joanne Sparker

God Bless & Good Luck
Kennett
North East Baltimore

1/01/2020
Happy New President's Day
Congrats President Biden

God bless the Staff Here
Please Stay Safe - Safe
J. Lee
Every Time I [illegible] my food I am coming back soon

TIME IS NOW
MADE
Danielle W[illegible]
Vince Blocker

Great food!
Great service!
I like coming here –
Harvey [illegible]

Every step counts
when every effort is earnest
and every intention true
Km

Be True to Yourself

THANKS 4 Being Here
Janaan Ali

THANKS AGAIN

Good Very Good!!
Tony Williams
Let it Be
Stay Good

Congrats To Owner of [illegible]
The Avenue Bakery
New Carmel Star Baptist Church [illegible]
James & Carol Turner.
Thank God and May He Bless You
Elliott [illegible] MD
May GOD Continue to give you Guidance in
Keeping your door open in 2K21 – Happy New Year! J. Lambert
Ja'Tecrah
"The NO Boundaries Youth"
Organizers
AKA → NBYO =)
Thank You for Keeping history
alive!
We appreciate it ♡!
Xiomara Strayhorn
(Norway + Atlanta GA)

Thanks
So much
For Serving
the Community. ♡♡
We really appreciate
your service to US!!

Thank
You all
for everything you are giving us.
The Franklin
Family
2020

God bless you –
Gayla Meekins

[illegible]

To The Owner's of The Bakery
Thank You For Your Love
of Helping People

The Blessings of the
Lord be upon you
and this wonderful
Bakery... Barbara Clark

15 August 2021

I remember when The Avenue Bakery was a dream.

I remember bringing over the 1st one of these books.

I remember pitching Dan Rodricks at The Baltimore Sun, and writing your 1st press release.

The Hamlin Family is Baltimore's beloved 1st Family of Popaye's Rolls

Love Youse

love us!!

xoxo

Jaynee Ann Jackson

10 years just zipped right on by!

WOW!!!

Thank you for Serving the Sandtown community

I was born on the 1100 Block of Woodyear St. my grandparents & their kids moved up from S Carolina. We have a close knit family. When me & my sibilings were born we lived with my grand parents and the smell of Schmidt Bakery was amazing. So thanks for bringing a bakery back to the Community. May God bless you all & your families Amen

Faud [Past Time] with God do Christ less Holy spirit

(KBJ)

GOD BLESS US ALL

PLEASE Save Our Souls

Skip was here!!
Ibtisaam Daniels was here feb 25, 2021
E.P. was Here
Bob @Freeland Construction supports The Avenue Bakery.
Thank you for the wonderful cakes & pies... will be ordering birthday cake from here...
K. Brown
Nia Jones
Co-Founder BPRB Black People Ride Bikes, Inc.
Marjaanah Matin was here! Feb 25, 2021
HiThere! What a wonderful place with beautiful smells!
Cheryl Crockett 2-27-21
Thur. Feb 26 2020
The bread pudding and coconut cake are delicious! DKD
MAY GOD CONTINUE TO BLESS YOU AND WATCH OVER YOU
How Amazing! Thank you for preserving our incredible History! God Bless! keep it up! Empower & Inspire!
Wendy 3/5/21
Love This Bakery!!
Hello My Name Lee 1st time Here The Smell when you walk in the Door is Awesome... Peach Cobbler Highly Recommended!! 2021
I got the Cherry Cream cheese Danish! It's so good! 3/4/21
Ibtisaam D March 4th 2021

11/3/21

3/11/2
Excellent Keep Up
The Great Business
Lonnie Norman

Perfection is When your
Satisfied With Anything
by [illegible]

Simply Marvelous
to me!!
Jenice Sheppard

Joseph Q. Curtis
Yusuf The Barber
Born 1959

Thanks for U

Thank you
for providing
pastries for the
VLP ☺
-Laura

3/12/2021

L. Young Your The BEST
Keep it up!!! ☺

Greater Youth
Christian Academy
Salutes this
Great Bakery.

3-13-21 - Coming in for Something
"yummy" / Delicious!! Roger / Sylvia

Blessings to
You for Excellence
in Community
Positive Youth
Expression
Dr. D. [illegible] Ph.D.

Val Jenkins
Hugs Don't Shoot
www Hugs Dont Shoot.org
3-13-2021

Bernard Lea
3/19/2021

God PLEASE Bless us all.. you Do This already.

Jesus I Pray in this world TODay

Walter

Quidman 3-14-2021 Smells so good ♡

Charles Cavenbaugh 4/1/21 414

Bless this Business God and those who Labor

The community is Pleased with your services thanks Grand Mom

Father Matthew 3.20.21 Best Bread Pudding PEACE

Calvin Dotson (Butch) House Hero 3/26/21

Ruben

ALAYAh

Amira & the [illegible] Family

Thanking you for your business and success in the African america community, Great Job ☺ May God continue to bless you and your Grand son. Love your rolls & cakes.

Thanks Mclean Kennedy

The Greatest Bakery in Baltimore Thank You!

We came from West Virginia love these rolls, cakes Oh my Goodness! Everything is delicious

We love You

3/27/2021

Dear Mr. Hamlin,
You are truly a asset to Pennsylvania Avenue. May God bless you and your family today and everyday,
Rhonda D. Lane

April 2, 2021

We really love this place

/2/2021
Jwanita Bunoz
Happy Easter
He Has RISEN

Cherise gordon
443-314-6027

I glad you have decided to remain on the Ave.
Mike Wooding

Wishing You All the Success.
You items are absolutely Delicious!
Bernadette Matthews

Congrats to you and yours Keep Striving!!

Kay Ferrell
April 3, 2021 Wishing you Success
Visit

We really enjoy All your Sweets.
Greater Youth Academy
Agape

Hortense Cannady
April 3rd
"I know I am going to enjoy"
"that bread pudding"

Abigail 040 was here! Enjoyed your rolls and cake! S. [illegible]

You establishment is an uplifting diamond providing wonderful treats. Keep shining! P3, Inc

So happy to have found this jewel hidden away. Bless you all for sharing your amazing talent gift of God

All The Blessings in the world
Thank You!!
Jesse Dorsher

Hallelujah

4-11-21
Love your Bake Goods Keep up the Great work

May the Most High Always show you favor [illegible]

Rose Acton K.

a beautiful day for beautiful words, good food and good music. honored thank you, Mr. [illegible]

I loved the tour! Baltimore is lucky to have you. -Ki [illegible]

Thank you [illegible]

Goodness Gracious God Bless you Guys

Sis. P.E. Patterson I Corin 1 to end

Thank you for the tour, the information, and the incredible baked goods! This was a real treat.
— Kevin Griffin Moreno 04/15/2021

Hi Family ~ Coming in for Something Home-made & Delicious!! SYLVIA 4-17-21

Stay safe. Be happy. Abdalla C. Islaah (BAM!) Baltimore area Muslims :)

Praise the Lord for He's Still in Control!

Stephanie Ruhle
NBC News
NYC — thank you for the magic

Charles Edmondson
Olet Cashner

Jesus I Pray!

all Praise due to Allah
Bro Kevin Muhammad
Vickie Coates 5-7-21

God Bless 5.28.21 S. Bates

a beautiful day for beautiful words, good food and good music. we thank you. mr. hamlin
Enjoyed your presentation 4/29/2021
Family Love 2021
I really love yall you make good roll & pastry keep up the good work and God Bless you!!
Charlie Edmondson
Jesus I Pray!
"These buns are so big!" -Sean Dunn 5/6/21
all Praise due to Allah
Thank you for the tour, the information, and the incredible baked goods! This was a real treat.
Hi Family - Coming in for Something Home & Delicious!!
5.28.21
Hey Mr. Hamlin, So proud to see your work. It's one of your oldest mentees, Marcia Ervin from Morgan. Much love!
Hi Hamlin Family - Coming in for Something Sweet & Delicious Sylvia
Thanks for all you are doing! Carol
Thanks! Great tour!
This was such an eye-opener for me!
Keep doing what you're doing for the community!!
Wanda Cooper
5/13/2021
These Danishes are sooo good!
5/20/21
Loved the tour & learning about area. Good luck on your work to revitalize Pennsylvania Ave, rebuild the Royal & create opportunities for young people - And thank you!
Sami
Black is beauty
beauty is Black and true
5/20/2021
Keep up the Good work
Mr. Hamlin,
You are a World Class tour guide, Baker & all around great asset to Baltimore. Beyond thank you for an amazing tour for us from Towson Unitarian Universalist Church. We had a wonderful experience
Love, Nina

Great PLACE
will Be BACK AND
Tell other. 4 SURE
VAN Edwards
5/23/21

Great Place
Friendly service. I will be
back.
T. Gray
5/23/21

Good place
to eat food i love it
Jimo

GOD Bless you, I HAVE TO
Come EVERY week AND Get
My Pie
BEST I EVER
HAD
5 29 21

Timothy Toh
Plz keep up
the Excellent
work we
need y'all

Thanks for the tribute
to our history!

5/6/21 DR Butler; Pauline Stewart.
Hallelujah!

5.11.21 Heather & Christian
with Nobis Project - Savannah, GA
Thank you! we look forward to coming back soon

06/12/2021
"God is Good/God is Great...
...let us thank you for this food!!!"
Louis B. Schrase

6/12/21 Blessings To You and your
Workers. I will Support Your
Business Thank You.

6/12/21 I'm so glad to catch you open
today. May God continue to
bless your business.

6/13/21 Blessings to all
BD

6/11/21
All the way
from Los Angeles, CA
Black Love + Support!
Megan Christi

AKA REDFOXX

6/12/21
He estado aquí en
este lugar maravilloso,
con buenas obras.

6/12/21
Calvin Dotson Jr

Praise God
Jesus I Pray in this World To Day!
6.12.2021

6/19/21
Came here with BLACK PEOPLE RIDE BIKES.
THE Apple Cobbler is AMAZING. ☺ Keep up the good work.
Allen [signature]

6/19/21 JUNETEENTH
Black People Ride Bikes

6/19/22 All about the smells. ☺

6/05/21 Thank you All for your wonderful SERVICE, been coming here for years Love y'all
Heavenly Cleaning Sv. llc

6/27 We're hooked!! Thank you for your service and the outstanding, delicious baking items!
Joan + Mark Campbell

6/26 —
Nubian Lodge No 132
WAS Here
And are coming Back
PM/WM 161

○ [illegible] from Bolton Hill

6/26/2021 Yvette Sweet

P.S. #130 II M. Banks – Fauntleroy

6/27/2021 Lady B WOLB 1010
1st time

6/27/2021 We Love

7/03/2021 Andrew F. Jackson III

7-03-21 Jess Dunlap & Amber Dunlap
KRIME
Krime Slugs in LOVE!! [illegible]
(OKAY) slugs love pie too!

Jeannie Everette
4311 Pimlico ROAD
443 570-5056

7/6/2021 Codetta Bake Shop ⊕

7/9/2021 [signature]
Love your bakery and the history lesson was excellent!!

7/9/2021 Sonya Askew-Williams
Braxton Williams Allen Hobbs
Paul Williams North Carolina
We were recommended to come here if we were ever in Baltimore and it was worth the journey. God's continued blessing be yours. Keep the history alive! ☺

7/10/21 Milroy B Harried
36 S. Paca St 415
21201

Towana Edison + Delores
VERY INFromtive

Debbie Trust
2116 E. Hoffman St
21213
"Love Everything in the Store"

Bridgett Morse 7/10/2021

George + Charlie Fuller 7/10/21
3717 Downy Dale DR
RANDALLSTOWN, MD 21133

Roddie Wood 7/10/2021

THANK you FOR your TIME & HOSPITALITY. [illegible] Ave Bay [illegible]

-443-831-7282-

Great Work

K.B. Taylor Jr.

Best Roll In Town 7/11/21

O.B.

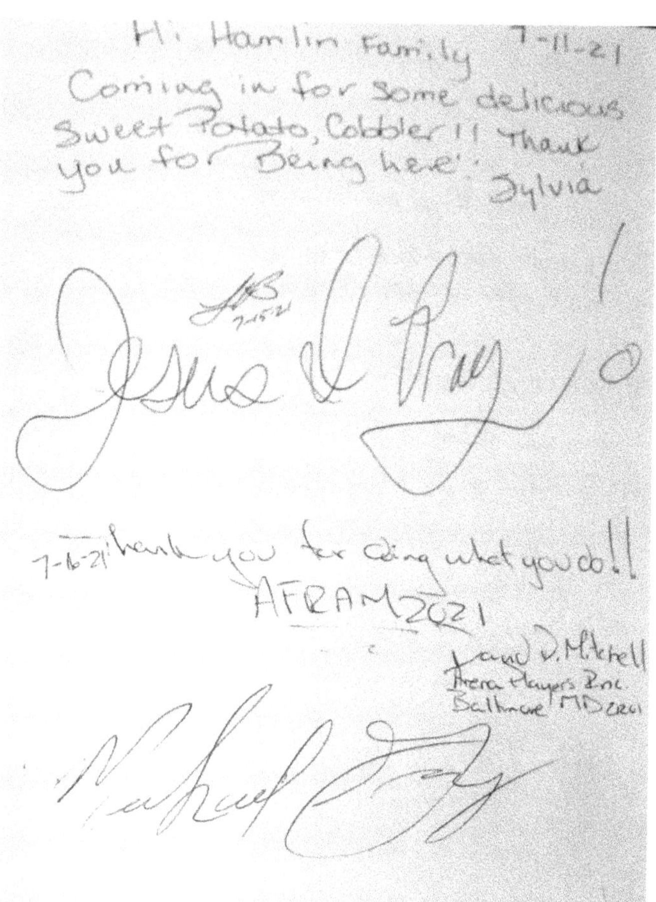

Hi Hamlin Family 7-11-21

Coming in for some delicious Sweet Potato, Cobbler!! Thank you for Being here! Sylvia

Jesus I Pray!

7-16-21 Thank you for doing what you do!! AFRAM2021

David D. Mitchell, Arena Players Inc, Baltimore MD 2021

July 16-21 DR Bulter / Pauline Stewart 1:15pm

-July 22 C. Mitchell Jackson

"I've loved the avenues baked goods for years, I'm so privileged to have met the owner and learned the history behind this very influential place!

July 23 - E. Reid

I've been comming here FOR 2 YEARS STRaight This is the best black bakery in th City. APPLE PIES + Glazed Crossonts. the best.

July 23 - Simon Lee

I love that food is what is bringing people here and change to this place

CAROL MCCARTHY (FRIEND OF DR. BUTLER)

+ ROBERT KEMPER (BUSINESS ASSOCIATES)

Sheila [illegible] we are proud to help provide the Pure Lights to Dr. Butler

CONGRATS LOVE ALL YOUR WORK!!!

July 23 - Jared Kinyua + Dr. Mel Bulter

I've enjoy popay rolls and the ten cent tour. Lots of history and lots of potential can't wait for the documentary and the memoirs.

July 23, Love You Ave Bakery, Quality Service, Great Fellowship and Wonderful Atmosphere.

Love, Gods Bloodwashed Min. Pastor James Boone

A WONDERFUL STORY + A DELICIOUS PLACE! TRISTRAM (GREAT BRITAIN)

Thank you so much for such a memorable experience! You are one of a kind & so is your bakery!

Thank you so much for being with Chastery

Wonderful! Best of luck & all blessings [illegible] Waters

One Person Can Always Make a Difference

My mantra has always been: *Whatever the mind can conceive and believe, it can be achieved.*

I want to pave the way for our young people to change their lives for the better. One of the lessons I always want to convey to them whenever they venture across our threshold is that with hard work, determination, and a plan, they can achieve their dreams!

The Avenue Bakery's grand opening took place on August 15, 2011, to a crowd of community residents, family and friends, elected officials, and the media.

Owning and operating The Avenue Bakery turned out to be my next chapter after leaving my job at the United Parcel Service (UPS). I retired from UPS in 2003 after thirty-five and a half years of dedicated service. During that time, I had learned and perfected many business and economic skills that translated into attributes for running The Bakery. It's another lesson learned that I convey to our youth of all ages. Waste not, want not, and use all the knowledge you've acquired.

I earnestly tell them how, except for having a baby, I've always been of the mindset that if *you* can do it—and *I* need to do it—then I'm going to give it a shot.

I'm grateful!

—James Hamlin

7/26/21
You are such an inspiration! Thank you for a wonderful visit. Julie Kramer
Ohio

Can't wait for the theater. Cake for now... best cake ever!
Flynn
SANTA FE, New Mexico

Great message, Great Food! - Ross Baker Crofton, MD

7/28/21 Liv Feld - Super BAKERY

hello from lafayette college!
erika Nally ありがとう!!
Emily Hockin

- Merci!!

Big Hi from Coppin State!

Just Great Stuff All Around. On Love

my Old Stompin Ground!!
Steve from
Morgan State University

James "Jim" you are a Wealth of Knowledge About the Way Pennsylvania Avenue has Been a Part of Baltimore for decades.
The Avenue Bakery is a Treasure!!
John Patti
WBAL News Radio 1090 & FM 105

Have A GREAT YEAR!! PEACE + BLESSINGS

Glad to help support you & to have you in our neighborhood. S.J.
7/31/21

I am so proud and pleased with you opening a black-owned and operated business. Thank you. Robin & Johnnie
(we love your chocolate cake and cinnamon roles)

Kentland Recreation Council
Landover, MD

with Love

Congratulations on being in business for almost 10 yrs. May you celebrate many more
Deidre Sterling
Eastern Shore MD.

Thanks for your service
Jeanne Carpenter

Delicious food - Thanks for staying open for us
Barbara Harris

Thelma C. HARLEY
LANDOVER MD 20785

Thrya
Balto / FLA
"The Best"

Ivette and Wendell Wheeler
Seoul, South Korea
Warrenton, VA
THANK YOU!

Kimberly Hendricks 2021
Looking forward to a taste of Pappy's

WASH. D.C.
Nice PLACE

Best Wishes & God's Blessings!

Freetown Sierra Leone
West Africa
08/12/2021

Jasmine Perez
08/19/2021
I like your Bakery & your worker may Allah Bless you and your family and worker

Aug 2021
As Salaam Alaikum & Thank You!
May the Creator continue to bless you for your good works!
Boston, MA

Happy Anniversary Peds!

"Happy Anniversary!"
Beatrice L. Kinyua

Happy 10th Anniversary
Love Alissa

Gertrude & Scott
Happy Tenth Anniversary.

HAPPY ANNIVERSARY
PEACE & BLESSING TO THE SUCESS OF YOUR ESTABLISHMENT.
2021 WILLIAMS FAMILY

Happy Anniversary!!
Arnold & Corinne Williams

Happy Anniversary

Jasmine Perez
HAPPY ANNIVERSARY JAMES Hamlin Allah Bless you my Brother and your Familye worker.

Happy Anniversary and many, many more
Kim Moir
Deborah Moir

Blessed & Happy Anniversary!!

HAPPY ANNIVERSARY

HAPPY ANNIVERSARY
BLESSINGS
Donna L. Smith 2021

Jasmine Perez
How is your Day TODAY
MAY ALLAH BLESS YOU.

Moussa Diallo
Bonjour à Vous
Tous

Jasmine Perez
How ARE Doing
hope everthings
is fine GOD
BIESS YOU
& YOUR

Great Service

God bless
our heritage

Great SERVICES

Calm N Ostrof
Grand Pastries

Happy Anniversary
Your UPS Son
Charlie Kurtz

GREAT TO SEE YOU (UPS)
ROY BROWN II

Amazing Work you are doing
Rev.
L. Wedington 2021

Great cakes in Baltimore
Lisa

GLORIA J. WILSON

Lovely Place
1st time
visit from
East Orange, NJ
Jersey
2021

Love Oh History
Khadyal
Stewart
2021
Diverse Training Sev.

Dillon

Peighton

Thank you. you can taste the
heart, soul, and love in every bite!
Marina

Kevin Porter
your cakes are delicious!
Thank you!

Jasmine Perez
ALLAH BIESS you
& YOUR Family I LOVE
YOUR COOKIES & Brownies

Thank's from the Smith & Lewis
Family Love, Love, Love,
you cakes & Pie

Tandi mayo UK4t
was here all the way
from NJ - and NY
Thank you
x44

This business remains
Integrity, Build Back
Better, Along with faith,
In community, and consumer.
Please don't STOP
your talent!
CRAIG Group Study.
2021-2022

Awesome Bakery

I Love Y'all
Officer T. Maddox

Have a blessed day
McElvian

Awesome Bakery Liz S.
9/23/2021
Mr. Hamlin's Grandson
I am so proud of your
Bakery in the African American
neighborhood. You are a great
person. I am very grateful for
you to be Elwood's best for
youth works
Rhonda D. Lane
Rhonda D. Lane

Dear
Awesome
Bakery
Thank you for all you
do to bring new life to the
history + music of your neighborhood.
Hugo, Karl, Sean
Reid Anfield
Portland, OR
PS. And thanks
for the rolls...

Tim +
Avenue Bakery
The community locally
and abroad appreciate what you
have brought and all that
you for the inspiration
-Will G Smith

Keep Doing
What You Do
For Our Communities
Mike Wooding
11/24/2021

Baltimore

ATL
in the house
Charleston

Tony ♡'s BMORE 12/3/21

Michael Debost
from Pennsylvania.
Thanks for the nourishment.
Good luck.

N.C. Durham

I came all the way from Durham, NC to purchase a variety of pies, cakes, and blue berry muffins. They are the BEST.

Naehali Williams

It is indeed a pleasure to have a Black business that is meeting the needs of our community.

May God's blessings flow like rain upon you!

Jackie T

Ronnie Dwane 7211

FIRST TIME FROM QUEENS, NY....

LOOKING FORWARD TO IT...! CAN'T WAIT TO BITE IN!

Been Hearing about this Bakery for a years. Finally Am in MD from N.J. to Sample the Goodies.

O. Handley

Didn't Knew this existed!!

So Glad we ventured out

W. Sh[illegible]

10/16/2021

Mr Hamlin,

Meeting you was indeed a pleasure. Thank you celebrating our history.

Sinerely,

Joseph Ampey

Excited to visit Avenue Bakery. Going to pick up a piece of cake for a friend having a birthday.
So happy to find you!
Cindy [illegible]

Ruby Drewery - got famous Rolls & Muffins

Angela Helm - Rolls/Apple 12 / Hdanagh Cake 3 / Pound Cake Whole

Angela Wilson - 1 slice pound cake, slice of upside down pineapple, 2 oatmeal cookies, 1 chocolate chip cookie,

Tim Barber & Ryan 2 doz Rolls Yum-Yum

TROY Munson October 16, 2021
THE AVENUE BAKERY

From this Area didn't Know you were here God Bless Gloria [illegible]

Best in town
LIZ

HI HOW ARE YOU
I LOVE YOUR COOKIES
MAY AllAH BlESS YOU
and YOUR FAMily
☺ XOXOXOX

NOTHING But The BEST

MAY ALLAH
BlESS YOU & YOUR
Family XOXOXO
☺

Kay Braxton

SHalom Brother
Keep up the Fight
Thank you for your
strength
Doran Talley

Keep up the Great
Work Joyce P. Brooks
From the Park Heights
Community...

Hey How ARE you today MAY GOD BlESS you & YOUR COOKies and CAKE'S everything LOVE it ☺ ♡ xoxoxo

Awesome Bakery. Love the historical concepts and I pray for much success! Stacia Dashiell

N.J.' City Worker

(Counselor) thx U We As A Community Are so blessed to have You And your Family!!! For Services & Great Experiences!!! ☺

Hi Family - 11-4-21 "stopping in to get something yummy" - thanks for being here for the Community. Your Neighbor Sylvia

I'm so Proud to have a BAKery Such As This On the West Side. Much Success + Blessings

Love + Peace Unto "U"

"nella ☺

Stuff is so Good Thanks Dan Dukes

Fatim

From DJ A.V. 11-5-21

Every Year Every Season

Mykel Hunter WEAA 88.9 Mornings w/ Mykel & Valencia Ohanian

God Bless!!

Jazzy

Jaya Fau

Lois Hamble

Grace Love Peace Thank you

Sami Ibtisaam 12/9/21

12-10-21
Food is Real Good
Like these People!!!

AREL was HERE Be Bless

Regina Buck Loves the food

Velma McCray God Bless Amen

Angela Hebron
apple Sauce Cake / Cookies / Pound Cake / Drink
Rolls

Thank you for your support of the Arts, the music and the people!!
All the very best! Dave from New Jersey

Looking forward to telling your story in Cuisine Noir magazine! ☺ Katia Hamas

Thanks for having me. The rolls are divine!!

Blessed to be here

12/19/21 My God bless you

12/16/21 My GOD is Soooo Good. GENO

12/17/21

12/17/21

CLARENCE SNAGGS Baltimore Community Lending 2022

God Forever 12/23/21

RONN

12/16/21 Delano & Bridget was here w/ Love

I Love This Place

Big Will & Babylove was here

Darrell "Golden Arm" Gough

01/30/2022 Paige Forte was here

Christopher Bevera
1/26/22
Coppin State University
Represent!!

Derrick Murray Sr.
2022 peace Blessings
and Reparations!!

It's all Good!
Eric Jones

Ms. Diane Bath
2/5/22
Thank you
with love

Love
2-4-22

Jim,
I'm glad you're
still here making
delicious baked
goods for our
community.
Best wishes always,
Linda Stewart

Paige,
Love Here

D.J.
from
City of Delta.

Jazzy Blue
"1992"

Bernard Lea
2/11/2022
Great Bakery

Best Bakery in Baltimore

Ray was happy to be here

Happy V day to you
D. Smith

Rev. Willie E. Ray

Shannon Sneed

Victor Clark, Jr.
"Great Job"
Let's build it!!!

Rev. Dr. Alfred Wells
Mark Wells
Great time @ 100th Anniversary
Royal Truth 2/15/22

Thanks for the difference you make in Baltimore!
Tom B.

Druid Hts CDC
Azalee Fisher

Bria Jones

Great time @ 100 Th
Anniversary

Mothers on
The Move

Great Memories
Sharon Burrus
Happy 100th

Reverend Elder Jackson
May the Good Lord
Bless You Real Good.

Drake Watson

Happy Anniversary
Coach John Moray
My Father had the Green Door
Restaurant, Dolphin + Pennsylvania

Randy Butler

Chavez

BryannaB ♡

Meluughn Wilter

Andrew Kingsley

George Produce
1102 Fremont Ave
Horse Stable "2022

Gregory G-MAN Nelson

Rufus
605 N. Magnolia Ave

Kenneth & Janie Booker Jwiorg

(The Counselor)

David Hill (Posse!)

Deborah Orlando, FL

Jayden

♡ Clara everett 3/9/22

Dinkk

Summers

Darwyn "Yum Yum" Brown

Butch Dotson

Khari fletcher

Jessica E. Jones Stone

Booker T. Washington 2/25/2022 ♥!

Komorra

Zymira B. ♡

was here

I like Donuts!

Aaron McKay

Kenzo ortiz

Mahayla Morrison

11-13-21

By K + Jim Stewart

Read on internet and it paid a visit. Looking forward to eating what we purchased. The owners daughter was very personable. He was one sick.

ROBIN LOVES JOHNNY

George Produce
1102 Fremont Ave
Horse Stable

Velma
LOVE
PP God Bless you

God Bless you

Best in town

Thank you!

2022

3/17/2022

Hi Mr. Hamlin,
Jewish Apple Cake
is simply scrumptious
Rhonda D. Lane

We love your
Rolls and
Cakes 3/19/22
Letitia Corey
God Bless you

March 19, 2022

Zula Crutchfield
Upper Marlboro Md.

Read about the place from
a friend. Purchased some rolls
& the bean Pie. Both were
great to eat. Back today to
purchase some more rolls & of course
the bean pie.
Thanks for this great experience
Zula Crutchfield

Pat Bailey
I have been some
Come

Mike Bell
Fort Washington, MD
Thank you!!

Alex Moret
was here
4/1/22

Brian Moses
3-31-22
Thank You

[illegible]
4/3/22

[illegible]

Habib Amir Abdallah Ali

Aaron & Chanae
4/3/2022

Every Sunday = My Fun Day
11 AM
"CREAM"

Claude + Beverly Simms - Our 1st Visit - 4/13/22

"ROCKY" "KEEP ON KEEPING ON"

City Wide Moving & Hauling LLC.

Leonard Stewart 4/14/22

"Florine Peaches Campher"

Calvin "Butch" Dixon 4.16.2022

Lloyd "Pappy" White 22 APR 2022 Patrick Pierce

L+R Whit 2022

This place is beautiful!

Shaniyah

I Love this place! May God continue to bless you! Kim

Simply so Amazing & Beautiful

Abigail was here 4 21 22

Iniko Carter

4/21/22

4/21/22

HEAF WAS HERE

WAS Here ON 4.22.22 DREXEL Taylor AKA Roggy LOVES THE BAKERY

Shandra was Here

love that + has so much heritage 4/22/2022

Love Your Rolls Judith Perkins 4/23/22

Melanie Barros thanks for everything that you do (New York City) 4/24/2022

(NY) - 4/24/22

Alexsys Culture - NJ 4/24/22

Love Angela 4/23/22

Thank you for your welcoming attitude Rachel (NY)

4/23/22 Felicia was here I love the Ace Bakery once a week is imperative

Thank you for the rolls - Jada (NYC)

Mariam Fortune I love it here! (4/24/22)

Yohealy Feliz (New York) - 4/24/2022

Thank you for being so welcoming - Max (NYC)

BALTIMORE RAVENS
HALL OF FAME
ED REED '19

THE GLORY DAYS OF MOVIE MATINEES AT "AVENUE" THEATERS
AREA THEATERS:
AMERICAN
CAREY
DIANE (CARVER PLAYHOUSE)
FREMONT
LENOX
LINCOLN #1
LINCOLN #2
MET
NEW ALBERT
NORTHWESTERN
PATTERSON
REGENT
ROOSEVELT
ROXY
ROYAL
SCHANZE
Theater entrance for African Americans aka "peanut gallery"
WHEN YOU DRINK A
Dr. Pepper
GOOD FOR LIFE!
A BITE TO EAT
CLARENCE MUSE
IN COLD BLOOD
NOTHING BUT A MAN
HALLELUJAH
PAUL ROBESON

Kim Loves the Bakery 4/24/2022

It's always a pleasure
Angela

Heard about your place and here I am.
Rhonda You

Heard about you in Aberdeen

This is How BLACK ESTABLISHMENT should be and we need to support them 100% times 100%
Charles C.

Heard about you from my daughter, came all the way from Connecticut to get the goodness! Long may you bake and prosper!
Dianne Daniels

Every time I come here it's a pleasure

I Love this Place Always

So Glad I MADE it Here!

B. Johnson

FIRST time Here

A very Impressive Development
Mary Shange

RONALD & Julia Mitchell

Ed Johnson Bolton House

Brian Henry
New Jersey

@rizzyink Was Here

CRIDER I LOVE IT

I absolutely love their goods

Sami 5/12/22

Army

Mr. Charles Bedd

(Balto City Heads) all the time!

Darrell V. (Owings Mills)

Rosalie Loved it here

Peters Family

Falicia Myers Lawson
27 May 2022

THE "RINEHART" FAMILY
LOVE, 5/27 2022

Jame Collins
&
Collins Family

Arianna & Zykiry

Keep pushing and stay Meddle

"KEEP ON KEEPING ON"
ROCKY #

Peace 2 your Bakery Best in Town

Bless The Businesses B MORE w/ That bless your patronage
learnt from K. M... Bus Leader US House of Representatives 6/3/22

Yummy Desserts!! ♡
6/4/22

God Bless your Legacy Tribute!
BARTINAS PARKER WAS A Hotel owner at the Base of the Avenue, it had a "speakeasy" Pool Room, & Resting place Rooms. He was the progenitor of the "Numbers" Games in the Community of Black folk & the Willie Adams worked for my great Uncle Bartinas riding a bike to transport #'s & any commodity associated with this legacy of cultural initiates. His son Casper Parker from near

Cooksville, Maryland was a sports promoter whose namesake "Parker" is inscribed at the Parker Gym in the Gary P. Arthur Center in Howard County. I even met Casper's wife Anna & Uncle Bartinas operated most of the pool halls around West Baltimore especially Sandtown and a lucrative Bootleg Liquor underground Enterprise, his part in a 1983 movie called "Children of a Lesser God" was filmed in Baltimore & is chronicled at our Enoch Pratt Library. Bartinas "passed for white" & made huge business strides & a magnanimous amount of $$ during the 1940's during the Avenue heyday era then.

Signed, Denise Parker, great niece of Bartinas Parker AKA "Uncle Bert."

Randallstown MD 21133

call me anytime for more historical fact finding...

My husband & I stopped by the bakery ... just to find out where it is. The bakery was closed but there was Jazz out back & I met Rosa Pryor. We had a Great Time. Joy + Keep Good. May God continue to bless your business

6/4/2022- "I will be back!" This is a wonderful, space! I feel the energy past & can't wait to spend more time here in the present! Love it DmB

6/4/2022 - FIRST TIME VISTOR AWESOME HISTRY WILL BE BACK! :)

Hello I stopped by my mother is Mary Robinson She loves your pies & Rolls (Sweet potatoe)

6/5/22 Great place to visit/history

Cynthia ... Very Good & BI

6/11/22 Brittany was here! Best Bakery ever Thank you

"KEEP ON KEEPIN ON" ROCKY!

6/8/2022 When in need of Conflict Resolution because you've made a mistake. Call OCPS for your conflict resolution needs. Always ready to support our community OCPS

"KEEP ON KEEPIN'S ON" ROCKY II

6/12/22 Dike Arymic Great Place!.!

6/12/22 One Love Favorite Bakery In The World & West Baltimore City

6/16/2022 Dianne Moore DRU Mondawmin Healthy Families, Inc.

God is good Roofs are us - michael

06-17-22 Jeffrey Long love The Bean Pies Keep it up

BLACK POWER!! ROCKY!!

6/18/2022 You are the Best! God Bless You!! Karen Sean

Been Known this business would be open for years to come thank you for letting Bmore be apart of your journey because of you my life will be forever sweet! XOXO Sweet Potato Pies Love Glow's Family

6.18.2022 God Bless you! I pray God continues to have His hand upon you. Love. Karen C.

Best Bakery!! Ever

06/22/2022 May God Continue To Bless This Wonderful Business, I Love What you're Doing For our Community. God Bless you my Brother

6/25/2022 – May GOD Continue to Bless This Bakery and our Community. Sending Lots of Love to All of our Kings & Queens. Charlie Thomas

Wishing you + yours all the Best, Amy Bl..

Thank you James & Belinda

27-08-2022 God Bless You all!!!

Myra Tolmin 6/25/22

DJ TRX BLACK POWER ROCKY

Great History thank you Jacque 6/26/2022

Great History and Presentation. This community! Bernard Lee

You are a Blessing to Ben Frederick – Baltimore

Best Bakery!! Ever Fresh Food! Daily Fatima Inwozer

Hello Baltimore! Cordelia Pottinger-Walters

Mr. Hamlin, Thanks for your contribution to the world & Baltimore. You are amazing.

Mr. Hamlin you are a true inspiration! Thank you!!!

J. Y. Best 2121 Winchester St 21216

Heads #15 Thx for good sweets!!

NO DOUBT MY ONLY STOP WHEN IT COMES TO SWEETS "BIG Mel"

The Avenue Bakery is Excellent! The rolls are home made like my mother use to make. They are very professional!

At last, I got here before you closed. The wheat rolls are the BOMB.. :) H. Norton

Thank you! For Preserving our Culture. A Willis-Lee

Thank you for your kindness!! We'll definitely return!!

7/9/2022 D. & D. Rogers

First Time Looking Good

I Love it

Vanessa Bradford Definitely a Baltimore Gem Eastside (Down the hill)

July 9th 2022

The Royal Squad Marching Unit Family.

Love the awesome Service you all are providing for the community.

Thanks for the delicious treats! :)

Hi Avenue Bakery:

Thank You for Providing something "Yummy for the tummy"

Sylvia

Nothing like Home Made love it!!!

Sonette

Good TREATS! :)

Nita

Great service and treats. They really help and emp[illegible] the Black Communi[illegible]

Velma mccray - kings[illegible]

I Love This Baker

God Bless you and family

Good stuff "Cakes"

Great Place

Tye + Company

Sahir was here ♡

Thank You for your work and all the amazing information.

Marie N'diaye from France ♡

An honor to meet you and take in all your efforts to remember and renew. Thank you for the informal tour today

Matt Testa

Peabody Institute

Thank you for sharing your time & stories with us - we love your rolls! I will be back with friends -

Marissa Scotti

Peabody Institute

What an amazing experience to be blessed with this amazing [illegible]

Thank you

[illegible]

Thank you for the tour and for the work you're doing to rebuild the business district of Pennsylvania Ave!

Sue Royer

Towson, MD

So blessed to have your leadership! Can't wait to dance at the Savoy!

♡ Breai from Baltimore

"Wherever you went, there was music on both sides of the street" - [illegible]

Thank you for sharing Old West [illegible] Baltimore and Pennsylvania Ave's LIVING history.

Andrea L. Morris

Peabody Institute

Thank you for your service and sweet treats

Ms. [illegible]

Thank you for the tour!

[illegible]

Amazing. Thank [illegible] all you do [illegible] community

[illegible]

Such an informative entertaining and enlightening tour. Thanks for sharing your enthusiasm [illegible]

[illegible]

Thank you for the tour! It was a wonderful experience!

[illegible]

1st Time Here love it. 7/23/2022

Cheyrita Meutchan Lanier will be back!!!

1st visit from Sarasota, FLORida and very excited to see you here for the community

Monique A Plair

759 116th CT NE

Bradenton, FL 34212

www.go-bu.com

mplair@go-bu.com

[illegible]

Wonderful The Lord Has Blessed us All! Keep Going!

[illegible]

God Bless You

Zion Baptist Church Philadelphia

J. Adams

Thank You

God Bless

[illegible] Lewis

Zion Baptist Church

Happy to be here♡
Love Ang

GREAT SERVICE,
GREAT FOOD
Lady Millard

Coach G♡
Coach G Academy, Inc

Linga Sa

Taylor Jd

Stacy Giselle♡

Kaliah S♡

Jayain☆

Haylin

The Stewart's
Love the Rolls

Amazing History and Tour. learned a lot on the tour. Keep Investing in us Because no one else will
Justin
Pruitt
Brewer

Best Rolls in Baltimore
To Niyah

2022 July 28

W Food

Rania
Alicia Black
Karim Amin

(Alicia – Thank You, 7/29/22)

Love It Thank You – Tanya 7/30/22

"BLACK POWER"
ROCKY

Rachael from Chicago! Best Wishes!

Beverly Boyd – Thanks for your amazing bakery

Tracy Warren
Indiana (Baltimore native!)

Dave & Kim Hacrell 7/29/22

Deliciousness Tamara

Lovelyadillz_3♡

Love the Cakes!!!

8/4/22 Linda & Andre Hinton

8-6-2022 Velma McCray God Bless
8-6-2022 Deborah J White 21214 Delicious!
8/6/2022 Kim, Deborah, Kamaron Moir

Thursday, August 18, 2022
11:05 this is the best entertainment/information
Dr. Charles Johnson
2436 P.O. Box
Ellicott City MD 21043
and good eats

8/20/22 Kirk Dailey
1344 N Willys
8/20/22 Ron + Carol Steen
8/20/22 Mr. Ms. Dyrums

Hello Ms Sandra
The first time I've ever played the Ot box

Ross family Peace & Blessings

8/25/2022 Salimah A. Hassan

Hello

08 25 22

8-26-22 B. Smith 8-26-22

Annette Hopkins
Willie Hopkins

8/26/22
Jerry & Deidre Petty
New Orleans, LA

8/26/22
Dionne McCray
Westminster, CA

8/27/22 – Aisha
8/27/22 Tim

8/28/2022 Dania
9/3 André Fisher DHCDC
9/3 Susie Dezurn BB
9/3 [illegible]

9/3 Brother [illegible]
9/8 Carrol Dixon
9/8 Brenda J. [illegible]
9/8 Linda Wheeler
9/8 Paula [illegible]
9/9 Reggie Waller

Sept. [illegible]
9/16 minikyun
9/16 Waykay
9/17 [illegible]
9/23/2022 [illegible]
9-24-22 [illegible]
Rachelle Bland
9/24 Maria Day
9/24 Dell [illegible]
9/24 Barry Powell
9/24 Joseph W. Simpson
9/25 Nevenah
9/25 Shana T. Giese
9/25/2022 Dwight B Barley Sr & Family

9-30-22 Kenneth Banks / Cynthia McCray
9-30- D/K/[illegible]
9/30/22 JOHN D. RUTOSKEY
10/1/22 Earlene Holland
10/2 Thomas Wells
Pauline Sanders

10/4 Liam Davis
Jacqueline Jones
10-4 Cheryl [illegible] Jackson
10-4-22 Diane Lewis
Ronald Lewis
10/4/22 NICOLE [illegible] HERITAGE CROSSING
10/4/22 Mark Shorter

Pastor Howard Graham
Like the New Covenant Fellowship Ministry
Thank you
Keep on Keep on
May the Lord Bless you!
[illegible]
10/8/22 Carolyn Washington
10-8-22 I'm blessed today Dawn Smith
10-8-22 I'm 60 yr young Sandtown born an raised. My 1st time in bakery. Cathie!
10-9-22 Lenny Harris
Sandtown all the WAY
BORN & RAISED

10/9/22 Earlene Holland
Thera Stevenson
Shaliya Hicks

10/9/22 Alice Thompson
I love this Place and all of it's history. Thank You.

10/9/22 Marcella Charles
So Amazing to see all this History here NOW!!

10-13-22- Best Rolls in town!
Love this Bakery ♡-

10.14.22 "BAMA" Akmal Saleem
"I'll Be Quite From Now On ..."

10/15/22 Debra Blakney
Historical site and interesting history
Place continue your mission.

10/16 Walking in for the 1st time!! Just the smell alone brought me. Plus it's nice 2 see black-owned companies in the area
Great job
Lyric ♡

10/14 Love this Place Kim Vice

10/16 Glad you are here! Melvina 1947 - 1977
The Avenue Pearl

10-16-22 I grew up in this nabohood And I was so thankful that yall open up right up the street from my Church St Peter Claver I try to come everytime I'm passing and see yall open
Laurene Pauling

11/13/23 November 13, 2023
What a wonderful surprise, walking into this small good bakery!

11/13/23
So happy to stumble upon this bakery. So happy to support a black owned business. Hope to see more of this in Upton.
Kelsey Smallwood

Catherine Trotter
It was a blessing to come here today and learn about our history. Your bakery is making a huge impact
- Baltimore

Gene Payne
I LOVE IT HERE...

I LOVE [sweet potato pie]

Thank You for the bread pudding. Delicious!!!
I especially enjoyed the walls full of history!
Nita Hunt

My first time here thank you for your service 10/21/23
Delicious!
Nikki Reynolds

Amy Agnew

Just like old days on East Balto Sunday

yummy and delicouse, as always! #1 to ME!

—Amani Brown

The Apple Cobler was slaming!

Snook

#15 always Here Balto City

Cake was very good

Dorothy Miller

Thanks you

THURSDAY FRIDAY SATURDAY SUNDAY
BECAUSE YALL OPEN MAKE THE BEST DAYS OF THE WEEK
KEEP UP THE GOOD WORK

Lamont..

Poppys Bakery
Greatest Bakery on East Coast!!!

Ricky 2022 the Best

Best Bakery Ever 2022

I love the Smell of BLACK EXCELLENCE!!! BAKE ON!

Rachael

Happy Thanksgiving from The Family Smyrna, DE

I love it Here

What a great experience! Thank you for all you do to keep History Alive!

D. Edwards '22

Best I love it

#Angelcrazy77 Love it

Blessings as you walk out your VISION

HOPE!

Peace & Blessings

I enjoy you all ♡ 10/30/22

-Akilah Muhammad

Amanda Hardy
Beautiful Time!

Joyce Sutton
I Love the Bakery 11/2022

awesome bakery!

Great experience! Thank you 4 the Awesome tour.

M Goggins

Great place

Dr. M

Nov 10, 2022 O Brown JR

Beautiful place with a beautiful person! love

Shantel Teal 11/22
All Good!!

Thank You!! Black Power

Greetings from Nicole & Dwight from CAJOU CREAMERY! ♥

Your rolls are perfect!

Nov. 17, 2022
Love all of the Great African American History.. and Justice for All!
Atlanta, Georgia 2022

THANKS FROM THE SWANNS

My first time will be back!!
7/8/2022

I Love it here, we come every weekend for the bread pudding!
7/9/22

Best Bakery

your shop is amazing!
keep on shining ♡
-Sievie Daniels

Gobble Gobble
Keep on Keepin ON!

xxxooo
Brenda Lorde

Amazing Rolls!
-Ralph Simpson (Austin, TX / Foster City, CA)

Yvonne Lee

kiss kiss

LaTawnda Smith - Baltimore "Cherry Hill" grown from Owings Mills 11/23/22

Best Wishes
[illegible] Brown 11/23/22 @ 1pm

THANK you for sharing
LINDA CLARK 12/21/22

First Time [illegible]

Jim, you are a staple in Baltimore! I moved here in 2015 and didn't eat a roll until 2019.. I ask myself what was I doing those other 4 years!!? Much love and continued success!
- Erick Ferris
WMAR-2 News

Best rolls in the country Not Just the city!
-Mike J

"You Get to Love this Place."

Stuart Wonders Open up more Winston Drive!!

Best of Wishes - Pitt Gord
TV Star
12/3/22

thank you for serving this community
God bless you always, Teresa Brunt Carraro
family
2022 Dec 31

winner. And, my husband ate two of the rolls as we drove back to our son's home.

I reread the page in The Tour Book on "The Avenue Bakery". Please use the enclosed check toward your fund raising for "The Royal Theater."

We look forward to returning to your shop.

Warm regards,
Leslie Hillel

MID-ISLAND NY 117
12 MAY 2021 PM 5 L

May 13, 2021

Dear Mr. & Mrs Hamlin -

My husband and I visited your bakery one day last week. We were in Baltimore to help with our grandchildren for ten days. We used the Book about 111 Things to do in Baltimore. Babe Ruth's orphanage was a bit disappointing. We couldn't find Dickeyville. Your bakery was the highlight of our touring.

Black History Month at The Avenue Bakery

. . . VOICES — TO BE CONTINUED!

www.ingramcontent.com/pod-product-compliance
Lightning Source LLC
Chambersburg PA
CBHW041533120626
46551CB00019B/2675
9798218477288